Unpacking international organisations

MANCHESTER
1824

Manchester University Press

1617 4252   32⁹⁵

European Policy Research Unit Series

Series Editors: *Simon Bulmer, Peter Humphreys* and *Mick Moran*

The European Policy Research Unit Series aims to provide advanced text-books and thematic studies of key public policy issues in Europe. They concentrate, in particular, on comparing patterns of national policy content, but pay due attention to the European Union dimension. The thematic studies are guided by the character of the policy issue under examination.

The European Policy Research Unit (EPRU) was set up in 1989 within the University of Manchester's Department of Government to promote research on European politics and public policy. The series is part of EPRU's effort to facilitate intellectual exchange and substantive debate on the key policy issues confronting the European states and the European Union.

Titles in the series also include:

Globalisation and policy-making in the European Union   Ian Bartle

The Europeanisation of Whitehall   Simon Bulmer and Martin Burch

The power of the centre: Central governments and the macro-implementation of EU public policy   Dionyssis G. Dimitrakopoulos

Creating a transatlantic marketplace   Michelle P. Egan (ed.)

The politics of health in Europe   Richard Freeman

Immigration and European integration (2nd edn)   Andrew Geddes

Agricultural policy in Europe   Alan Greer

The European Union and the regulation of media markets   Alison Harcourt

Mass media and media policy in Western Europe   Peter Humphreys

The politics of fisheries in the European Union   Christian Lequesne

The European Union and culture: Between economic regulation and European cultural policy   Annabelle Littoz-Monnet

Sports law and policy in the European Union   Richard Parrish

The Eurogroup   Uwe Puetter

EU pharmaceutical regulation   Govin Permanand

Regulatory quality in Europe: Concepts, measures and policy processes   Claudio M. Radaelli and Fabrizio de Francesco

Extending European cooperation   Alasdair R. Young

Regulatory politics in the enlarging European Union   Alasdair Young and Helen Wallace

Unpacking international organisations

The dynamics of compound bureaucracies

*Jarle Trondal, Martin Marcussen, Torbjörn Larsson
and Frode Veggeland*

Manchester University Press
Manchester and New York
*distributed in the Unites States exclusively
by Palgrave Macmilla*

Copyright © Jarle Trondal, Martin Marcussen, Torbjörn Larsson and Frode Veggeland
2010

The right of Jarle Trondal, Martin Marcussen, Torbjörn Larsson and Frode Veggeland to
be identified as the authors of this work has been asserted by them in accordance with the
Copyright, Designs and Patents Act 1988.

Published by Manchester University Press
Oxford Road, Manchester M13 9NR, UK
and Room 400, 175 Fifth Avenue, New York, NY 10010, USA
www.manchesteruniversitypress.co.uk

Distributed in the United States exclusively by
Palgrave Macmillan, 175 Fifth Avenue,
New York, NY 10010, USA

Distributed in Canada exclusively by
UBC Press, University of British Columbia, 2029 West Mall,
Vancouver, BC, Canada V6T 1Z2

British Library Cataloguing-in-Publication Data is available

Library of Congress Cataloging-in-Publication Data is available

ISBN 978 0 7190 9541 2 paperback

First published by Manchester University Press in hardback 2010

This paperback edition first published 2014

The publisher has no responsibility for the persistence or accuracy of URLs for any external or third-
party internet websites referred to in this book, and does not guarantee that any content on such
websites is, or will remain, accurate or appropriate.

Printed by Lightning Source

Contents

Figures

Tables

Abbreviations

AD	Administrator (European Commission)
AST	Assistant (European Commission)
CDR	Career Development Review
CFDP	Common Foreign and Defence Policy
CFSP	Common Foreign and Security Policy
DDG	Deputy Director-General
DG	Director-General
	Directorate-General (of the European Commission)
EC	European Community
ECB	European Central Bank
EU	European Union
GATT	General Agreement on Tariffs and Trade
GS	General Secretariat
IO	International organisation
IR	International relations
ITO	International Trade Organization
NPM	New Public Management
OECD	Organisation for Economic Co-operation and Development
SNE	Seconded national expert
TAD	Trade and Agriculture Directorate
WTO	World Trade Organization

Authors

Jarle Trondal is Professor at the University of Agder department of political science, and at ARENA – the Centre for European Studies, University of Oslo. His main fields of research are comparative international bureaucracy, the emergent European executive order, and the Europeanisation of domestic branches of executive government.

Martin Marcussen is Professor at the University of Copenhagen department of political science. His main fields of research include central banking, social constructivist theory, governance networks, the OECD, and economic and monetary integration in Europe.

Torbjörn Larsson is Associate Professor at the University of Stockholm department of political science. His main fields of research include EU committee governance, the European Commission, public administration, and Swedish government and governance.

Frode Veggeland is Senior Researcher at the Norwegian Agriculture Economics Research Institute and at ARENA – the Centre for European Studies, University of Oslo. His fields of scholarly interest include food safety policy, the Europeanisation of domestic core-executive institutions, the WTO, and multilevel governance.

Foreword

This book introduces international bureaucracy as a key field of study for public administration and also rediscovers international bureaucracy as an essential ingredient in the study of international organisations. The questions posed by this book are to what extent, how and why international bureaucracies challenge and supplement the inherent Westphalian intergovernmental order based on territorial sovereignty. To what extent, how and why do international bureaucracies supplement the existing international intergovernmental order with a *multidimensional* international order subjugated by a compound set of decision-making dynamics? The ambition of this book is to rediscover international bureaucracies as a key engine of international organisations in particular, and as one important component of modern public administration more generally. The book explores the compound nature of international bureaucracy by comparing three such institutions: the European Commission, the OECD Secretariat, and the WTO Secretariat.

This book is the result of six years of co-operation between the authors. The project was launched in 2003 with the idea that international bureaucracy should be given more systematic scholarly attention and with a wish to compare everyday life inside international bureaucracies. The project was titled 'DISC – Dynamics of International Secretariats'. The initiative to compare international bureaucracies was partly triggered by claims in the literature of the *sui generis* nature of the European Commission compared to other international bureaucracies. This claim, we believed, was often put forward without systematically comparing the European Commission with other international bureaucracies, and thus, it was more often claimed than tested. Prior studies of the OECD and the WTO also indicated that the *sui generis* claims of the Commission should be challenged, substantiated and partly modified. This book adds to the comparative literature on international organisation particularly and to the wider field of public administration with fresh and original empirical observations from the life inside international bureaucracies.

During the 2003–9 period the research group has met several times in Brussels, Copenhagen, Kristiansand and Oslo to discuss and write. We have benefited extensively from the excellent infrastructure provided by the Larsson family in Brussels, by Martin Marcussen in Copenhagen, by Jarle Trondal in Kristiansand, and by ARENA in Oslo (the Centre for European Studies, University of Oslo). The process of writing this book has been firmly co-ordinated among the authors. All the authors have written in every chapter and the book is thus truly multi-authored. The need to ease the burden on each author, however, means that some authors have had the main responsibility of certain chapters. In order to make the book as coherent as possible and also in order to make the arguments as solid as achievable, all chapters have been internally reviewed by all authors through the whole writing process. Among the most enduring discussions in the research group has been how to operationalise different decision-making dynamics within international bureaucracies and also how to disentangle them. The second continuing theme of discussion during the project period has been how to theoretically account for what we see. How do we best theoretically anchor the compound dynamics within international bureaucracies?

The project has been supported over the years by financial allowances from the Joint Committee of the Nordic Social Science Research Councils, from the Norwegian Research Council, and from ARENA. Thanks should also be given to the CONNEX network (Connecting Excellence on European Governance) for providing opportunities to present and discuss earlier versions of the book at several conferences and workshops. Different sections of the book have been presented at several CONNEX conferences, the Norwegian Political Science Association, the European Consortium for Political Research and the European Union Studies Association. We have benefited greatly from discussions with Michael Bauer, Morten Egeberg, Hussein Kassim, Morten Øgård, Anchrit Wille and two anonymous referees who provided valuable comments on several draft versions of this book. We are also indebted to Simon Bulmer for thorough comments on the very last draft of the manuscript. During the production of the book the editorial team at Manchester University Press has been most helpful. Without their support and backing we would not have been able to finalise this manuscript. The authors would also like to thank Hege Haugland, Lene Jeppesen, Zuzana Murdoc and Anders Siegumfelt for much-needed research assistance, and Melinda Hill for improving our language. Last but not least, we are most grateful to those officials at the European Commission, the OECD Secretariat, and the WTO Secretariat who gave of their scarce time to this project.

Jarle Trondal, Martin Marcussen, Torbjörn Larsson and Frode Veggeland
Kristiansand, Copenhagen, Brussels and Oslo

Part I

Introducing and theorising international bureaucracy

Part I

Introduction to the basic
arguments

1

The bureaucracy of international organisations

International bureaucracies are compound systems of public administration that blend departmental, epistemic and supranational
decision-making dynamics. The intergovernmental dynamic is seen to be
less essential within international bureaucracies. The fact that the
departmental dynamic seems to be overwhelmingly present does not mean
that other dynamics are absent; rather, the departmental logic seems to be
the basis and maybe even the precondition for the two other dynamics to
play out. This world of multiple behavioural dynamics is depicted in this
volume as being organised around concentric circles where *the
departmental dynamic serves as the foundational dynamic* at the very
centre of bureaucracy. Behavioural dynamics within international bureaucracies are activated fairly independently of the larger international
organisation in which these bureaucracies are embedded. This book also
illuminates the fact that the mix of behavioural dynamics within
international bureaucracies is organisationally contingent and more
complex than assumed by the theoretical orthodoxy of the study of
international relations (IR). International bureaucracies seem to share
important behavioural dynamics due to the *organisational characteristics*
of these bureaucracies.
  International bureaucracies constitute a distinct and increasingly
important feature of public administration studies. However, the role of
international bureaucracies has been largely neglected in most social
science sub-disciplines. This lacuna perhaps reflects a more general gulf
between various social science sub-disciplines, such as public administration and organisation theory (March 2009), as well as comparative
public administration scholarship and research on international organisation and administration (Heady 1998: 33; Jörgens et al. 2009). This
book takes a first step into a third generation of international organisation (IO) studies. Paradoxically, this requires that the study of
international organisations is somehow 'normalised', i.e. that a public
administrative turn comes to characterise IO studies (Trondal 2007a).

Comparing cases of international bureaucracy will arguably move the study of international bureaucracy towards 'normal science'. 'Even if there is only one [Commission], we should study this case carefully and in a comparative fashion' (Schneider 2008: 279). Until now studies of international bureaucracy have largely lacked comparative designs. For example, the study of the European Commission has been criticised for the 'N=1' problem (Warleigh-Lack and Phinnemore 2009: 216). There has also been a tendency in the literature to assume that international bureaucracies can somehow be understood by reading their formal mandates and legal provisions. This book argues that one of the defining features of international bureaucracies is their compound nature consisting of multiple behavioural dynamics, role definitions and identities among the incumbents. Since the study of national administration has a long tradition of studying the lives and day-to-day routines of national civil servants, such a perspective, if applied to international bureaucracies, would imply a normalisation of IO studies – a so-called public administrative turn (Trondal 2007a). Despite the obvious differences that exist between national and international bureaucracy, a third generation of IO studies would be based on long and extensive experience and theoretical development within the area of public administration studies. This requires that new questions be asked and new concepts applied to the field of IO research.

Some scholars (e.g. Rosenau 1997) picture the nation-state as weakened, hollowed out and fragmented due to the advent of international bureaucracies. Others argue that international bureaucracies merely strengthen and integrate the nation-state as a coherent Westphalian system of territorial sovereignty (e.g. Biersteker 2003; Moravcsik 1998). Moreover, some picture international bureaucracies as a key motor in the transformation of nation-state institutions (Cowles, Caporaso and Risse 2001; Wessels, Maurer and Mittag 2003). Others argue that the effects of international bureaucracies are moderate and are associated with the evolving dynamics of domestic change (Andersson 2002; Olsen 2003a). Conflicting assessments of these kinds represent more than standard academic turf-battles with regard to the transformation of political orders (see Hurrelmann et al. 2007). We are in fact facing complex, puzzling and poorly understood relationships between the nuts and bolts of international bureaucracies and policy making within domestic governments.[1] Understanding the *modus operandi* of international bureaucracies is essential in order to better understand how decisions are shaped within international organisations and also how and to what extent international organisations transform domestic government(s) and governance. The emergence of relatively independent international bureaucracies may profoundly transform the executive branch of government in Europe (e.g. Graziano and Vink 2007).

The pertinent question targeted by this book is to what extent, how and why international bureaucracies challenge and supplement the inherent Westphalian intergovernmental order based on territorial autonomy (Gourevitch 2003; Kegley and Raymond 2002: 192; March and Olsen 1998; Rosenau 1996). To what extent, how and why do international bureaucracies supplement the existing international intergovernmental order with a *multidimensional* international order subjugated by a compound set of decision-making dynamics? In order to approach these large-scale questions, this book focuses on the following research questions:

- Firstly, what behavioural dynamics predominate in the everyday decision-making processes within international bureaucracies? More specifically, *to what extent* are intergovernmental behavioural dynamics transcended or supplemented by supranational, departmental and/or epistemic behavioural dynamics within international bureaucracies?
- Secondly, under what conditions do different behavioural dynamics dominate within international bureaucracies? More specifically, *under what conditions* are intergovernmental dynamics bypassed by supranational, departmental and/or epistemic behavioural dynamics within international bureaucracies?

The ambition of this book is to rediscover international bureaucracies as a key engine of international organisations in particular, and as one important component of modern public administration more generally. The book has two main objectives:

1 Firstly, the book systematically compares behavioural dynamics within a carefully selected number of international bureaucracies. The focus is on studying these dynamics within international bureaucracies at the actor level – that is, by studying the behaviour and roles as perceived by the officials themselves. The book outlines a conceptual map of four generic behavioural dynamics that are likely to be evoked by these officials: intergovernmental, supranational, departmental and epistemic dynamics (see below). Essentially, the Westphalian international order dominated by the intergovernmental dynamic is challenged to the extent that international bureaucracies embed supranational, departmental and epistemic dynamics in everyday decision-making processes. Admittedly, there are no guarantees that these dynamics always materialise in the actors' behaviour and ultimately in the decisions reached by international organisations. However, they serve as cognitive and normative frames for action, rendering it more likely than not that particular decision-making

dynamics are associated with certain behavioural patterns (Aberbach, Putnam and Rockman 1981: 86; Van Knippenberg and Van Leeuwen 2001: 250).

2 Secondly, the book illuminates some causal factors that may help to explore the conditions under which different behavioural dynamics are manifested in the behavioural and role perceptions of the incumbents of international bureaucracies. Essentially, we do not propose to 'test' the four dynamics outlined above in a rigorous manner. They serve more as 'searchlights for illuminating empirical patterns in our data' (Aberbach, Putnam and Rockman 1981: 20).

What is international bureaucracy?

International organisations penetrate ever more areas and levels of national government. Evidently, the international political scene has become increasingly organised in the post-Second World War period, reflected in the upsurge, institutionalisation and impact of international bureaucracies (Finnemore 1996; March and Olsen 1998). There are currently around 5,000 international organisations, many of which have semi-autonomous institutions in addition to plenary assemblies (Bauer and Knill 2007: 14). In a world of international organisations there is a rising number of 'unelected bodies' that complement the traditional branch of government at the domestic level based on elections (Vibert 2007). The task of international bureaucracies has become increasingly that of an active and independent policy-making institution and less a passive technical servicing instrument for the plenary assemblies (Lemoine 1995: 28). International bureaucracies are important, though not omnipotent, centres of gravity of most contemporary international organisations and serve partly as a new branch of government.[2]

International bureaucracies consist of the permanent secretariats of international organisations. They are organisationally separate from the plenary assemblies of international organisations and have a formal autonomy vis-à-vis the member states. The autonomy is often codified in staff regulations. International bureaucracies typically have fixed locations, they have a formalised division of labour vis-à-vis the plenary assembly, they have regular meetings, and they are staffed mostly with permanent personnel recruited on the principle of merit, although sometimes supplemented with a more flexible set of contracted temporary staff (seconded officials). One essential element of international bureaucracies is that the staff have sworn an oath of undivided and primary *loyalty* towards the international bureaucracy. With respect to the formal organisation of international bureaucracies, they are mostly vertically-specialised bureaucracies, often with an administrative leader at the top. The European Commission (the Commission) is *sui generis* by also having a political umbrella at the top with the College of Commissioners and their Cabinets. Even more important, the Commission is unusual in being organised outside the Council of Ministers and thus formally independent of member-state preferences and the inherited intergovernmental order. The Commission is the hub in a multilevel union administration that spans levels of governance, and has gained administrative capacities to support its formal independence vis-à-vis the Council (of the European Union) and the European Parliament, for example with respect to the initiating and implementation of legal acts (Curtin and Egeberg 2008). This particular institutional role of the Commission being an autonomous international executive serving as part of a quasi-federal European executive order was also envisioned by Jean Monnet (Duchêne 1994).

International bureaucracies are also horizontally specialised bureaucracies, resembling the ministerial organisation of the member states where different policy portfolios are linked to separate ministers. Beyond purely administrative functions such as arranging meetings, translation, legal assistance etc., some international bureaucracies also increasingly enjoy initiating and implementing functions vis-à-vis the plenary assembly and monitoring functions concerning member states' implementation of decisions. They are also important in integrating external institutions (such as member-state ministries and agencies, and other international organisations) into their own decision-making process through committees and boards (for example the Commission's web of expert groups). For example, within the EU, executive functions such as policy initiation, policy formulation and policy making are increasingly transported from national governments to international bureaucracies.[3] International bureaucracies contribute to initiating, formulating and influencing the policies and politics of international organisations, and to the administrative continuity and institutional memories between the ministerial meetings. Essentially, international bureaucracies have increasingly become political secretariats for the international organisation. However, despite being created by the states, the international bureaucracies are not necessarily instruments of these states.

Historically, it was the creation of international secretariats that transformed 'a series of conferences into an organization' (Claude 1956: 194). An early example of a permanent international secretariat was in the League of Nations (although this was largely staffed with seconded national officials without a primary loyalty to the secretariat, and also overly staffed with personnel carrying out technical servicing rather than policy making) (Lemoine 1995: 18; Mathiason 2007: 28). What is key to the *de facto* existence of international bureaucracies is that its officials should act relatively independently of the member states and be loyal to the international bureaucracy. The first international bureaucracy to

dictate that its officials should be internationally loyal was the League of
Nations, which in 1920 claimed that:

> the members of the Secretariat, once appointed, are no longer the servants
> of the country of which they are citizens, but become for the time being
> servants only of the League of Nations. Their duties are not national but
> international. (League of Nations 1920: 137)

Whereas most international-relations approaches view international
organisations as black boxes and an epiphenomenon to inter-state
relations, this study unpacks the executive arms – the bureaucratic
interior – of international organisations, and does so comparatively. The
Commission is no longer depicted as a unique case among international
bureaucracies. The goal is to analyse the similarities and differences in the
internal working of international bureaucracies. The literature on international organisations has only recently started conceptualising and
empirically illuminating the inner core of international bureaucracies (see
Barnett and Finnemore 2004; Reinalda and Verbeek 2004b). However,
'to date, we do not really know how to conceptualize international
organizations and how to deal with the organizational components' of
international bureaucracies (Gehring 2003: 13). This book offers an
organisation-theory approach in order to conceptualise the compound
nature of international bureaucracies, and provides a comparative
empirical analysis of the behavioural dynamics within three such
bureaucracies – the Commission, the OECD Secretariat, and the WTO
Secretariat. The book thereby challenges claims like 'comparing the
Commission with international secretariats ... would certainly be of very
limited usefulness' (Christiansen 1996: 77).

One rationale for comparing the selected international bureaucracies is
that they share some basic organisational features as public inter-state
bodies that are organised according to well-known organising principles
from domestic executive institutions. However, these three international
bureaucracies differ in many respects. Most importantly, they differ with
respect to their degree of independence vis-à-vis the member states (see
above). Moreover, they also vary with respect to the size and
heterogeneity of membership (global vs. regional), their main outputs
(hard law vs. soft law), and the top leadership of the administrative
apparatus (administrative vs. political). A second rationale for studying
international bureaucracies generally and the selected international
bureaucracies in particular is the idea that everyday behavioural dynamics
inside international bureaucracies reflect *less* the international
organisations in which they are embedded and much more the
organisational variables of the international bureaucracies themselves.
Previous studies of management reforms within different international
organisations suggest that the international organisation as such is of

limited relevance in order to explain reforms of their international bureaucracies (Bauer and Knill 2007: 194). Hence, it is time to unpack the black box of international bureaucracies.

Executive politics in Europe is in transition, arguably moving towards a European Administrative Space (Curtin and Egeberg 2008). One essential characteristic of this executive transformation is the increased integration of national ministries and agencies on the one hand and international bureaucracies on the other. The transformation of public administration is seen in the literature as the spread of second-generation New Public Management reforms (e.g. Christensen and Lægreid 2007), as reforms of international organisations (Bauer and Knill 2007), and as the increased integration of the public administrations of international organisations and domestic government systems (Egeberg 2006). This study contributes to this literature by analysing the compound nature of international bureaucracies. Whereas most of the previous studies of international bureaucracies have been single-case studies, this volume presents a comparative analysis of three selected international bureaucracies. This book, however, does not study the historical routes, roots and reforms of international bureaucracies as has been done elsewhere (e.g. Bauer and Knill 2007; Mathiason 2007).

How can we *explain* the compound nature of international bureaucracies? Theoretically, this book suggests a middle-range organisation-theory approach to explain the everyday behavioural dynamics of international bureaucracies. This approach advocates that the internal dynamics of international bureaucracies may be accounted for by analysing their

- organisational components;
- recruitment procedures;
- relationships with external institutions;
- demographic composition of personnel.

The advanced argument suggests that these organisational characteristics foster the emergence of compound behavioural dynamics among the incumbents (see Table 1.2 below).

This introductory chapter is organised as follows:

- The first section outlines and substantiates the compound nature of international bureaucracies.
- The second section provides a short literature review of past and more recent studies of international bureaucracies.
- The final sections present the methodology and data that underpin the book, followed by a description of the structure of this volume.

The compound nature of international bureaucracies: a third generation of study

Domestic public administration is traditionally established to prepare and implement public policy. Historically, the study of public administration has been limited to the study of domestic administrative systems, notably reforms and politics within domestic ministries and agencies (e.g. Christensen and Lægreid 2007). A 'public administration turn' in the study of international organisations, particularly in the study of the Commission (Trondal 2007a), has recently directed increased attention to the reforms and dynamics of the 'ministries' and 'agencies' of international organisations.

With this volume we are basically drawing the contours of a third generation of research on international organisations. In the first generation, the main lines of debate concerned whether or not international organisations were effective decision-making forums. There seemed to be general agreement that the most important actors on the world scene were nation-states. While some would argue that these nation-states could reap immediate benefits from international co-operation in the form of reduced transaction costs, others would argue that when the salience of policy issues was raised, i.e. when issues were politicised, they were primarily dealt with in purely bilateral forums. In other words, multilateralism is good when it is harmless. In that first generation, there was not much interest in what was going on below the intergovernmental surface. International organisations were mainly dealt with as black boxes, with the distinct characteristics of international bureaucracies being ignored. Therefore, in the second generation of research on international organisations, attention was directed at the international bureaucracy, highlighting the fact that bureaucracies at an international level could be expected to be just as compound as any other bureaucracy at a national level. In the second generation, the field of international organisation research was opened up for public administration scholars. This development can be described as a public administration 'turn' in international organisation research (Trondal 2007a). To discover that international bureaucracies can have identities, resources, authority and interests of their own is, of course, an important development (Barnett and Finnemore 2004). However, when seen from a purely public administration point of view, this seems to be a less novel discovery.

Therefore, the purpose of a third generation of international organisation research is to go one step further by studying the criteria for and the patterns, dynamics, conditions, varieties and dynamics of international bureaucracies. In the second generation of study, the challenge was to bring international bureaucracies back into the study of international politics and to argue that bureaucracies matter in their own right. The third generation of studies is mainly interested in studying *how* they matter. The fact that international bureaucracies are compound systems on their own account requires that we analytically treat them as such. There is no one way of doing that. In the same way as a broad spectrum of public administration tools exists for studying the organisational dynamics of national public administrations, we would expect in a third generation of research on international organisations that multiple research strategies are applied to highlight different aspects of the international bureaucracies – their structures, resources, authority, relations, functions etc.

Whereas the second generation of international organisation studies viewed international bureaucracies as complex systems, this volume adds two elements:

- Firstly, by outlining explicitly *what components* make up the compound systems of international bureaucracies.
- Secondly, by suggesting *conditions under which* each component is more likely to be mobilised than others.

Whereas the second generation of international organisation research largely applied *either/or* theorising, this study suggests that a *both/and* approach should be applied. Such an approach tends to view the everyday decision-making processes in international bureaucracies as compound (Olsen 2007b). This view reflects the 'growing recognition of human and social complexity' in recent integration theory (Geyer 2003: 19). The idea of compound administrative systems is not new. 'This view of political order harks back to a tradition from Plato, Aristotle, Polybius and Thomas Aquinas and their ideas about how "mixed" orders and combinations of competing, inconsistent and contradictory organising principles and structures may co-exist and balance interest, values and claims to power' (Olsen 2007a: 13–14). However, the *study* of compound administrative systems signifies a fairly new scholarly turn (Olsen 2007a: 13) and it tends to see administrative systems as combining and balancing 'a repertoire of overlapping, supplementary and competing forms' (Olsen 2007b: 22–23). This classical tradition in the study of public administration argues that robust and legitimate administrative systems should balance several competing dynamics sequentially and/or simultaneously (Jacobsen 1960; Olsen 2007a). Multidimensional orders are considered more robust against external shocks and therefore preferable to uni-dimensional orders (March and Olsen 1989; Vibert 2007). Conceptualising public administration as compound systems is based on the assumption that international bureaucracies rest on the mobilisation of multiple complementary sets of institutions, actors, interests, decision-making arenas, values, norms, and cleavages (Schmidt

2006). The empirical yardstick thereof is the mobilisation of intergovernmental, supranational, departmental and epistemic behavioural dynamics among the officials of international bureaucracies. In essence, the transformation of international bureaucracies has to do with the shifting mix of co-existing everyday behavioural dynamics within international bureaucracies.

Recent literature has assumed that the Commission represents a critical case of transformation beyond the Westphalian political order. It is argued that if we do *not* observe transformational dynamics within the Commission we should not expect similar dynamics within other international bureaucracies (Johnston 2005). This assumption is challenged in this volume by advocating that international bureaucracies are multidimensional administrative apparatuses, embodying contradictions and dilemmas that are difficult to resolve and that affect how decisions are made. International bureaucracies are seldom unidimensional as suggested by realist and neo-liberalist theoretical orthodoxy, stressing the intergovernmental nature of international organisations. This book challenges this theoretical orthodoxy by seeing international bureaucracies as compound systems of public administration. They are not merely neutral tools used by member governments to fulfil predetermined preferences; they are also Weberian rule-driven bureaucracies, epistemic communities of professional experts, and socialising institutions that transform nationally oriented officials into community-minded supranational officials (Checkel 2003; Haas 1992; Lemoine 1995). International bureaucracies are multidimensional organisations that should be analysed by fine-grained operational accounts in order to understand their diverse *modi operandi*. They live with inbuilt tensions between at least four behavioural dynamics:

1 An intergovernmental dynamic;
2 A supranational dynamic;
3 A departmental dynamic;
4 An epistemic dynamic.

This book argues that these actor-level dynamics may be complementary rather than contradictory (cf. Herrmann, Risse and Brewer 2004). As suggested by early contingency theory (Thompson 1967: 44), integration research (Pentland 1973: 196) and recent neo-institutional approaches (Olsen 2007a: 13), bureaucracies tend to combine and integrate a multidimensional set of organisational components and decision-making dynamics. We suggest that a compound system of public administration manages to integrate a multidimensional set of behavioural and role perceptions. Behavioural and role perceptions are generalised receipts for action as well as normative systems of self-reference that provide *spontaneous* codes for behaviour and feelings of allegiance to organised communities (Bevir, Rhodes and Weller 2003: 4; Mayntz 1999: 83). Ultimately, such perceptions may guide the actual behaviour of actors because roles provide 'conceptions of reality, standards of assessment, affective ties, and endowments, and [...] a capacity for purposeful action' (March and Olsen 1995: 30; Selden 1997: 140).

An *intergovernmental* dynamic has several elements (see also Chapter 9): firstly, an official is guided by an intergovernmental dynamic if s/he acts in accordance with formal or informal instructions or mandates issued by the member state from which s/he originates. Secondly, officials may operate as a 'Trojan horse' into the international bureaucracies on behalf of the member state(s). This was clearly the perception in the UN Secretariat in 1952 and 1953 when the US government accused several UN officials of being communist representatives (Claude 1956: 207). The third element of the intergovernmental dynamic focuses on the self-perceptions of the officials. An official is intergovernmental if s/he is guided by a loyalty to the home government, has a preference for national interests, and/or enjoys close contact with his or her home base.

A *supranational* dynamic focuses solely on the self-perceptions of the officials. Supranationalism at the level of actor denotes actors' feelings of loyalty and allegiance to the international bureaucracy as a whole and/or their feelings of loyalty and allegiance to the international organisation as a whole. A supranational role implies a 'shift of loyalty' and a 'sense of community' that is integral and endogenous to actors' self-perceptions (Deutsch et al. 1957: 5–6; Haas 1958: 16; Herrmann and Brewer 2004: 6). A supranational role perception denotes that a shared system of rules, norms, principles and codes of conduct is inducted, internalised and taken for granted by actors. This is consistent with the 'type II socialisation' as suggested by Checkel (2005: 804) whereby actors acquire a collective interest and a positional 'organisational personality' inside the international bureaucracy that is distinct from the national, professional and departmental roles previously internalised (Searing 1991: 1249; Simon 1957: 278). They identify personally with the international bureaucracies in which they are employed (Wagenen 1971: 17).

A *departmental* dynamic predicts the civil servants of international bureaucracies to be 'neutral, intelligent, generalist professionals who advise ministers' (Richards and Smith 2004: 779). In short, officials evoking a departmental dynamic tend to evoke an inward-looking behavioural pattern geared towards their 'own' organisation. The officials are expected to evoke classical Weberian civil servant virtues – being guided by formal rules and procedures in everyday decision making, being party-politically neutral, attaching identity towards their unit and division, and abiding by the administrative rules and proper procedures of their international bureaucracy (Barnett and Finnemore 2004: 167). This is the Westminster model that sees officials as neutral, permanent and loyal to the agency (Richards and Smith 2004: 783). The 'departmental officials' 'share the belief that there is a concrete distinction to be made between activities that are inherently controversial (and hence "political") and those that are noncontroversial or technical' (Pentland 1973: 74). We thus expect officials to be guided by the formal rules, routines and procedures of the international bureaucracy in which they are employed. Their role perceptions and loyalties are also directed towards the international bureaucracy, and the officials tend to perceive themselves primarily as representatives of their portfolio and/or unit.

Finally, an *epistemic* dynamic predicts that the staff of international bureaucracies enjoy a great deal of behavioural discretion and are influenced by external professional reference groups (Wilson 1989: 60). They are assumed to prepare dossiers, argue and negotiate on the basis of their professional competences and to legitimate their authority on scientific competences (Haas 1992). Their behaviour is expected to be guided by considerations of scientific and professional correctness and the power of the better argument (Eriksen and Fossum 2000). Their role perceptions and loyalties are primarily directed towards their expertise and educational background as well as towards external professional networks. This is the 'expert official' who is institutionally independent of any constituencies and is a high-flying and mobile technocrat. International bureaucracies dominated by an epistemic dynamic challenge institutional unity by being loosely coupled with the international bureaucracy. Epistemic organisations are typically porous and open institutions staffed by government actors from different external expert institutions such as domestic agencies, universities, research institutions etc. The officials are driven by a so-called 'technical self-determination' (Pentland 1973: 74).

Table 1.1 summarises the proxies introduced above to assess the compound nature of international bureaucracies.

Arguably, the behavioural dynamics of international bureaucracies can be considered compound to the extent that the intergovernmental dynamic is supplemented or replaced by different mixes of supranational, departmental and/or epistemic behavioural dynamics. The focus of this study is thus on the end-point of actor transformation rather than on the process of it (Alderson 2001). Moreover, a mutual relationship between actors' behaviour and roles is assumed: acting in certain ways makes actors better equipped to play particular roles, and by playing these roles the actors may over time take them for granted. Roles that are taken for granted may affect the roles that are played and the behaviour evoked. We also suggest that actors are strongly transformed if they activate supranational, departmental and/or epistemic behaviour and role

Table 1.1 The compound nature of international bureaucracies

An intergovernmental dynamic	A supranational dynamic	A departmental dynamic	An epistemic dynamic
Mandated by domestic government institutions	Loyalty to the 'mission and vision' of the international organisation as a whole	Loyalty towards the international bureaucracy and/or their own portfolio/dossiers	Discipline loyalty
Loyalty to the nation-state and the home government		Mandated by department and unit rules	Professional discretion and room for manoeuvre
Guided by domestic preferences and concerns	Mandated by the leadership of the international bureaucracy	Guided by departmental preferences and concerns	Guided by professional preferences and considerations
	Preferences for 'the common good'		Contacts with professional experts
Co-operation and conflict lines follow territorial boundaries that *transcend* the borders of the bureaucracy	Contacts and co-ordination with the leadership of the international bureaucracy	Co-operation and conflict lines follow organisational boundaries *within* the bureaucracy	Co-operation and conflict lines follow professional boundaries that *transcend* the borders of the bureaucracy
	Co-operation and conflict lines between 'organisational visionaries' and 'non-visionaries' *within* the bureaucracy		

perceptions in a more or less *routinised fashion* (Beyers and Trondal 2004; Zurn and Checkel 2005). In summary, actor transformation implies that the compound set of roles and behaviour evoked by civil servants is less biased by their country of origin than by their supranational, departmental and/or professional affiliations respectively. They become less focused on defending fixed national positions than on discovering and pursuing what is perceived as the 'common good' (the supranational dynamic), acting in accordance with existing rules, roles and administrative routines (the departmental dynamic), and pursuing behaviour and roles that are perceived as scientifically correct (the epistemic dynamic).

Data and methodology

The empirical observations presented in this book aim to illustrate how the four independent variables outlined in Chapter 2 are associated with the decision-making dynamics of the personnel. The purpose of this book is to *illustrate* the predicted relationships between these four variables and the behavioural dynamics among the incumbents of international bureaucracies. This book has mainly explorative ambitions and does not give a systematic variable-by-variable test. In order to arrive at robust conclusions this book offers comparative studies of several international bureaucracies. Studying more than one international bureaucracy serves two purposes: firstly, studying several cases makes it easier to assess the compound nature of international bureaucracies as the robustness of the conclusions is improved by including observations from several laboratories; secondly, comparative studies make it easier to assess the impact of *various* organisational variables, thus illuminating the validity of the organisational approach outlined in Chapter 2.

The empirical observations presented and the conclusions drawn benefit from synchronised comparative studies of permanent and temporary officials in the Commission, the WTO Secretariat and the OECD Secretariat. The study is synchronised in the sense that the same interview guide has been applied to all three bureaucracies. The full list of questions that were used in the interviews is listed in the Appendix. As mentioned above, two administrative sub-units were selected in each of the three international bureaucracies. Firstly, we selected the Trade Department (or its equivalent) as a sector (purpose) organised department in all three cases. Secondly, we selected the General Secretariat (or its equivalent horizontal co-ordinating units) as a horizontal department which is organised according to the principle of process. When selecting officials for interviews in these departments we took care to include respondents from high, medium and low levels in the hierarchy. Essentially, only officials at the level equivalent to the 'A-level' were interviewed. Appointments at this level usually require a university degree.

The interviews were carried out during 2006 and 2007 in Brussels, Geneva and Paris. All interviews were taped and fully transcribed. The book is illustrated with rich quotes from these interviews. All interviewees are treated with full anonymity. Consequently, quotations from particular interviews are referred to in the following way throughout this book: (Commission 2, WTO 15, etc.). In addition to interviews with permanent officials, the project also includes interviews with temporary officials in the Commission and also in the OECD Secretariat. The WTO Secretariat rarely hires temporary officials on short-term contracts. By contrast, the OECD Secretariat hires officials on temporary contracts almost exclusively. Consequently, the OECD officials listed in Table 1.3 are all

Table 1.2 Number of interviewees among permanent officials, by formal rank

	Top level (Director-General, Deputy Director-General or equivalent)	*Medium level (Director, Head of Unit, deputies or equivalent)*	*Low level (Adviser, counsellor, case handler, analyst, officer or equivalent)*	*Total*
The Commission	1	9	14	24
The OECD Secretariat	0	10	18	28
The WTO Secretariat	2	4	13	19
Total	3	23	45	71

temporary officials (see also Chapter 4). The Commission, by contrast, consists mostly of permanent officials with life-long careers. This group of officials, however, is supplemented by some contracted officials, whom we have interviewed. This empirical record on temporary officials represents the most extensive study on seconded officials in international bureaucracy to date (see also Abrams and de Moura 2001; Trondal 2007a; Van Knippenberg and Van Leeuwen 2001; Wessels 1998). Empirical research on temporary government officials is generally rare. This study benefits from three separate but highly co-ordinated studies of Commission secondees. The first study consists mainly of Swedish, Danish and Norwegian secondees (Trondal 2006). Based on similar methodology, this first study was replicated twice on secondees from the Netherlands (Trondal, van den Berg and Suvarierol 2008). This replication applied the same questionnaire and interview guide as in the original study on Nordic secondees. In summary, these data include three surveys (N=169) and three in-depth qualitative interview studies (N=50) on secondees. The mean response rate in the surveys is 73 per cent. Despite covering only a minor selection of Commission secondees, the organisational approach outlined above does not predict significant variation in decision-making dynamics between secondees of different national origins (see Trondal, van den Berg and Suvarierol 2008).

Table 1.3 gives an overview of the 121 interviews conducted in the project.

The questions posed in the interviews were strongly directed at measuring the *perceptions* of the officials with respect to their behaviour (i.e. their contact patterns, the importance assigned to different institutions and sub-institutions etc.), their roles and their identities. In this usage of

Table 1.3 Number of interviewees, by administrative unit

	Trade units	General Secretariats	Other units	Total
The Commission				
Permanent officials	18	6	0	24
Temporary officials	0	0	50	50
The OECD Secretariat	16	12	0	28
The WTO Secretariat	19	0	0	19
Total	53	18	50	121

the interview data, the interviewees are utilised as respondents. This book thus follows the suggestion of Cox and Jacobson (1973: 22) that 'attention must be given to their attitudes and perceptions and more broadly to process. Attitudes and perceptions are crucially important factors affecting actors' behavior.' In other words, the behavioural dynamics of international bureaucracies are studied by the perceptions and experiences among the officials themselves. The perceptions of officials are crucial because the choices made by these officials are often guided by their perceptions. Studying the perceived behavioural dynamics of officials is based on a 'reputational approach' (Jacobsen 2007). Without the ability to study the 'objective' dynamics of organisations, we are left studying how actors perceive it. Admittedly, there are no guarantees that these dynamics always materialise in the actors' behaviour. However, they serve as cognitive and normative frames for action, rendering it more likely than not that particular behavioural dynamics are associated with certain perceptional patterns (Aberbach, Putnam and Rockman 1981: 86; Van Knippenberg and Van Leeuwen 2001: 250). In addition to using interviewees as respondents, they are also utilised as informants in this book. Informants provide inside observations and analyses from within international bureaucracies. In this regard, we are less interested in the 'life worlds' of the interviewees than in the observations these actors make from the international bureau-cracies more broadly. This usage of the interviewees is particularly relevant in Part II of the book where we analyse the macro-, meso- and micro-levels of international bureaucracies.

One note of caution is needed when studying human perceptions. This book presents quotes from the interviews 'as they are', i.e. as they were spoken by the interviewees. However, care is needed in the interpretation of quotes. For example, it is possible that the interviewees respond according to what they think is expected and not according to what they truly mean. It is difficult to control for sources of error such as these in data material. However, the variation in responses indicates that honest responses have been given. The quotes are primarily used as illustrations of behavioural dynamics appearing in international bureaucracies and not as tests of such dynamics in the strict sense of the term. Moreover, there is always the possibility of perceptional errors occurring both in the actors and in the observers. Sometimes interviewees may be unaware of particular perceptions or of biases in these perceptions. Similarly, observers may find it difficult to interpret human perceptions because perceptions are often open to multiple interpretations. Moreover, potential errors may occur in the transfer of perceptions from the actor to the observer because of misunderstandings from the observer. This may add to the problems of interpreting human perceptions. In our interviews, some observations reported by our interviewees turned out to be ambiguous in the sense that they can be subsumed under several decision-making dynamics (cf. Table 1.1). Hence, some quotations might be interpreted according to several dynamics – for example both according to a departmental dynamic and a supranational dynamic. In some cases, therefore, the same observation may reflect different underlying dynamics. Our solution to these potential analytical errors is to try to be explicit about the possibility of multiple interpretations and the ambiguity of the reported observations.

Structuring the volume

This volume is organised into four main parts. In Part I, Chapter 2 outlines the theoretical approach suggested in the book. Part II presents the three international bureaucracies at the three levels of analysis: the *macro-level*, the *meso-level* and the *micro-level*. The macro-level of international bureaucracies consists of the *de jure* and *de facto* functions and roles as well as the wider institutional environment in which the international bureaucracies are embedded. The meso-level of international bureaucracies consists of the organisational components of international bureaucracies, particularly the horizontal and vertical specialisations of the services. Finally, the micro-level of international bureaucracies represents the recruitment and staff of these organisations. In addition, the chapters in Part II provide supplementary descriptive information on international bureaucracies with respect to organisational size, administrative resources, recent reforms and administrative transformations, strategies and administrative policies. In Part II of the book, the Commission is presented in Chapter 3, the OECD Secretariat in Chapter 4, and the WTO Secretariat in Chapter 5.

Part III of the book presents and analyses the empirical results from the project. Each chapter in Part III is organised according to the analytical template outlined in this first chapter: Chapters 6 to 9, respectively, explore the departmental dynamic, the supranational dynamic, the epistemic dynamic and finally the intergovernmental dynamic within international bureaucracies. In summary, Part III explores empirically the compound nature of international bureaucracies.

In Part IV, Chapter 10 concludes by summing up the main observations of the book, draws theoretical lessons and suggests some roads for future research on international bureaucracy. Chapter 10 also draws implications from the observations provided in the book with respect to questions on the autonomy, accountability and efficiency of international bureaucracies.

Notes

1 Among the puzzling observations is the fact that the volume of institutional change within the European Union seems larger than the corresponding volume of institutional change within the member states (Wessels, Maurer and Mittag 2003). Hence, transformational processes at the nation-state level seem imperfectly associated with transformational changes at the EU level.
2 In the EU, Christiansen (2001: 49) demonstrates the increased 'actorness' of the Council Secretariat, particularly within the field of Common Foreign and Security Policy (CFSP). Studies also show that the Commission's power of initiative tends to be weakened during turbulent institutional periods, for example during the Enlargement process and the Convention process (e.g. Sverdrup 2000).
3 For reasons of simplicity, we use the term international organisation to describe the OECD and the WTO as well as the European Union. These three organisations all have nation-states as their members.

2

On the principles of organisation of international bureaucracies

Beyond single-case studies there is a surprising dearth of theoretically informed comparative studies of the *internal dynamics* of international bureaucracies (Barnett and Finnemore 1999; Checkel 2003; Gehring 2003: 4; Gould and Kelman 1970; Johnston 2005; Mouritzen 1990; Reinalda and Verbeek 2004b; Rochester 1986). International bureaucracies – and particularly international civil servants – are the invisible actors in international organisations (Mathiason 2007; Yi-Chong and Weller 2008: 35). '[N]ormative claim-making and abstract theorizing have outrun carefully designed and methodologically sound empirical studies' (Checkel 2004: 1). More recent research on governance in international organisations also pays scant attention to the bureaucracies of these organisations (e.g. Hawkins et al. 2006; Karns and Mingst 2004). One explanation for this lack of scholarly attention to international bureaucracies is the gulf between the literature on international organisations, which has been mainly dominated by rationalist scholars, and public administration literature, which has been informed by organisational and institutional approaches (Trondal 2007a). A clear example of this gulf is the recent book by Acharya and Johnston (2007), which makes a comparative analysis of international organisations without exploring their administrative systems. Rationalist accounts of international organisations – both the realist, neo-realist and liberalist variants – treat the secretariats as an epiphenomenon of the interaction among states. Studies of international organisations have been mainly preoccupied with reporting and analysing the more visible interplay of states rather than the back-stage activities of the secretariats (Rochester 1986). One notable exception is the growing volume of studies of the Commission and to some extent reports on the UN Secretariat. The everyday decision making of international bureaucracies has been of less interest than studying the voting behaviour of states in the general assemblies (Hix 2008), analysing the great leaders of international bureaucracies such as the General Secretary of the UN (Chesterman 2007;

Cox 1969: 202; Rochester 1986) and studying the organisational reforms of international organisations (Bauer and Knill 2007).

One characteristic of the first generation of international bureaucracy studies was their neglect of the compound nature of bureaucracies (see above). The literature was overly descriptive – describing the administrative history of singular international bureaucracies and also analysing the great leaders such as the UN General Secretaries (Jordan 1971). The early international bureaucracy literature was also dominated by single-case studies of individual agencies underneath the international bureaucracy (Claude 1956). The 1960s and 70s also saw several studies of international organisations that treated them as hubs in international networks and regimes rather than as organisations and institutions in their own right (e.g. Nye 1975). Regime analysis tended to view international secretariats as intervening variables that 'somehow affect regime outcomes', but they did not analyse such secretariats as bureaucracies with independent impact (Bauer 2006: 26). Moreover, past research on international bureaucracies has focused more on the functions they perform – such as preparing meetings and documents, providing technical assistance etc. – than on the organisational dimension of the bureaucracy dynamics (see Haftel and Thompson 2006).

The regime literature downplayed the organisational dimension of international organisations, and the role of international organisations was seen mainly as facilitating the regimes (Gehring 2003: 11). The seminal work of Cox and Jacobson (1973: 428) reflected this lack of organisational focus in international bureaucracy studies, concluding that 'international organizations facilitate the orderly management of intergovernmental relations without significantly changing the structure of power that governs these relations'. Recent regime literature, however, attributes a larger and more independent role to international bureaucracies in providing independent, substantive inputs to decision making and/or amplifying outputs (see Underdal 2008: 198).

The dearth of comparative studies of international bureaucracies is paralleled by a general lack of comparative studies of domestic administrative systems. Most comparative studies of domestic administrative systems are country-by-country studies (e.g. Bekke and van der Meer 2000; Christensen and Lægreid 2002; Olsen and Peters 1996). The only international bureaucracy that attracted early scholarly attention was the Commission (e.g. Coombes 1970; Michelmann 1978). This attention has been mainly targeted at studying Commission history, reform, recruitment patterns and decision-making processes (e.g. Bauer and Knill 2007; Egeberg 2006; Trondal 2007a). Many books on the Commission are also textbooks rather than fresh empirical contributions to the field (e.g. Cini 1996; Edwards and Spence 1997). Moreover, few scholars have systematically compared the Commission with other international bureaucracies. Hence, the *sui generis* claim that the Commission is not comparable to any other international bureaucracy has been mostly assumed and not sufficiently tested. This book argues that the Commission is just one example of an international bureaucracy, albeit a crucial one.

Two main bodies of literature have combined theoretical innovation with the empirical testing of the everyday decision-making dynamics of international bureaucracies. The first strand of research was the functionalist and neo-functionalist studies of the Commission and the UN Secretary, inspired by Ernst Haas (e.g. Alger 1963; Ernst 1978; Wolf 1973). The second body of research is the more recent institutionalist and social constructivist literature on organisations such as the EU, the Council of Europe and NATO (e.g. Checkel 2005; Zurn and Checkel 2005). However, even recent literature on international bureaucracies lacks a truly comparative design and is overly focused on the UN Secretary (Mathiason 2007). Neither the early neo-functional nor the more recent institutional scholarships have systematically studied the executive arms of international organisations. Nor have these bodies of literature emphasised the relationships between the generic organisational properties of international bureaucracies and the behavioural dynamics of the personnel (Kratochwil and Ruggie 1986: 761). Hence, there has been a lack of three kinds of international bureaucracy studies:

1 Comparative studies of international bureaucracies.
2 Studies with an actor-level focus that explore everyday decision-making dynamics within international bureaucracies.
3 Studies with an organisational focus that explore how the formal organisation of international bureaucracies impacts on the everyday decision-making dynamics of international bureaucracies.

Notably, existing studies have not solved the enduring puzzle as to whether supranational loyalties among the officials of international bureaucracies are the result of pre-socialisation at a national level (Hooghe 2005) or of re-socialisation processes within the international bureaucracy itself (Trondal 2007b). This study demonstrates not only that supranational loyalties among the officials of international bureaucracies reflect the *organisational* embedding of the officials within the international bureaucracy itself, but also that processes of pre-socialisation (for example within international universities) and re-socialisation within the international bureaucracies play a certain role in this respect. The most robust test of the *organisational* dimension of supranationalism is the fact that the national officials seconded to the Commission, evoke supranational roles shortly after entering the Commission, and also that this supranational role is significantly reduced when the official leaves the Commission (Trondal, van den Berg and Suvarierol 2008).

The principles of organisation

This book is influenced by the organisational and neo-institutional theory turn in political science. These approaches see political and administrative life as contextualised and embedded. This turn contributes to introducing organisational and institutional variables to the study of international bureaucracies. We believe that organisational theory is a powerful tool for approaching such organisations. Political processes and political systems cannot be adequately understood or explained without including both the organisational dimension(s) of executive orders (Olsen 2007a) and the organisational principles structuring international bureaucracies.

Students of international bureaucracies tend to adopt neo-liberal, realist and principal–agent approaches in order to understand the baseline dynamics of international organisations (Hasenclever, Mayer and Rittberger 1996). Basically, these accounts focus on patterns of co-operation and conflict among states and see international bureaucracies as neutral vehicles for maximising state preferences and for lowering transaction costs among state actors. However, recent studies of international bureaucracies have made a combined 'institutionalist and constructivist turn' and have rediscovered questions of actor socialisation, complex learning and cognitive framing of norms and rules (Checkel 2005; Trondal 2007a). International bureaucracies are pictured as more than empty vessels and neutral arenas in which state representatives gather (Finnemore 1996: 35). An equivalent rediscovery of institutions was made in the field of organisation theory over 20 years ago (March and Olsen 1984). The independent variables outlined below benefit from these organisational and institutional schools of thought. One additional criterion for selecting the independent variables for this book is how successfully they have survived past empirical tests.

The principles of organisation provide a codified and normative embedding of organisational members. In order to understand the process whereby actors adopt particular behaviour and roles, one has to unpack the normative structures embedded in these principles of organisation. Actors are boundedly rational with limited computational abilities. Formal organisations provide cognitive and normative shortcuts and categories that simplify and guide the actors' choice of behaviour and roles (Simon 1957).[1] Organisations provide cognitive maps that simplify and categorise complex information, offer procedures for reducing transaction costs, and give regulative norms that add cues for appropriate behaviour as well as physical boundaries and temporal rhythms that guide actors' perceptions of relevance with respect to behaviour and role (Barnett and Finnemore 1999; March and Olsen 1998). Organisations also discriminate between what conflicts are activated and what conflicts are de-activated (Egeberg 2006). By organising civil servants into permanent bureaucracies within international organisations, a system of 'rule followers and role players' is established above and beyond domestic executive institutions (March and Olsen 1998: 952).

Four organisational variables are discussed in the following, specifying conditions under which the officials of international bureaucracies are likely to adopt intergovernmental, supranational, departmental and/or epistemic decision-making dynamics in a more or less routinised way (Zurn and Checkel 2005).

Organisational properties of international bureaucracies

The first independent variable considered is the core organisational properties of international bureaucracies. Formal organisations are normative structures 'composed of rules and roles specifying, more or less clearly, who is expected to do what, and how' (Egeberg 2003a: 117). Stein Rokkan (1987: 212) argued that political institutions are often two-dimensional, organised along one territorial and one functional axis. One central organising principle of the General Assemblies of international organisations is their territorial organisation of political geography, mirroring the spatial structuring of state sovereignty. In contrast, the organisation of international bureaucracies typically mirrors the policy sectors covered by the organisations and the processes used to support these policy sectors. Robert W. Cox and Harold K. Jacobson (1973) saw the organisational similarities between national executive institutions and international bureaucracies. According to Wagenen (1971: 5 – original emphasis), '[t]he *similarities* overwhelm the differences between national and international administration'. Most executive organisations, both domestic and international, are horizontally organised according to the principles of purpose and process (Gulick 1937). The argument here is that international bureaucracies organised by purpose and process are likely to accompany behavioural and role perceptions that are departmentally and epistemically oriented respectively, and not biased by territoriality. Hence, due to the formal organisation of international bureaucracies, the territorial principle of Westphalia is likely to be transcended by departmental and epistemic behavioural dynamics.

The behaviour and roles evoked by the officials of international bureaucracies are thus likely to be affected by the *formal structure* of the services, which is the *horizontal* specialisation into departments and units, and the *vertical* specialisation of the hierarchy of international bureaucracies.

Firstly, consider the vertical specialisation of international bureaucracies. Executive organisations are typically vertically organised according to a specialised structure of rank. One proxy of the vertical organisation of international bureaucracies is the formal rank position of the personnel. Arguably, officials in top-rank positions are likely to represent the organisation as a whole (thus evoking a supranational role), whereas officials in bottom-rank positions are more likely to represent their unit (evoking a departmental role) and professional expertise (evoking an epistemic role) (Mayntz 1999: 84). The Commission, the OECD Secretariat and the WTO Secretariat are all vertically organised. The argument suggested here is that vertically specialised international bureaucracies have the potential for *disciplining and controlling* civil servants by administrative command and individual incentive systems like salary and promotion (Egeberg 2003a). Hence, vertically specialised international bureaucracies are likely to have a stronger impact on incumbents' behaviour and role perceptions than less vertically specialised international bureaucracies (Bennett and Oliver 2002: 425; Egeberg 2003a: 137; Knight 1970).

Secondly, with respect to the horizontal specialisation of international bureaucracies, the department and unit structure of administrative systems is typically specialised according to two conventional principles of organisation: purpose and process (Gulick 1937). Firstly, formal organisations may be specialised by the major *purpose* served – such as research, health, food safety etc. This principle of organisation tends to activate patterns of co-operation and conflicts among incumbents along sectoral (departmental) cleavages (Egeberg 2006). Arguably, organisation by major purpose served is likely to bias behavioural dynamics towards a departmental logic where preferences, contact patterns, roles and loyalties are directed towards portfolios, departments and units. This mode of horizontal specialisation results in less than adequate horizontal co-ordination *across* departmental units and better co-ordination *within* units (Ansell 2004: 237). The Commission administration – with its Directorates-General (DGs) and units – is a prominent example of this horizontal principle of specialisation (Egeberg and Trondal 1999). The Commission is a horizontally pillarised system of government specialised by purpose and with fairly weak organisational capabilities for horizontal co-ordination at the top through presidential command (Dimitrakopoulos and Kassim 2005). As officials spend most of their time and energy on organisational sub-units, they are expected to make affective ties primarily towards their sub-unit and less towards the organisation as a whole (Ashford and Johnson 2001: 36). Hence, the officials of international bureaucracies are likely to activate behavioural and role perceptions that reflect their affiliations towards units and divisions to a larger extent than their affiliations towards the international bureaucracy as a whole.

One observation highlighted in previous research is that actors' roles are likely to be transformed in highly issue-specific situations (Zurn and Checkel 2005). One reason may be that actors tend to be granted a great amount of leeway and autonomy in horizontally purpose-specialised organisations. Specialisation by purpose may accompany the emergence of epistemic communities of sector experts who enjoy shared understandings of causal relationships between means and ends, worldviews, roles and norms of appropriate behaviour. Arguably, the horizontal specialisation of international bureaucracies by purpose may accompany a need for exclusive and professional competences in order to act effectively within them. Moreover, such expert communities are less bound to territorial borders and are often loosely tied to particular organisations (Haas 1992). Participants in such networks often have life-long commitments and careers attached to them, accompanying the emergence of epistemic expert roles among such officials (Haas 1990: 42; Hasenclever, Mayer and Rittberger 1996: 209). This argument implies that the WTO Secretariat, the OECD Secretariat and the Commission may activate an epistemic behavioural dynamic due to their horizontal organisational issue-specificity. This argument also implies that epistemic dynamics are likely to be stronger within the specialised divisions of international bureaucracies (for example within Commission units) than at the helm of these bureaucracies (for example within the College of Commissioners).

A second principle of horizontal specialisation present within most international bureaucracies is the principle of the major *process* utilised – such as general secretariat, administration, legal services, personnel services etc. (Gulick 1937). This horizontal principle encourages the horizontal integration of functional departments and the disintegration of the major purposes served. Within the Commission the internal services such as the Legal Service, the DG for Translation and the General Secretariat illustrate the process principle. For example, the processes provided by the General Secretariat aim to integrate the different sector DGs into one coherent Commission apparatus. The process principle is likely to accompany departmental behaviour among the staff focused on the functions of the unit. For example, officials in the Commission's General Secretariat are likely to develop an inter-DG picture of their work by activating a 'helicopter view' of the whole Commission. Officials employed in process-organised units such as the General Secretariat, however, are less likely to activate an epistemic logic. This stems from the lack of specialised attention devoted to particular policy areas (as for example in DG Trade of the Commission) and the more generalist orientation of the officials. Arguably, organisation by major process is less conducive to epistemic behaviour than departmental behaviour among the incumbents.

In different parts of this book attention is directed particularly towards the sub-structures of international bureaucracies, which are the units organised by purpose (trade) and units organised by process (the general secretariat in all three international bureaucracies). One reason for selecting trade departments and the general secretariats of these international bureaucracies is that they illustrate the two organisational principles presented above and that there is a lack of research on these sub-units. Even a key institution such as the General Secretariat of the Commission remains surprisingly under-explored (Kassim 2004b). Officials embedded in purpose-organised units – such as DG Trade in the Commission – are likely to evoke strong departmental (portfolio) and epistemic (expert) behavioural dynamics. On the other hand, officials located in the general secretariat of international bureaucracies are less likely to employ an expert (epistemic) dynamic and more likely to emphasise the departmental role of integrating the different services of the whole international bureaucracy. Moreover, officials in the general secretariats are also more likely to evoke the supranational role by acquiring an overarching identification with the international bureaucracy as a whole. General secretariats typically have horizontal tasks of co-ordinating the work of the whole international bureaucracy as well as vertically integrating the administrative and political levels of the international bureaucracy – which is most relevant in the Commission. These organisational functions are likely to foster supranational perceptions among incumbents because their portfolios cover larger terrains of the international bureaucracy as a whole.

In addition, international bureaucracies may have a complementary territorial component in their organisational structure. For example, the very fact that civil servants of international bureaucracies are sometimes recruited from member-state governments contributes to a *de facto* territorial component by their *de facto* national origin. We do not expect the nationality of staff to significantly affect their perceptions of behaviour, roles and identities. However, the staff's national origins may sometimes be supported by territorial organisational components inside the international bureaucracies – such as when the administration is internally organised according to geographical desks. The geographical specialisation of administrative units may foster the enactment of an intergovernmental behavioural dynamic among the personnel in everyday decision-making processes. For example, civil servants in the Council of Ministers are shown to have fairly strong intergovernmental orientations, although these are supplemented with departmental and supranational orientations (Egeberg, Schaefer and Trondal 2003). The territorial organisation of parts of Whitehall, for example the Welsh Office and the Scottish Executive, may foster some degrees territorial preferences among the incumbents and an emphasis on territorial variation and exceptionalism (Griffiths 1999). Smith (2001) shows that officials from the Scottish Executive who are seconded to the Commission tend to reinforce existing (largely intergovernmental) dynamics rather than being transformed into European Mandarins (Eppink 2007).

Recruitment procedures

The perceptions of officials within international bureaucracies regarding their own decision-making behaviour, roles and identities may be greatly affected by the procedures applied to recruit the staff. Different procedures for recruitment tend to bring in different people and keep them more or less autonomous vis-à-vis past constituencies (Cox 1969). This book considers two basic recruitment procedures: recruitment may be based on a merit principle as in most Western democracies, or on a quota principle or other systems of patronage or *parachutage* as in the top echelon of the American civil service (Ingraham 1995: 9). While the merit principle recruits permanent civil servants on the basis of competence and past achievements, the quota principle typically recruits officials on more temporary contracts on the basis of, for example, professional, sectoral or territorial mandates (Ingraham 1995: xix). The autonomy of international bureaucracies is arguably strongly dependent on the recruitment procedures adopted because different procedures for recruitment tend to affect actors' decision-making behaviour and role perceptions differently (Mouritzen 1990: 39). Recruitment to the Secretariat of the League of Nations, the UN Secretariat, the NATO Secretariat, the first High Authority of the European Community and many other international bureaucracies relied heavily on the recruitment of temporary officials from the member-state governments. Today, international bureaucracies are more inclined to recruit officials on the basis of merit into more or less permanent positions, and the inner core of the international bureaucracies is less dependent on 'participant subsystems' composed of temporary officials (Cox and Jacobson 1973).

This book argues and demonstrates that the behavioural perceptions of officials within international bureaucracies are better explained by considering the way the officials were recruited than by who is paying their salaries. We thus challenge claims suggesting that supranational loyalties are contingent 'on whether one is paid by one's country of origin or by the organization' (Reinalda and Verbeek 2004a: 20). Whereas the merit principle is a recruitment tool for building autonomous executive institutions with permanent officials, the quota principle is less able to safeguard the establishment of permanent, continuous and autonomous government institutions (Bekke and van der Meer 2000: 281–282; Ingraham 1995: xix). The argument advanced here is that, *ceteris paribus*, the merit principle applied to international bureaucracies fosters supranational, departmental and epistemic roles and behaviour more effectively than the quota principle because there is no inherent territorial logic in the meritocratic principle (Bennett and Oliver 2002: 418). This principle is in essence blind to nationality. The principle of merit secures both the autonomy of international bureaucracies as far as recruitment is concerned and non-territorial loyalties among the incumbents. Whereas the merit principle is central to the Commission as well as to the WTO Secretariat, the quota principle is more active in the OECD Secretariat. The quota principle is conducive to the emergence of an intergovernmental dynamic among the staff. The national connection is upheld under the quota principle, securing a staff loyal to the domestic constituency. Intergovernmental organisations typically employ the quota principle and different systems of secondment in order to uphold the geographical balances of posts and territorially loyal delegates, such as in the NATO and the UN Secretariats (Bennett and Oliver 2002: 413; Mouritzen 1990; Reymond and Mailick 1986).

Studying officials in international bureaucracies sometimes implies studying officials who have had previous careers in national institutions prior to entering the international bureaucracies. One can assume that previous careers in national institutions make officials sensitive to national concerns. One can also assume that officials with previous careers in domestic sector ministries and agencies are receptive to sectoral preferences of domestic origin. International civil servants with previous careers in national institutions are particularly evident among the officials of international bureaucracies who are seconded on short-term contracts. The WTO does not employ seconded personnel to the same extent as the Commission and the OECD Secretariat. In the WTO, permanent positions are the rule. Officials are recruited on the basis of merit, and personnel tend to remain in the WTO once they have entered. In the OECD, a large and increasing number of the employees are seconded consultants and researchers. Furthermore, in the OECD apparatus the term 'permanent' has lost its significance since 70 to 80 per cent of staff are employed on time-limited contracts. The whole OECD Secretariat may be considered a 'contracted administration'. It can be assumed that seconded officials are less likely to become supranationally oriented than permanent civil servants, and are more likely to evoke an intergovernmental dynamic.

Organisational affiliations
The third independent variable considered is the characteristics of the actor relationships that may develop between organisations and within organisations. Both rationalist and cognitive accounts of international organisations 'have been rather silent on the role of domestic factors' (Hasenclever, Mayer and Rittberger 1996: 221). This study stresses the fact that international bureaucracies serve as parts of complex webs of organisations, including other international bureaucracies, member-state institutions, private organisations etc. Different international bureaucracies may have institutionalised mutual relationships because of overlapping jurisdictions, overlapping members and histories of co-operation (Cox and Jacobsson 1973: 382; Haas 1990: 27).

Civil servants of international bureaucracies have typically multiple institutional affiliations – both nationally and internationally – that pose multiple cognitive frames, incentives and norms of appropriate conduct (March and Olsen 1998). We assume that the behaviour and role perceptions of officials are a product of their *primary* (international bureaucracies) and *secondary* (external) organisational affiliations. A primary affiliation means that officials are employed in the organisation, are paid by the organisation, give loyalty to the organisation and use most of their time and energy in that organisation. A secondary affiliation means those organisations that officials are affiliated to in addition to their primary organisation, and thus they are *not* permanently employed by, paid by or give primary loyalty to that organisation. They use only partial time and energy within secondary organisations. This line of argumentation assumes that there is a hierarchy of organisational memberships. The demands that these affiliations pose may conflict, thereby inducing role and behavioural conflicts among the officials (Barnett 1993). For example, most Commission officials as well as officials of the WTO Secretariat use the majority of their time and energy within their DGs and units (Commission) and specialised divisions (WTO Secretariat), and less within other institutions. This implies that their portfolios are likely to govern their behaviour and role perceptions more strongly than external (secondary) institutions. The status of primary and secondary affiliations may thus be measured by the length and intensity of affiliation to each of them. One effect of intensive and long tenure within international bureaucracies is that these institutions become 'real' in a social psychological sense to the officials. Both students of EU institutions and students of mass opinion conclude that actors tend to develop multiple identities, and that supranational, national and professional identities supplement each other. Different roles are activated in different situations, and they become partly meshed and blended into each other over time (Lewis 2000; Risse and Maier 2003; Trondal 2004a), although the relative primacy of organisational affiliations is expected to impact on the role selection among staff.

There is an inbuilt tension between a logic of recency and a logic of primacy. While the logic of recency implies that recently evoked roles and behaviour are likely to be evoked again (March 1994: 70), the logic of primacy implies that roles and behaviour that are evoked within primary institutions tend to be enacted in secondary institutions as well. Arguably, the logic of recency may trump the logic of primacy if actors engage for a long time and interact intensively within secondary (external) institutions. The logic of recency is also likely to affect actors' behaviour and roles if there is a sufficient temporal gap between the primary and secondary affiliation. Hence, the amount of time spent in the secondary institution and the amount of time passing between occupation in the primary and the secondary institution may condition the relative importance of the logic of recency and the logic of primacy (Johnston 2005). Consequently, permanent officials of international bureaucracies are likely to be affected by a logic of primacy whereas officials of international bureaucracies on temporary contracts are more likely to act on the premise of a logic of recency.

Finally, the logic of primacy is conditioned by the *properties of actor interaction*. Actors may have dense, moderate or low levels of interaction across organisational tiers. Interaction may also be formalised or based on informal codes of conduct. Role change often follows from long-term and informal interaction, often involving face-to-face encounters (Lewis 2003; Olsen 2003b: 18). However, empirical studies challenge the assumption that the *length* of participation among the officials of international bureaucracies accompanies a re-socialisation of them (e.g. Ernst 1978; Trondal 2001). Transactionalists and functionalists have argued that intensive and face-to-face interaction between state agents leads to the development of common identities and roles, and a shift towards a greater alignment with the international organisation (Deutsch et al. 1957). Internalisation and social learning of roles seem to occur through the *intensive* repetition of role and action. Direct and intensive experiences of international bureaucracies increase the likelihood that civil servants evoke roles and behaviour consistent with the shared norms and values of the international bureaucracies (the logic of primacy). Jean Monnet believed that 'men are changed by what they do' (quoted in Duchêne 1994: 376).

Consequently, the tenure of civil servants is likely to mould their behavioural and role perceptions. Arguably, senior officials with life-long service are more likely to evoke supranational and departmental behaviour and roles than newly recruited officials (Mourtizen 1990: 44). Findings suggest that loyalty towards any international bureaucracy is assumed to be a function of the official's length of service (Reinalda and Verbeek 2004a: 20).

Demographic characteristics
Finally, organisations are composed of actors with demographic characteristics (e.g. education, tenure, age and nationality) that may guide actors' perceptions of their own behaviour, roles and identities. It can be assumed that the demographic profiles of officials are likely to penetrate their behaviour in weakly organised and institutionalised situations. This argument gives the following prediction: *ceteris paribus*, highly educated civil servants within porous expert organisations are more likely to evoke roles as independent sector experts than roles as national representatives (Cortell and Peterson 2003: 6). Moreover, officials of international bureaucracies with an international education and with a multinational family background are more likely to be supranationally oriented than

officials with mainly a national education and family. This is due to their parental and educational pre-socialisation prior to entering the international bureaucracies. Finally, young civil servants are more likely to become guided by supranational and epistemic behavioural patterns than older civil servants who have been subject to domestic pre-socialisation for longer periods of time.

Note

1 By contrast, informal structures contain non-codified normative structures.

Part II

International bureaucracies

3

The European Commission

The Commission systematically excludes territorial preferences, institutions and concerns from its agenda-setting processes. Departmental, supranational and epistemic behavioural dynamics are likely to reflect the organisational components of the Commission services. This chapter introduces the Commission organisation and personnel. As will be shown in Chapters 6 to 9, the Commission is indeed a compound system of international bureaucracy, balancing departmental, epistemic, supranational and to some extent intergovernmental dynamics in everyday decision-making processes. The conditional mobilisation of each of these dynamics is arguably attributable to the Commission organisation. The Commission is a multi-standard organisation that combines and balances several partly conflicting and poorly integrated concerns by its organisational corpus and personnel. This chapter also shows the Commission as balancing and integrating an autonomous civil service staffed mainly by permanent officials, although supplemented by temporary short-term contracted personnel from the member states.

This chapter is organised as follows. The first section explores the *macro-level* of the Commission, i.e. the core functions and roles that the Commission performs as well as the wider institutional environment within which the Commission is embedded. The next section unpacks the *meso-level* of the Commission, i.e. the formal organisation of the Commission services with respect to both horizontal and vertical specialisation. The Commission is pictured as balancing several organisational principles, notably the principles of purpose and process. Particular attention is paid to two DGs that illustrate each of these competing principles of organisation. Firstly, the principle of purpose is illustrated by DG Trade. Secondly, the principle of process is shown by the General Secretariat. The succeeding section introduces the *micro-level* of the Commission – the Commission personnel. Focus is directed towards the distinction between permanent and temporary Commission officials. Some final comments are also made with respect to recent reforms of the Commission.

The macro-level: the institutional environments of the Commission

Almost all books list some five or six core functions and roles that the Commission performs, with the exact number depending on how the functions and roles are defined. Some of these functions are clearly stated in the treaties guiding the European Union while others are the result of how the EU system operates and its relations with its organisational environment.

The function that is often mentioned first is that of initiator of new EU legislation. The Commission has something of a monopoly when it comes to initiating new legislation, especially within the EC framework, while in other areas the initiating power is shared with the member states. No new legislation can be adopted by the Council and the Parliament unless the Commission has put forward a proposal. However, what may look like an important function, that of formally initiating new proposals, is somewhat diminished when the origin of many initiatives is taken into account. In fact, a closer look reveals that as many as 80 per cent of all initiatives can be traced back to a source other than the Commission (Larsson and Trondal 2006). It is often either the Parliament or the Council that is behind a Commission initiative, both having the right to 'encourage' the Commission to put forward a proposal on a certain topic or to further explore certain aspects in different policy areas.

A second function of importance is as the executor of EU policy. Despite the fact that in many areas the actual implementation of EU legislation and policy is carried out by the administrations of the member states, the Commission supervises, evaluates and – with the assistance of the member states – adopts implementing provisions. In this way, the Commission plays an administrative and management role, especially in areas such as trade, competition and agriculture (Sverdrup 2007).

A new component of this function is the increasing number of EU-level agencies, all under the supervision of the Commission but with varying degrees of autonomy. What was some ten years ago just a handful of bureaux or agencies located in a few member states is today a mosaic of organisations of well over 30 entities spread across more than 15 member states. The execution and implementation of EU policies has over the years increasingly become a question of managing the work of EU agencies rather than just the internal work of the Commission and its relations with the member states' administrations (Groenleer 2006; Trondal and Jeppesen 2008).

A third role for the Commission is to represent the EU in negotiations with third countries and in many international organisations. In the ongoing WTO negotiations on world trade the EU is, for example, represented by the Commission and not by the member states. On other occasions involving international organisations the Commission can appear as an additional 28-member state with its own seat (Bàtora 2008).

A fourth role is to act as the guardian and the conscience of the treaties and the *acquis communautaire*. Should the Commission find that a decision has been taken that is not in conformity with EU regulations, it is up to the Commission to warn, penalise and eventually bring companies, member states and even EU institutions before the European Court of Justice (ECJ). A fifth role, sometimes seen as part of the fourth, is to be the 'engine' of the EU, the force that propels the co-operation between the member states forward. Originally this role was aimed at further and deeper integration, while today it is perhaps more about maintaining the pace of integration and making it more efficient. Finally, the sixth role is to be the mediator helping the member states and the EU institutions to reach common agreements and decisions.

The roles and functions of the Commission are carried out in a system with at least three political and administrative dimensions. First of all, the Commission has to act within the boundaries drawn by the member states. Secondly, the Commission is one part of the system of EU institutions as defined by the treaties. Thirdly, the Commission increasingly plays an active part in the international political arena.

The member states and the Commission

In the first dimension, the Commission has to manoeuvre between the interests of the different member states and the tensions between them. The traditional rivalry between the bigger member states – especially France, Germany and the United Kingdom – is one factor to take into account. Historically speaking, the Germany–France axis has been a decisive factor in maintaining progress and change in the European Union, and the efficiency of that alliance has affected the performance of the Commission over time (Dinan 2004).

Another tension is between large member states and smaller ones, which is usually most clearly visible when new treaties are to be signed. However, what is large and what is small may often be ambiguous and may vary from one policy area to another: a small state can have 'large' interests in a specific policy area and the other way around. Therefore, it is often difficult to identify more permanent divisions between and coalitions among the member states. However, it is often said that there is a special relationship between the smaller member states and the Commission, where the smaller states tend to side with the Commission in exchange for its support against the large member states. The small member states often see the Commission as the referee, i.e. the most important player on the field who makes sure that every member state, especially the large ones, sticks to the rules of the game. On other occasions, northern Europe with its tradition of output-oriented public administrations opposes southern Europe where the public administrations have a more legalistic profile. New member states, especially the most recent ones, can also be found plotting against the older member states.

The relationship between the Commission and the member states is perhaps best described in terms of interdependency, although of a very complicated type. It is often analysed in terms of a two-tier game where the member states try to use (and sometimes abuse) the European arena for their ambitions in the domestic arena. On some occasions member states will try to transfer their domestic agendas to the European level with the help of the Commission in order to solve domestic problems (Larsson and Trondal 2006).

However, on the whole the Commission tries to cultivate close co-operation with the governments and administrations of the member states since it needs their support for the preparation of drafts for new legislation and is dependent on national administrations for the execution of EU legislation. Consequently, the institutional links between the Commission and the member states are numerous, the most important one of which is the Commissioner. Each member state has one Commissioner, and although they are officially forbidden to receive or demand instructions from the government or from anybody else, the Commissioners may be the eyes and ears of the national governments vis-à-vis the work of the Commission. This is a communication channel that can go both ways: a Commissioner may not only inform its own government of what is going on in the Commission and explain EU decision and policy to the public, s/he may also inform the Commission of his or her own country's policy and ambitions (see Chapters 6 to 9).

However, being a player in this game is also about handling different types of interested groups and sub-governments. To many of the non-governmental organisations and sub-governments in the member states, the EU level – and particularly the Commission – offers a complementary or alternative source of influence for authoritative decision making and legislation. Likewise they are a potential source of alternative information to the Commission regarding national government business – a way to balance influence exerted by member states' governments. The EU and the Commission operate within a multilevel system where not only national governments but also different forms of sub- and non-governmental actors are considered to be important participants (Bache and Flinders 2004; Loughlin 2001).

An institutional three-party game
EU policies are shaped by a three-party game in which the key players are the Commission, the European Parliament and the Council of the European Union. However, in reality it is often a four-party game since

the European Court of Justice has a role to play. The relations between these institutions are organised in a power-sharing setting where all institutions have exclusive powers in certain areas, and in others the influence and the responsibility is shared. Originally the dynamic three-party game between the Commission, the Council and the Parliament was to a large extent a two-party game because the European Parliament had significantly less influence. Later on, as the Parliament became a real player, the Commission had to find constructive solutions to problems and to compromise when the Council and the Parliament disagreed. This role as an honest broker has perhaps diminished over the years since nowadays, as a result of the introduction of the co-decision procedure, the Parliament and the Council often find workable solutions without the help of the Commission (McElroy 2006). Nevertheless, the Commission is almost always involved in discussions between the Parliament and the Council, and until the Conciliation Committee is called in it can always withdraw its original proposal.

Although based on a power-sharing system, an important aspect of the three-party power game is the unbalanced construction of the whole system, giving more formal powers to the Council than to the other two parties. This means that the Parliament constantly tries to establish new procedures or new practices in order to enhance its own influence. This ambition is also partly true of the Commission, but here it is more a question of maintaining the influence and power given to it in the twentieth century. In fact, during the first decade of the twenty-first century the established influence of the Commission has been under strong attack which has forced the Commission onto the defensive (Kassim 2008). It is also clear that many of the new powers given to the Parliament during the last 20 years have been at the expense of the Commission. However, it is important to remember that many of the restrictions imposed on the Commission by the Parliament are in reality aimed at the Council, which is regarded by the Parliament as its main opponent.

The international arena

The Treaty of Rome gave the European Union (specifically, the European Community) and the Commission an important role in the international arena when the competences on trade matters and trade policy were transferred to the Community level. Today, within areas of exclusive Community competences, the Commissioner for Trade represents the EU in the WTO negotiations and thus speaks with 'one voice' on behalf of the EU27. However, before negotiations between the Commission and third countries are held, extensive discussions among the member states have defined the mandate and the guidelines for the Commission. The member states also closely review and follow the negotiations that take place, and the agreements finally reached have to be adopted by the Council. In this area, the role of the Commission is to help to define and protect the common interests among the member states vis-à-vis international organisations and large industrial states, such as the US and Japan, and rising new markets and competitors, such as China, Brazil and India (National Intelligence Council 2008: 29–35).

In areas of legally exclusive competences such as in trade policy the Commission acts as a true Community government by representing the member states in international negotiations – for example G8 and OECD. In areas of shared competences the Commission and the Presidency of the EU may act as an additional and complementary voice to the member states. Thirdly, the Commission also has a role to play in areas such as foreign (CFSP) and defence (CFDP) policy. However, the legal competences of the Commission and the Commissioner of External Relations in the CFSP and CFDP are limited and the corresponding role of the Council is larger – chaired by the High Representative. Close co-operation between the High Representative in the Council and the Commissioner of External Relations is a well-established practice, and gradually a special service is being developed merging the two functions and offices into one. However, the exact organisation and function of this new post is still pending the outcome of the ratification of the Lisbon Treaty.

The different functions and roles of the Commission and the different settings within which they are performed give rise to conflicting pressures on the Commission that may trigger departmental, intergovernmental, supranational, and epistemic roles and behaviour among the Commission staff.

The meso-level: the Commission organisation

The Commission was established in 1957 under the leadership of President Hallstein, who succeeded the High Authority under the presidency of Jean Monnet (1952–1957). Organising the Commission into 'vertical columns' was Hallstein's idea (Dumoulin 2007a: 221). Following Hallstein's ideas, since 1957 the Commission has been horizontally organised with a total of nine DGs numbered from I to IX. Émile Noël, the long-term Secretary-General of the Commission, recalls that President Hallstein had clear ideas about the organisation of the Commission; he wanted a 'great administration', both strong and hierarchical (Dumoulin 2007a: 221). Today the number of DGs totals 42.

At the very outset, President Hallstein emphasised the autonomy of the Commission, both in the recruitment of staff and in the day-to-day functioning of the services (Bitsch 2007a: 60). The autonomy of the Commission, however, did not mean that it should be politically neutral:

Mansholt felt that, as a Member of the Commission, he also had to be impartial, of course, but that did not mean remaining neutral: 'to serve the interest of Europe, it is essential to express political opinions. In its absolute independence, the Commission itself will judge what that meant'. (Van der Harst 2007: 174)

An essential component of the Commission organisation from its early beginnings to the present day has been the horizontal division of the work by portfolio. Hence, the organisation of the Commission according to the portfolio logic emerged very early on as an organisational solution inside the Commission (Bitsch 2007b: 190). The horizontal structuring of the services in a series of DGs has been described as organising the Commission into separate 'baronies' or 'fiefdoms' (Kassim 2008: 652).

Political orders and administrative systems are hybrids and inconsistent collections 'of institutions that fit more or less into a coherent system' (Ansell 2004: 234; March and Olsen 2006). Organisations tend to accumulate conflicting organisational principles over time through horizontal and vertical specialisations (Olsen 2007a). This is clearly also perceived by Commission officials today. One of our interviewees reports that:

Each enlargement has brought to the Commission administrative structure some richness. Originally, it was conceived very much like the French system, but it has lost a lot of it throughout the years. There is a series of systems, it is very hybrid. (Commission 2)

When specialising formal organisations, like the Commission services, horizontally, two conventional principles have been suggested by Luther Gulick (1937). Firstly, formal organisations may be specialised by the major *purpose* served – such as research, health, food safety etc. This principle of organisation tends to activate patterns of co-operation and conflict among incumbents along sectoral (departmental) cleavages. Co-ordination and contact patterns tend to be channelled *within* departmental portfolios rather than between them (see Chapters 6 to 9). Arguably, organisation by the major purpose served is likely to bias decision-making dynamics towards a departmental logic where preferences, contact patterns, roles and loyalties are directed towards portfolios, DGs and units. This mode of horizontal specialisation results in less than adequate horizontal co-ordination *across* departmental units and better co-ordination *within* units (Ansell 2004: 237). The Commission DG and unit structure is a prominent example of this horizontal principle of specialisation. The Commission is a horizontally pillarised system of government specialised by purpose and with fairly weak organisational capabilities for horizontal co-ordination at the top through presidential command.

The different sector DGs are mainly organised according to the main purpose of the policy sector covered, such as DG Trade. Within the policy areas covered by the Commission, it is mostly regulated through hard law while also supplemented by more soft methods of regulation (the open method of co-ordination). The Commission only marginally makes distributive and re-distributing decisions due to its fairly small budget. Budgetary decisions are mainly made within the areas of competitiveness and cohesion (40 per cent) and natural resources (43 per cent). In several areas the Commission shares competences with the member states – notably within foreign and security policy and within justice and home affairs. In the core areas of the internal market the Commission often enjoys more exclusive competences. As will be shown below, DG Trade has largely exclusive competences within its area of jurisdiction.

The so-called horizontal DGs are organised according to different *functions*, such as the General Secretariat (GS). The Formal Rules of Procedure adopted by the Commission in 2000 claim that the Commission shall act collectively and adopt annual work programmes that set clear priorities for action. It is the GS and the President that have the obligation to co-ordinate the activities of the different services underneath. Moreover, the ambitions of the current President of the Commission are to foster a more horizontal co-ordination of the services, contributing to increased presidentialisation of the core executive of the Union (see Poguntke and Webb 2005).

One essential part of the presidentialisation of the Commission administration is the role of the political level of the Commission consisting of the College of Commissioners and their Cabinets. As a direct effect of EU enlargement, the membership of the College of Commissioners has grown from originally six to 27 at present (2009). Recent research shows that the increased size of the College has accompanied a more departmental behaviour among the Commissioners – being increasingly focused on portfolio concerns and less on issues that cross-cut their portfolio. Issues that cross-cut the DGs are increasingly handed over to the Commission President. The ambitions of President Barroso have increasingly been to provide 'political guidance' to the institution (Kurpas et al. 2008: 32) Recent research also demonstrates that the personal advisers of the individual Commissioners – the Cabinets – have become increasingly multinational. The standard portrayal of the Cabinets was that they were national enclaves and points of access for the member states (Michelmann 1978). A study of Egeberg and Heskestad (2009) demonstrates that the demographic profile of Cabinet members has become increasingly multinational – even beyond the formal prescriptions. In sum, the political level of the Commission has become increasingly presidentialised, and also increasingly departmentalised and multinational by a strengthened portfolio logic inside the College.

The Commission administration is vertically specialised into three main levels: the Director-General is the top administrative leader of the DG, and below the Director-General are the Directors and the Heads of Unit. The hierarchical structure of the Commission administration is depicted in Figure 3.1.

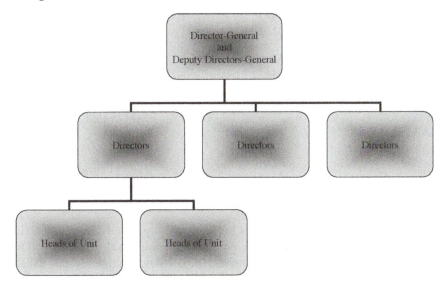

Figure 3.1 Hierarchical structure of the administrative level of the Commission services

Since 1 May 2006 the Commission personnel has been divided into two main ranks: 'administrators' (ADs) and 'assistants' (ASTs). The focus of this study is on the ADs – because they carry out the policy and regulatory decision making in the Commission. Working as an AD requires 'a level of education which corresponds to completed university studies of at least three years attested by a diploma' (Article 5 (8) (96)). The lowest level of Administrator is AD 5 while the Director-General is designated as AD 16. Roles classified as B, C and D grades under the old system are now categorised as AST.

Although by some standards the Commission is a rather small administration, it is formally a strongly hierarchical organisation with clear distinctions between the Director-General, Directors, Heads of Unit and operating officials. Duties and responsibilities are clearly associated with formal rank. The Commission contains a plethora of administrative sub-units below the Commissioner and Cabinet level. The DG structure of the Commission has been described as a 'semi-autonomous organisation with hierarchical management structures', contributing to the compartmentalisation of the Commission services (Edwards and Spence 1997:

Table 3.1 The old and new grading scales of Commission Administrators (AD)

Old grading system	New grading system	Posts (described according to the new grading system)
A1	AD 16	Director-General
A2	AD 15	Director-General/Director
A3	AD 14	Director/Head of Unit/Adviser
	AD 13	Head of Unit/Adviser
A4	AD 12	Head of Unit
A5	AD 11	Head of Unit
A6	AD 10	Head of Unit
	AD 9	Head of Unit
A7	AD 8	Officer
A8	AD 7	Officer
	AD 6	Officer
	AD 5	Officer

Source: Spence 2006: 540

104). As such, the Commission is horizontally organised according to the Germanic *Ressortprinzip* which emphasises ministerial autonomy (DG autonomy) vis-à-vis other ministries (DGs) (Stevens and Stevens 2001: 38). The *Ressortprinzip* tends to strengthen 'silo thinking' within each ministerial domain and to hamper inter-ministerial (inter-DG) co-ordination and co-operation.

In summary, the Commission is horizontally organised into 24 purpose-organised DGs. In addition, the Commission houses 18 DGs for internal and general services, mostly organised according to the principle of process. Each DG is internally organised into directorates and units that compete for influence and resources and that develop idiosyncratic sub-cultures, *esprit de corps* and institutionalised perceptions of appropriate problems, solutions and expertise (McDonald 1997; Shore 2000). This book demonstrates that the decision-making dynamics in the Commission are fostered by the vertical and horizontal organisational structures of the services. Consequently, officials of different ranks in the Commission hierarchy as well as officials in different DGs employ different decision-making behaviour, role perceptions and institutional identities (see Chapters 6 to 9). Figure 3.2 provides a simplified visual picture of the main organisational components of the Commission. Vertically, the figure shows the distinction between the political level (the College of Commissioners and the Cabinets) and the administrative level (headed by the Director-General and Deputy Director-General(s), and subsequently led by Directors and Deputy Directors, and finally Heads of Unit and Deputy Heads of Unit). Horizontally, the figure depicts the difference between two competing but complementary principles of organisation – process and purpose – as well as the vertical hierarchy from the helm of the Commission all the way down to the web of Commission expert committees.

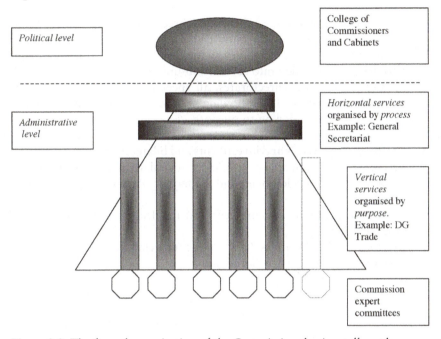

Political level	College of Commissioners and Cabinets
Administrative level	*Horizontal services* organised by *process* Example: General Secretariat
	Vertical services organised by *purpose.* Example: DG Trade
	Commission expert committees

Figure 3.2 The formal organisation of the Commission, horizontally and vertically

DG Trade
To illustrate a DG organised by major *purpose* we have selected DG Trade. One key argument for selecting this particular DG is due to its policy compatibility vis-à-vis the OECD and WTO Secretariats. Methodologically speaking, the policy sector (trade) is thus kept constant throughout the analysis and the policy area may thus not interfere with the observations reported in the three international bureaucracies. This DG is one of the Commission DGs that is granted – *de jure* although not necessarily *de facto* – exclusive competences within several of its areas of jurisdiction. DG Trade has the following main functions:

- to define (and reappraise) the trade interests of the European Community;
- to negotiate bilateral, regional or multilateral agreements;
- to monitor and ensure the implementation of international agreements;
- to devise and monitor internal or external policies which have a bearing on the Union's trade and external investments;
- to ensure consistency between the EU's commercial policy, the EU's

general external relations policy and the contribution of the EU to global economic governance;
• To provide society with updated information.

DG Trade is vertically specialised into three main administrative layers with the Director-General, currently David O'Sullivan (2008), at the top of the administrative hierarchy. Below the Director-General level are nine Directorates, each divided into several sub-units. Horizontally, DG Trade is organised into seven Directorates, all specialised mainly according to the principle of purpose. The following are the Directorates of DG Trade that are specialised according to purpose:

• Directorate B (Services and investments and bilateral trade relations);
• Directorate C (Sustainable development and bilateral trade relations);
• Directorate D (Development and Economic Partnership Agreements (EPAs));
• Directorate E (Public procurement and intellectual property, bilateral trade relations)
• Directorate F (WTO affairs, OECD and food-related sectors)
• Directorate G (Market access and industry).

DG Trade also has two Directorates that are organised according to process:

• Directorate A (Policy co-ordination);
• Directorate R (Resources management).

As outlined in Chapter 2, we predict that the departmental dynamic will prevail within units organised according to the process principle. In summary, however, we expect officials in DG Trade to combine the departmental and the epistemic dynamic due to: (i) the uppermost purpose organisation of the DG vis-à-vis other DGs, and (ii) the internal horizontal specialisation of the DG (directorates) according to purpose. Secondly, the highly issue-specialised units within DG Trade make it also likely that officials will enact the epistemic dynamic. The issue specificity of the portfolios of DG Trade, together with the legal competences of this DG, renders it likely that officials will evoke so-called silo thinking – reliance on intra-DG contact patterns, emphasising preferences for trade, and having a strong loyalty towards the DG as well as towards the trade area. Officials in DG Trade are likely to co-ordinate less with officials in other DGs/policy areas than with fellow colleagues within their own DG/policy area.

DG Trade has approximately 587 officials divided into 253 Administrators, 214 Assistants, and 120 temporary officials of different kinds. Of the total workforce of DG Trade some 20 per cent is thus hired on temporary contracts (Statistical Bulletin of Commission Staff 2008). Hence, the main workforce of DG Trade consists of permanent officials hired through competitive exams into life-long careers.

The General Secretariat (GS)

The GS has been selected to represent a *process*-organised DG. The GS was installed in 1958 as a small executive secretariat of the President of the Commission. It was soon described as 'the engine room of the Commission's administration' and as the 'guardian of the Community doctrine' (Bossuat 2007: 211–212). It is considered by many – including some GS staff – as the *primus inter pares* among the DGs today. While the GS numbered no more than 20 officials in 1958 (Kassim 2004b: 51), it has grown substantially and at present (2008) totals approximately 580 officials. Historically, the GS has been a fairly small secretariat of the President of the Commission. Most recently, notably under the Barosso Commission, the size of the GS has made it begin to resemble a DG in its own right – being more clearly vertically separated from the political level of the President – although the GS reports directly to the President of the Commission. The increased size of the GS may contribute to augmenting the behavioural autonomy of the officials of the GS, and may reduce the level of interaction with the political level of the President. This increased size of the GS reflects both the increased legislative activity of the Union over time, and the increased size, differentiation and complexity of the EU institutions and decision-making processes, as well as the increased number of days spent in meetings in the different Union bodies. The need to 'keep the house in order' has grown (Kassim 2004b: 56). As in the Commission writ large, GS officials are divided into Administrators and Assistants. In the GS the number of Assistants is greater than the number of Administrators. Moreover, approximately 28 per cent of the GS workforce consists of external staff on temporary contracts (Statistical Bulletin of Commission Staff 2008).

The GS is organised mainly by *process* with the main task of ensuring the overall coherence of the Commission's work – both in shaping new policies and in steering them through the other EU institutions. The functions of the GS include:

- preparing weekly Commission meetings;
- supporting the President with respect to prioritised policy areas;
- defining and designing the Commission's strategic objectives and priorities and shaping cross-cutting policies;
- co-ordinating, facilitating, advising and arbitrating between different DGs;
- liaising with the other European institutions, national parliaments and non-governmental organisations and entities;

- overseeing the execution of Commission decisions in the services;
- ensuring that EU laws are applied correctly by the member states.

The GS is often pictured as 'the brain' of the Commission services (Edwards and Spence 1997: 110). One key function of the GS is to keep an eye on the Commission's operation as a whole – providing a 'helicopter view' (Commission 2). Its organisational function is to be the main interlocutor between the college and the services. The role of the GS has gradually changed from being an executive secretariat of the President to becoming more of a political secretariat of the Commission as a whole. The inter-service co-ordination role of the GS has also changed over time, from the time of Noël to the present day (Kassim 2004b). This role of the GS is also reflected in the competences of the personnel in the GS, with a high presence of generalists rather than specialists as we see in DG Trade (Kassim 2004b: 56). The increased importance of the GS is echoed in the following reflection: 'As one former Commission President, Delors, noted, a visit to the Secretary-General's office before taking up one's responsibilities became part of the routine for incoming Commission Presidents and commissioners' (Kassim 2004b: 57).

The overall organisational mission of the GS has over time been to represent the institutional memory of the Commission, but also increasingly to hammer out the core policy priorities of the Commission writ large. The ambitions of the current Barroso Commission is to make the GS more into a presidential office, hierarchically superior to the services. 'Today's Secretariat General has a clear focus on the core tasks of planning, inter-institutional relations and co-ordination' (O'Sullivan 2006: 100). The presidentialisation of the Commission is also codified in the Nice Treaty:

> The Commission shall work under the political guidance of its President, who shall decide on its internal organisation in order to ensure it acts consistently, efficiently and on the basis of collegiality. (Article 217 (1))

The increased presidentialisation of the GS is echoed in the enhanced role for prime ministers and prime ministers' offices at the domestic level (Poguntke and Webb 2005). This tendency is also reflected in the post-New Public Management reforms where increased focus on the horizontal and vertical co-ordination of the administrative apparatuses is emphasised in order to regain control and reduce the 'siloisation' of the public sector (Christensen and Lægreid 2007: 11).

Following a recent reorganisation in 2005, the GS is now horizontally divided into eight Directorates each headed by a Director. These Directorates are specialised according to *process*:

- Directorate A (Registry);

- Directorate B (Relations with civil society);
- Directorate C (Programming and administrative co-ordination);
- Directorate D (Policy co-ordination);
- Directorate E (Resources and general matters);
- Directorate F (Relations with the Council);
- Directorate G (Relations with the European Parliament, the Ombudsman, the Economic and Social Committee, the Committee of the Regions and the national parliaments);
- Directorate H (Institutional affairs).

Each Directorate is vertically specialised into three or four units. In total the GS has 26 units underneath the Directorates. At the top of the administrative hierarchy of the GS is the Director-General (at present Catherine Day) and two Deputy Directors-General. Compared to the average size of Commission DGs, the GS is a fairly small administration.

The organisational role of the GS is to reduce tunnel vision and 'vertical silos' among the different sector DGs. As such, the role of the GS reflects the 'whole of government' reforms among domestic core executives which aim at reducing the level of 'departmentalism' of the administrative apparatus (Christensen and Lægreid 2007). At the same time, the GS also has a preparatory role vis-à-vis the College of Commissioners. The GS is installed both to co-ordinate the services downwards and to prepare decisions within the College of Commissioners upwards.

Commission organisation and reform

While the Commission is mainly organised according to the principles of purpose and processes – as shown above in DG Trade and the GS – the Commission also embodies a territorial principle of organisation as well as a party political component. Territorial concerns are embedded into the Commission services by the recruitment of *de facto* national officials (which is particularly evident in the case of temporary contracted officials from the member states (seconded officials)) notably among Administrators, Cabinets and Commissioners. The party political component is organised into the College of Commissioners, particularly because Commissioners have become increasingly political heavyweights and because of the creeping parliamentarisation of the College (MacMullen 1997; Nugent 2006). In summary, the Commission is a 'multi-organisation' horizontally specialised according to two main principles of organisation (Christiansen 1997), contributing to 'sending ambivalent signals to Commission officials' (Hooghe 1997: 105).

Faced with an increasing agenda overload, one supplementary strategy available to the Commission in addition to building administrative capacities in-house is to import a large number of external specialists and experts when preparing initiatives and drafting new legislation. Importing external expertise may take many forms, and according to the Commission it means:

> including both scientific knowledge and that derived from practical experience. It may also relate to specific national or regional situations. Expertise may be brought to bear at any stage in the policy-making cycle, although different forms of expertise may be needed at different stages. Sometimes experts and representatives of interested parties are brought together in single groups. Sometimes they interact by way of workshops or other deliberative mechanisms. In addition, complementary expertise may be gathered during open consultation such as the publication of green and white papers. (European Commission 2002)

It is often claimed that the Commission is a small bureaucracy, considering its assigned portfolio and number of civil servants, and therefore needs assistance from outside expertise in order to prepare dossiers to the Council and the Parliament (e.g. Stevens and Stevens 2001). Even if the picture of the Commission as a small administrative apparatus heavily dependent on outside knowledge and resources is accurate, the Commission occasionally has sufficient internal knowledge to modulate proposals without the help of external expertise. However, superior knowledge to solve identified problems is usually not enough to get proposals through the later stages of the policy-making cycle; equally important is information on how the member states and important interest groups may react. For that reason the Commission usually needs to disentangle in advance what kind of resistance the member states and different interest groups may potentially mobilise (Larsson 2003). In other words, the Commission is not only dependent upon external expertise in a certain area but also on assessing the likely obstacles that lie ahead in terms of competing preferences represented by the member states and societal interests. Therefore, the Commission has developed several techniques (procedures) to import expert advice during the early stages of the policy-making process.

There is a whole army of expert groups assisting the Commission in initiating and drafting proposals. Few contemporary international bureaucracies have institutionalised a committee system that integrates external expertise and national civil servants to the same extent as the Commission. Updated estimates count as many as 1,237 Commission expert groups, but they are unevenly distributed among the different Commission DGs. Comparing the size of the Commission workforce and the expert committee system, Gornitzka and Sverdrup (2008: 13) state that '[i]n fact, there is about one expert group per eight persons working as an official in the European Commission'. Expert groups exist primarily in the policy domains of the Commission. There are considerably fewer expert groups in the internal services – such as in the General Secretariat. Notably, the Commission expert committees tend to strengthen the sector segmentation of the DGs for two reasons. Firstly, as depicted in Figure 3.2 previously, expert committees are typically subordinated directly under single DGs, and most committees only report to their parent DG and seldom to other DGs. Secondly, most expert committees are single-task entities, thus largely mirroring the portfolio organisation of the DGs (Gornitzka and Sverdrup 2008).

Following the resignation of the Santer Commission (1999), the Commission has undergone the most extensive organisational reforms since its inception in 1957. The reform has been partly inspired by New Public Management (NPM) measures. The goal has been to 'create a modern and efficient public administration based on the principles of efficiency, transparency and accountability' and on principles of 'good governance' but supplemented by 'Weberian-bureaucratic' ideas (Ellinas and Suleiman 2008; see also Chapter 6 and Wille 2007: 37). The internal reforms of the Commission have been perceived by many as the most far-reaching reform since the creation of the High Authority in 1952 (Kassim 2008). The recent reforms as well as the management problems facing the Commission seem to be a reaction to the enduring characteristics of the Commission organisation. As early as 1979 the Spierenburg report made the diagnosis of a 'lack of cohesion within the College, an imbalance between Commissioners' portfolios, worrisome organizational fragmentation at College and administrative levels, an inefficient distribution of staff compared with responsibilities, and a problematic career structure' (Bauer 2007: 56). Many of the same organisational diagnoses were identified more than 20 years later by the Santer, Prodi and Barosso Commissions (Bauer 2007). One ambition underpinning recent Commission reforms has been to increase vertical and horizontal co-ordination and coherence within the Commission – thus reasserting the centre (Jordan and Schout 2007). Ambitions to strengthen the central powers of the GS mirror the presidentialisation of politics at the member-state level centred on the centralisation of powers inside the core executive (Poguntke and Webb 2005). Presidentialisation in the case of the GS has to do both with increased steering and co-ordination ambitions as well as with the increased organisational power and autonomy of the Commission President and the Secretary-General. This trend, however, only supplements the existing horizontal specialisation and 'siloisation' of the services and the increased parliamentarisation of the College of Commissioners. As seen above, the 'siloisation' of the services is increasingly supported organisationally in the College where Commissioners interfere less in other portfolios (Kurpas et al. 2008). Compound systems of public administration – like the Commission – tend to balance and combine rival organisational components such as these (see Chapter 1).

The Kinnock reforms, which have been extensively analysed elsewhere (e.g. Bauer and Knill 2007; Kassim 2004a and 2008), have introduced a more linear career structure, promotion linked to merit and a new pension fund. Central to the ambition of reasserting the centre of the Commission has been installing obligatory mobility among the staff – intra-service mobility as well as inter-service mobility. All officials have been given the benchmark of staying within the same position for two to five years. As commented on by most of our interviewees, a key element in the reform package has been the creation of a new appraisal system – Career Development Reviews (CDR). 'Officials can now accumulate their points and are promoted when they reach a certain threshold' (Knill and Balint 2008: 674). Ban (2008) gives a more thorough assessment of the CDR system. At present, each Commission official receives an appraisal every year. However, most of our interviewees think that the CDR system has had a modest impact on their own decision-making behaviour (see Chapter 6). One explanation may be that there are often 'very weak ties between any specific behaviour and the actual reward', and that the precise thresholds that officials have to meet in order to be promoted are shifting, ambiguous and often set after the appraisal process (Ban 2008: 7). In addition, the process of allocating points is extremely complicated.

Re-engineering a large Commission apparatus, however, is not done overnight, partly due to staff union resistance and path dependencies inside the Commission services. Despite ambitious policies to modernise and reform the Commission during the first decade of the twenty-first century, the results so far have been modest. The key organisational principles of the Commission have remained largely unchanged during the Kinnock reforms and thus resistant to efforts towards a radical organisational redesign. By 2008 the pressure to reform the Commission apparatus has largely vanished from the office of the President of the Commission.

The micro-level: the Commission personnel

Commission officials enjoy great powers, notably by being centre-stage in the agenda-setting process of the Commission (Larsson and Trondal 2006). The real power of Commission Administrators is to turn hotly contested issues into 'A points' on the desk of the College of Commissioners (Eppink 2007: 141). To illustrate this power, the industry Commissioner Guenter Verheugen (2006) recently claimed that:

> the whole development in the last 10 years has brought the civil servants such power that in the meantime the most important political task of the 25 Commissioners is controlling this apparatus. (EUobserver 2006)

In several respects the Commission shares a number of similarities with national core executives both with regard to formal structures and to personnel (Egeberg and Trondal 1999; Lequesne 2000; Stevens and Stevens 2001: 166). Despite Jean Monnet's early vision of creating a small Commission mostly hired on secondment contracts and intentionally not exceeding 200 officials, the current Commission houses around 35,000 officials. Of the workforce of 35,000 Commission officials, only the Administrators (totalling approximately 12,000) are studied in this book. Divided by the number of DGs in the Commission, there are on average about 300 Administrators per DG (Statistical Bulletin of Commission Staff 2008). The most notable expansion of the Community admini-stration, however, is found at the level below the Commission – the EU-level agencies (totalling over 30 at present (2009)).

The Commission personnel increased from 280 officials in 1953 (the High Authority) to 680 in 1957. When the Hallstein Commission was established in 1957 the original estimate was that the Commission needed some 1,000 to 2,000 officials, and already by December 1958 there were 1,051 officials (Bitsch 2007a: 58; Dumoulin 2007a: 219). The staffing of the first Commission was completed by 1961. The number of officials reached 2,892 in 1967 – at the time of the merger of the three Commissions – and by 1972 the Commission had a total of 5,778 officials (Dumoulin 2007a: 220). Whereas by 1953 the Commission was dominated by short-term contracted officials from the member states, today the Commission is mostly staffed by permanent officials with long-term careers. For example, in 2000, 19 out of 22 Directors-General had tenure within the Commission of more than 10 years (Georgakakis and Lassalle 2007: 12). Since the last enlargement, more than 4,000 new civil servants from the new member states have joined the Commission (Kurpas et al. 2008: 46). Figure 3.3 gives an approximate overview of the development of Commission staff over time.

Figure 3.3 depicts the enormous increase in staff in the Commission from its inception to the present day. Whereas the Commission started out in 1957 as a small club of highly dedicated temporary officials, today it houses around 35,000 career officials of which over two-thirds are employed in life-long positions. The largest increase in staff occurred after 1990, partly due to the increased workload caused by the Commu-nitarisation of ever more policy areas and partly due to the enlargements in 1995 and more recently.

Table 3.2 clearly shows that the Commission is supplemented by a considerable number of temporary officials in addition to its permanent core staff. In total, 31 per cent of the total Commission workforce consists of temporary officials. For our purposes, however, it is mainly the seconded staff that are of interest because they serve at the level of Administrators, mostly at the AD 5 level according to the new grading

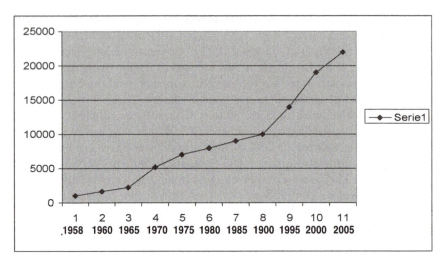

Figure 3.3 Staff numbers estimates, 1958–2005

Sources: Dumoulin 2007a: 220; Stevens and Stevens 2001: 15

Table 3.2 Composition of Commission officials, 2008

Type of official	Number	Totals
Permanent officials		
Administrators (AD)	12,494	
Assistants (AST)	12,113	
Total permanent		*24,607*
Temporary officials		
Contract agents	5,764	
Seconded national experts (SNEs)	1,113	
Others	4,388	
Total temporary		*11,265*
Total Commission officials		**35,872**

Source: Statistical Bulletin of Commission Staff 2008

system (see Table 3.1 above). The High Authority of 1952 was largely staffed by secondees from the member-state governments, and the intention of its first President (Jean Monnet) was that the High Authority should rely on a seconded, flexible staff of top experts (Duchêne 1994: 240). The first Hallstein Commission (1958–62) was also largely staffed with fixed-term contracts. 'Each member of staff received a contract in the form of a letter of recruitment, known at the time as a *lettre de Bruxelles*' (Dumoulin 2007b: 253). However, contracted officials (secondees) have never come to dominate the Commission staff although their number steadily increased in the 1990s, particularly under the Delors Commission, to 1,108 secondees (10 per cent of the present Commission AD staff) (Statistical Bulletin of Commission Staff 2008). Today temporary officials provide the Commission with additional expertise, supply learning across levels of government, secure the Commission with a more flexible workforce hired through a fast-track recruitment system (the 'submarine procedure'), and provide national officials with extra EU experience. According to one current Dutch secondee:

> Seconded officials bring an external perspective to the Commission, a new zest. [The Commission] no longer thinks that the *concours* is the only right way of recruiting people or that candidates who passed the *concours* are better than civil servants from the member states. [The Commission] can continue to build bridges to the member states. At the end of the day, both sides profit because [the secondment system] brings in fresh knowledge. It is a link that provides much better insights. [The Commission] draws in people with a very different experience. (Commission 20)

Secondees typically work at the AD 5 level in the Commission and always below the Head of Unit level. They are normally recruited to the Commission to supplement DGs with much-needed specialist knowledge. As Commission policy makers, secondees are subject to the everyday balancing acts between competing concerns, interests and institutions. From the outset, seconded officials have a double allegiance since they are employees of their home organisation (financially and officially) but they work under the instructions of the Commission. Seconded national experts (SNEs) are obliged to behave solely in the interests of the Commission and not to accept any instructions or duties from their home government. Moreover, they do not have the authority to represent the Commission externally or to enter into any commitments on behalf of the Commission.[1] According to Article 7:1a of the new Commission rules for SNEs (2004), 'the SNE shall carry out his duties and shall behave solely with the interest of the Commission in mind'. At the same time SNEs 'shall remain in the service of their employer throughout the period of secondment and shall continue to be paid by their employer' (Article 1:2).[2] This double role is exacerbated by the fact that the whole secondment system is based on the assumption that SNEs return to their home organisation following the termination of their secondment contract (Trondal 2004a). Moreover, according to the new Commission rules for SNEs, SNEs do not have the same formal rights and obligations as permanent A staff (European Commission 2004: Article 6). Thus, SNEs are detached partly from their home government and partly from the Commission.

Permanent Commission Administrators should act loyally to the

Commission at all times. A Commission official should act according to the portfolio assigned to him/her in the Commission, and not pay attention to personal interests (Article 11a (96)) or external incentives such as gifts or favours (Article 11 (96)). The Staff Regulations that established a genuine permanent European civil service were laid out in the Treaty of Rome, although they were added to the Treaty after it was formally signed in 1957. According to Hubert Ehring, 'I attended the signing of a Treaty which still included blank pages. [...] It was only after the signing that they filled in the blanks with the Staff Regulations, Privileges and Immunities, things like that' (Dumoulin 2007b: 251). The obligations of Commission staff are clearly codified in Staff Regulations Article 11 (96):

> An official shall carry out his duties and conduct himself solely with the interests of the Communities in mind; he shall neither seek nor take instructions from any government, authority, organisation or person outside his institution. He shall carry out the duties assigned to him objectively, impartially and in keeping with his duty of loyalty to the Communities.

One organisational measure to secure the loyalty of members of the organisation is to install formalised recruitment procedures. The recruitment of Commission officials is dominated by the principle of merit but supplemented by different quota systems, mostly into temporary positions. According to the Commission Staff Regulations:

> Recruitment shall be directed to securing for the institution the services of officials of the highest standards of ability, efficiency and integrity, recruited on the broadest possible geographical basis from among nationals of member states of the Communities. (Article 27 (77) (96))

Despite the concern for a geographical balance of Commission personnel, there is no national bias (quotas) in the recruitment procedures to permanent posts. Even the recruitment to the Commission's top management has eliminated nationality as a formal criterion (Hooghe and Nugent 2006: 160). The meritocratic system was recently strengthened in the Staff Regulations with respect to internal promotion (Coull and Lewis 2003). A recent study of top Commission officials (Directors-General, Directors and Heads of Unit) demonstrates that a vast majority of these officials think that recruitment to the Commission is 'fully merit-based' (Ellinas and Suleiman 2008: 716). Recruitment to the Commission on the basis of the merit principle is based on competitive exams – the *concours*. The result of the *concours* forms the reserve list from which DGs can recruit for a vacant post. When vacant posts are available, however, the policy is first to look for internal candidates within the services before consulting the reserve list. The details of the *concours* are described elsewhere (e.g. Edwards and Spence 1997: 73). The key aspect of the *concours* is that it is blind to nationality and to pressures from national governments. This recruitment procedure is thus helping to safeguard the independence of officials entering the Commission. Whereas Egeberg (2006) demonstrates that Commission officials are overly recruited on merit principles, Wille (2007: 41) claims that nationality still plays a role in the recruitment process particularly at the more senior levels. The role played by nationality in the recruitment process, however, is more often claimed than empirically demonstrated (see also Edwards and Spence 1997: 82). The recent study of Ellinas and Suleiman (2008) shows that the recruitment practice in the Commission has become less nationally based and ever more autonomous. This recruitment procedure secures the Commission high-calibre staff. Recruiting officials with lengthy university studies is conducive to the emergence of an epistemic decision-making dynamic among them. Whereas most officials arriving at the Commission in the late 1950s came from the member-state governments, today the majority of officials arrive more or less directly from higher education. 'Universities were not only a rich breeding-ground for the talent recruited by the Community institutions, they were also a natural pool of potential young trainees, or *stagiaires*' (Dumoulin 2007b: 247).

SNEs are not recruited to the Commission through an open competition process to vacancies based on a written test, but through a more opaque process described by Stevens and Stevens (2001: 87) as a 'submarine approach' or as an entry to the Commission services through the back door. In the Commission, initiatives to launch vacancies and the final selection of relevant candidates to SNE contracts are co-ordinated by the Director or Head of Unit in the relevant Commission DG (EEA 2002: 4). SNE vacancies are usually made public by informing the Permanent Representations of member states in Brussels, which subsequently contact the respective national authorities. The recruiting Commission unit receives the applications of SNE candidates from the member states, makes a shortlist and selects SNEs, usually as the result of an interview. Moreover, it is the Commission that determines the job description for each SNE (administered by DG Admin), based on initial information from the member states about particular preferences among particular SNEs. The vast majority of SNEs seem to be recruited on the initiative of individual Commission DGs as well as on the basis of personal initiatives by individual SNEs (Statskontoret 2001: 17, 34). Reflections on the recruitment of SNEs are reported as follows by the Head of Unit in DG Trade (Commission 8):

> Now it is very strictly organised. We have to publish a profile. Even if I want a German speaker, I have to spread this profile, this vacancy, throughout all MS [member states] via the Permanent Representations here in Brussels. They then distribute that internally to the relevant ministries. There is an administrative deadline for applying which I do not determine.

Q: Are you in control of the initial call?

Yes, I formulate the terms of my call, the profile I am looking for. After two months I then get applications. If someone has not replied within the deadline, he's out. So it is quite strictly regulated. But I make the choice then. I make the choice who I want to interview, who I recruit. Or sometimes I don't want to recruit anybody from that lot. But, of course, what I try to do is influence the recruitment in the sense that I call ministries saying 'Look, I need a good official to do this or that, do you have any candidates?'. Parallel, of course, you use your network.

Q: Corresponding ministries at the national level, corresponding to this DG?

Yes. And to the tasks you want to leave to this SNE.

Arguably, because the 'submarine' procedure for the recruitment of SNEs is not the responsibility of the central staffing service but is instead heavily governed by the individual DGs, it is conducive to departmental behaviour among the SNEs (see Chapters 6 to 9).

The Kinnock reforms introduced several measures to 'modernise' the Commission. Two key measures are the staff rotation system and the CDR system. Firstly, Commission officials are now expected to rotate every fifth year. One ambition has been to increase the innovation capacity of the Commission by circulating their staff internally. Another ambition has been to reduce the so-called 'silo thinking' that comes from the formal organisation of the Commission (see above). One potential effect, however, is that the institutional memories in the different DGs may be reduced by internal staff mobility (Wille 2007). According to one official in DG Trade:

> I have occupied at least six or seven positions in this DG. So there was a lot of internal mobility within the DG [Trade]. I know very few people who have stayed inside a DG for more than four years. (Commission 8)

Thus, the average tenure of permanent officials and temporary officials (SNEs) at the unit level may sometimes be surprisingly similar. There may even be examples of units where SNEs have longer tenure than most permanent Administrators. However, despite the great ambitions of the Kinnock reforms, the assessments of the reforms are less glorious (see Kassim 2004a). These reforms have not only contributed to NPM-related measures but have clearly also contributed to strengthening bureaucratic elements in the services through an expanded body of control and verification procedures (Ellinas and Suleiman 2008: 709). At present, about 9 per cent of the Commission's total body of officials engage in financial management, control and audit activities (European Commission 2007: 11).

Despite the attention devoted to Commission reform, and despite the ambition of creating a flexible and rotating pool of Commission officials, the Commission structure and the power vested in the services still very much affect the distribution of positions inside the Commission. According to one official:

> The Commission is yet to be really flexible in re-allocating people to new priorities. Posts are fixed within a unit, within a directorate. No Director will give up his post. I mean, it is a question of power. (Commission 22)

Hence, the great hopes from Kinnock are sometimes dashed within the services. Experiences with reforms of the promotion system are reported with reference to the new assessment system installed by Kinnock (the CDR). Our interviewees demonstrated that assessments of this system vary concerning its effect on the behaviour of Commission officials, and assessments also vary among officials at different hierarchical levels within the Commission (see also Ellinas and Suleiman 2008: 707). The CDR system seems partly to accompany strategic and self-serving manoeuvring among officials. The annual reviews of the performance of the officials are managed by the Head of Unit but are partly controlled by the Directors. They are considered time-consuming and costly, but also as a process that increases mutual information between officials and the leadership (see also Wille 2007: 46). '[I]ncrease in transparency came at the cost of cumbersome procedures that overburden managers' (Ellinas and Suleiman 2008: 719). Opinions on the CDR tend to be associated with rank in the Commission hierarchy. Officials at the Head of Unit level or above tend to have more favourable attitudes towards the CDR than officials below the Head of Unit level. One Head of Unit claims that:

> Actually, I was a supporter of the CDR when it was introduced three years ago; for different reasons. Firstly, it contained self-assessment by officials, which I thought was very useful because, as a Head of Unit, I discovered quite a lot through the self-assessment. Then there was the definition of objectives for colleagues, which I thought was also very good. People should be clear about what they are supposed to do, and what the criterion for success is. And I found the system of points reasonable. You know there are three aspects we have to assess: performance, competence and conduct. My experience is that the original ideas have been a bit lost along the way to implementation. The Head of Unit was supposed to be at the centre of the system. But in the end we were given so many constraints that we had no freedom at all to allocate the points. Plus there was a double system of points: the merit points given by the Head of Unit and the priority points. And there we lost control totally. (Commission 8)

A Director in DG Trade assesses the CDR in the following way:

> If you take into account this scoring system, it allows one to operate a kind of predictable evolution of a career. It certainly has many advantages, it also has some disadvantages; it is true that people are sometimes frustrated vis-à-vis their expectations. (Commission 12)

Among fellow Administrators the attitude towards the CDR seems to be a combination of frustration with the system and a view that the CDR has no profound effects on the behaviour of officials.

> The CDR system was well designed, but has been badly implemented. The CDR has not steered people's behaviour, for the worse or the better ... I don't think it made any difference, because the people who are in DG Trade are naturally quite dynamic and competitive people. They are people who derive a significant degree of their personal happiness and satisfaction from competition-related activity. In the end I think most people find motivation in themselves. You are by nature motivated or not motivated, but on the margin, OK, it can have an impact. It certainly is an encouragement if you get a good report and if your boss describes in black and white your merit. (Commission 21)

According to another official in DG Trade:

> I have never witnessed a colleague changing his work performance and habit because of or thanks to the CDR, probably because there are other reasons – hopefully – than just the CDR for working in the Commission. (Commission 5)

However, despite the fact that the CDR system does not seem to profoundly alter Commission officials' everyday decision-making behaviour, most officials report that the system has contributed to increased conflicts and frustration:

> The CDR is a very conflict-prone system, because it is a system that is meant to create competition. But the conflict with CDR is probably much more between the Head of Unit and the job-holder.
> Q: Has the Commission become a 'hierarchy-of-fear'?
> I think it is a fair criticism of the new system, that it creates competition between people. (Commission 22)

The Kinnock reforms thus have had effects on the attitudes of many Commission officials and sometimes on the atmosphere at work, and also on the amount of work devoted to annual staff evaluations:

> The Kinnock Reforms [...] had implications on everybody, not on the work but on the way we are paid and promoted. That has probably changed dramatically. The first staff evaluation that started in 2003 has indeed added enormous amounts of work for all the managers. (Commission 14)

The strong criticism that has been directed towards the Kinnock reform has made the Commission rethink this reform only after a few years of operation, and it has already suggested modifications of the system from 2009 (Ban 2008: 11). The intention is to simplify the CDR system, speed up the appraisal processes, and set the threshold in advance of these processes. The future will show how this modified CDR system will be received within the Commission. However, this book suggests that neither the CDR nor the rotation system seems to have profoundly affected the way Commission officials work on their everyday files (see Chapters 6 to 9).

A compound Community administration

The Commission occupies a pivotal role as the key executive institution of the EU. The idea of establishing an autonomous community executive was codified in Article 157 in the Treaty of Rome and subsequently integrated into the Staff Regulations. A considerable part of the output crafted by the Commission is initiated, drafted and put on the agenda at the administrative level. Hence, to understand Commission decision making one has to unpack the organisational machinery of the Commission – including its staff. This chapter has pictured the Commission as a mature core-executive institution within the EU, albeit a core executive with several competing organisational forms. Notably, the Commission is a strongly vertically organised executive with a compound mix of horizontal principles of organisation.

The Commission is horizontally specialised according to both the principle of purpose (DG Trade) and the principle of process (the GS). Arguably, it is expected that officials embedded into DGs that are organised differently will adopt different decision-making behaviour, roles and identity perceptions (see Chapters 6 to 9). Notably, DGs organised by purpose, as in DG Trade, are likely to adopt a 'silo logic' by emphasising the departmental and epistemic dynamics. On the other hand, DGs organised by process, as in the GS, are more likely to adopt a departmental dynamic characterised by officials adopting a 'helicopter logic' emphasising inter-service co-ordination and co-operation. We also expect officials in different vertical positions within the DGs to employ different decision-making behaviours. As such, the Commission is indeed a compound machinery of international bureaucracy.

The Commission is staffed mainly with permanent officials, but supplemented by a large group of contracted temporary officials. Whereas previous literature on the Commission has mainly studied the permanent officials, this book also includes some observations on the temporary Commission officials. Assuming that the Commission organisation impacts on the behaviour, roles and identities of its officials, a crucial test-bed thereof is the temporary officials who have a more ambiguous and indeed a shorter affiliation to the Commission services. A long-lived assumption in the literature has been that the 'secondment system would tend to produce an unmanageable cacophony' of officials loyal to the national civil service (Cox 1969: 208). For example, the Spierenburg Report § 110 argued that '[t]he Commission should ensure that the use made of national experts does not rise significantly above its present level, or again the risk is run of distorting the European character of the administration'. This book strongly challenges such claims (see Chapters 6 to 9).

Notes

1   In 2004 the Commission formalised new rules on the secondment of national experts to the Commission (Commission Decision C(2004) 577 of 27 February 2004).
2   Additional financial allowances are granted by the Commission. They include a daily allowance and either removals costs or an extra monthly allowance.

4

The OECD Secretariat

Many years ago the Organisation for Economic Co-operation and Development (OECD) was primarily an 'economic' organisation. Although many people will associate the OECD with its thorough economic analysis and frequent warnings regarding real estate bubbles, overheated labour markets, financial crises and unsustainable public spending, the OECD frames public discourse on a wide range of supplementary themes. Few people know, for instance, that the OECD is a leading actor on areas such as energy security, third world development, environmental sustainability and public sector management. In fact, today it is quite difficult to point to any area of activity where the OECD does not play some sort of inspirational and analytical role.

The broad scope of the organisation can be seen as both an advantage and a weakness. Originally the OECD that replaced the Organisation for European Economic Co-operation (OEEC) in 1961 was thought of as an alternative producer of independent policy ideas. The organisation's first Secretary-General, Thorkil Kristensen, was convinced that the OECD even had a democratic responsibility to renew public debates and enhance their quality by providing evidence-based analysis. Only a truly independent international organisation employing the most skilled policy analysts in the world would be able to play such a role in the modernisation of our societies. It was seen as a clear advantage that the OECD could cope with more than one policy sector, thereby avoiding traditional silo thinking. At that time, it was simply assumed that the organisation would be fully independent from its member states and that it would be financially and organisationally capable of providing the kind of qualified interdisciplinary, cross-sectoral research-based input required for national reform processes.

Yet the broad scope of today's OECD can also be seen as a sign of weakness. Looking at the pluralist landscape of international economic organisations, it is a fact that the core service of the OECD – comparative economic analysis – is being provided by a multitude of competitors. Over recent years, the OECD has attempted to reinvent itself, to find a *raison d'être* among equals. In addition, the OECD member states have gradually established their own analytical capacities, making them less dependent on OECD analysis. So what is the future for the OECD? Will it develop to become a gigantic commentator organisation that will always be able to provide a rapid and an authoritative headline in the news media? Will it specialise as a consultancy organisation that can be paid for its services? Or will it make a last effort at becoming a science organisation that provides the kind of basic research upon which everything else is based? At present, the organisation has not taken an unequivocal step in any of these directions. The OECD is still in search of an identity. This provides a very interesting context for studying the ways in which the OECD Secretariat defines itself, its role and its future.

This chapter has three sections and a conclusion. At the macro-level, the historico-political context of the OECD is discussed. At the meso-level, the committee structure is central; this is where politics meets international bureaucracy. At the micro-level, the secretarial dynamics are spelled out. It is concluded that the OECD is overstretched in more than one sense and in search of a role.

The macro-level: the shadow of the member states

The OECD is no different from any other international organisation in that it has both a 'political' and an 'administrative' organisational level. By 'political' we simply refer to the fact that the OECD can be thought of as a member-state-driven organisation, which is dependent on inputs and demands emanating from its 30 member states.[1] Inputs are broadly defined in terms of financial contributions but also in terms of ideas, administrative support and political authority. The number of members of the OECD has grown quite considerably, particularly since the end of the Cold War. In the media, the OECD used to be known, and often still is known, as the rich-countries' club. In statistical databases, a distinct category called 'the OECD world' used to exist in contrast to the 'developing world' or the 'underdeveloped world'.

So far, the number of issues on which there is a basic consensus among OECD members has been large, making the OECD a quite harmonious organisation in terms of membership. The basic purpose of the organisation is stated in Article 1 of the OECD Convention from 1960, which obliges the OECD to support economic growth, to boost employment, to raise living standards, to maintain financial stability, to assist other countries' (in addition to its members') economic development and to contribute to growth in world trade. Although over the years the world views of the member states have to a very large extent tended to converge, the means to achieve these objectives have, of course, varied in substance and scope, and the ability of the OECD to reach beyond its own borders can be questioned. Such convergence has fostered an understanding of the OECD as a unitary actor on the global scene. In the respective decision-making and co-ordinating forums – the annual Ministerial Council and the regular meetings both in the Council constituted by ambassadors from the permanent delegations in Paris and in the Executive Committee – interactions used to be characterised by flexibility, mutual understanding and a minimum of friction. This allowed for the gradual development of a deeply ingrained aspect of a distinct OECD method: mutual trust. A high level of trust between member states sharing a certain world view has been the basis for consensual decision making, mutual supervision and organisational learning.

With the end of the Cold War, a large number of other countries soon managed to fulfil the criteria for OECD membership: a belief in and a consolidated practice of a market economy and a liberal democracy. Thus, in the 1990s negotiations were undertaken with six countries (Mexico, the Czech Republic, Hungary, South Korea, Poland and the Slovak Republic) which consequently became new members of the OECD family, raising the number of OECD insiders from 24 to 30. Almost in parallel with this first wave of enlargement, the OECD Secretariat was confronted with quite drastic demands for reform, basically meaning that the expansion of membership would not be matched with an expansion of resources. At the same time, it proved to be impossible to break with the established practice of seeking consensus when decisions were made.

Thus, during the 1990s the OECD engaged in extensive enlargements and was met with demands for reforms – just like most other inter-state organisations that functioned as the first world's ideological bulwark against the so-called communist second world during the Cold War. At the same time, it became common practice inside as well as outside the organisation to openly question the *raison d'être* of the OECD. Now that the implicit geo-political function of the OECD had essentially dis-appeared, what was left for the organisation to do? Was it enough to provide a forum for the rich world in which a narrow set of countries could co-ordinate their thoughts and to produce surveys, reviews and comparative data on an increasing number of issue areas? Or should the organisation refrain from only studying the internal business of the OECD family and increasingly engage in outreach, thereby turning a basically introvert image into an image of an organisation with global responsibility?

In discussing the identity problem of the OECD it soon became clear that most of the services that had traditionally been provided by the OECD had now been overtaken by other international organisations, public as well as private. The OECD used to be the sole provider of high-quality comparative data and analysis, and it used to be the only rich country club that systematically engaged in multilateral supervision and bench-marking. During the 1990s it became clear that a whole range of other international organisations had copied the OECD method with success. Taken together, these developments left the OECD with no alternative than to prepare for new ground to be covered. This new ground turned out to be the broader global arena, on which a series of new power actors had turned up. So-called developing economies had become superstars, emerging economies and major actors on the global scene. Consequently, in December 2007 the OECD started accession talks with Chile, Estonia, Israel, Russia and Slovenia. In addition, the OECD offered a so-called 'enhanced engagement' with a view to possible membership to Brazil, China, India, Indonesia and South Africa. If successful, the planned road map will lead to a major change in the political set-up of the OECD. The idea of an 'OECD family' characterised by trust and common world views may be at risk, and the ideal of making decisions through consensus may become illusionary thinking. With the next wave of enlargement, the OECD arena will essentially become identical to the arena of other world organisations such as the WTO, the Bank for International Settlements (BIS), the World Bank, and the International Monetary Fund (IMF). The OECD shares with the WTO and the BIS the fact that the size of their bureaucracies is small, but in contrast to these two other 'small' organisations the OECD is supposed to cover a lot more issue areas. The OECD continues to be a multi-purpose organisation like much larger organisations such as the World Bank and the IMF. The most marked difference, however, still concerns the fact that the OECD contributes to global governance, not by possessing a funding capacity like the BIS, the World Bank and the IMF, nor by possessing a regulatory capacity like the WTO, but mainly by producing ideas and 'the better argument' (Marcussen 2002).

Over the years, the Ministerial Council of the OECD has indeed been able to sign various conventions (six in all) such as the anti-bribery convention and the model tax convention. To this should be added a number of recommendations (163), declarations (23), decisions (21) and some other regulatory instruments that all lean towards the soft category of governance instruments (Figure 4.1). However, compared to other international organisations, of which the EU, of course, sticks out as being the extreme example of a hard law producer on an international level, the OECD is not a regulator in the traditional sense (Marcussen 2004a).

It is primarily by producing regular country reviews (process supervision) and by producing data and comparative analysis in the form of 'outlooks' and 'at a glance' reports that the OECD makes a difference (Table 4.1).

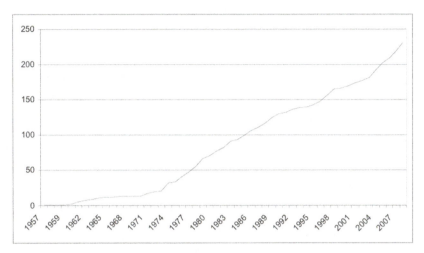

Figure 4.1 Accumulated OECD legal acts in force

Source: OECD legal acts database

Table 4.1 Examples of OECD's analytical activities in terms of regular reports

Outlook series	At a glance series
Science, Technology and Industry Outlook	Education at a Glance
International Migration Outlook	Agricultural Policies in OECD
Employment Outlook	Countries at a Glance
Agricultural Outlook	Health at a Glance
Economic Outlook	OECD Regions at a Glance
Environmental Outlook	Development Aid at a Glance
World Energy Outlook	Pensions at a Glance
Information Technology Outlook	Space Economy at a Glance
Communications Outlook	Society at a Glance

Since the existence of reports, analysis and data does not in itself produce a visible impact, a central feature of the OECD method is to make 'practical men' meet on neutral OECD territory. Essentially it is the socialising process of producing these reviews that makes a difference (Marcussen 2004c). This is where the OECD Committee structure comes into the picture. Over the years, an extended system of inter-state meeting places has developed in Paris (Figure 4.2).

Each time a member state has expressed a wish that the OECD should deal with a new issue area, a committee has been established. In carrying out its duties, the various committees have continuously created working parties and networks within their respective areas of interest. These new bodies have typically found it useful to establish even more additional bodies, such as working groups, task forces and expert meetings.

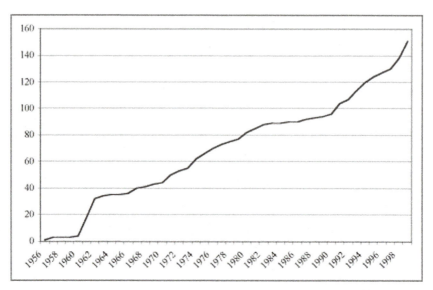

Figure 4.2 Number of inter-state bodies at work in the OECD framework

According to such a dynamic, it should not be surprising to discover that the OECD at present hosts well over 200 different bodies in its committee structure.

The mushrooming of inter-state bodies takes different shapes in different sectors. It is interesting to note that the classical OECD area – 'economics' – has limited itself to creating five central bodies for member-state interaction, whereas 'newer' areas such as 'environment', 'taxes', 'science' and 'education' have created dozens of additional bodies. Table 4.2 illustrates clearly that the number of OECD committees and other inter-state bodies varies considerably from area to area. In addition, it shows that these many and varied forms of inter-state meeting arenas have been categorised according to what appears to have been a rather random and ad hoc practice.

Thus, it is in the encounter between different nationalities that new ideas are being presented, operationalised, translated and, finally, brought home to a special national context. The overall idea behind the OECD method is to develop and diffuse ideas through national reform entrepreneurs at a relatively decentralised level of operation (Marcussen 2002). To exemplify how such an inter-state committee structure may look, it is instructive to list the extended and quite complex pattern of committees and other bodies that are served by the Trade and Agriculture Directorate in which a considerable number of the interviews for the present volume have been conducted (Figure 4.3). The frequency and intensity of meetings in different committees and other bodies vary to a

Table 4.2 OECD committees and other inter-state bodies, 2008

	Committees, governing bodies and steering groups	Boards, forums, centres, programmes	Working parties, joint meetings and networks	Working groups and task forces	Schemes, meetings, experts	Number of bodies
Nuclear Energy Agency	8	2	6	15		31
Environment	2		8	16		26
Science, Technology and Industry	5	1	13	7		26
Trade and Agriculture	4		13		8	25
Financial and Enterprise Affairs	5		9	11		25
Council	10	12				22
Tax Policy and Administration	1	5	6	9		21
Education	5	2	3	10		20
Employment, Labour and Social Affairs	3		4	3	8	18
Public Governance and Territorial Development	2		14			16
The International Energy Agency	3	3	3	5		14
Development	1		8			9
Economic Policy	2		3			5
Statistics	1		3	1		5
Entrepreneurship, SMEs and Local Development	1	2				3
Joint Subsidiary Bodies to the Co-ordinated Organisations	1					1
Total	54	27	93	77	16	267

high degree, but it is in the work of the committees that the idea of a member-state-driven organisation is most clearly unfolded.

The meso-level: politics meets administration

Clearly, there are important links between the 'political' level related to the Council, the Executive Committee and the many sub-committees, and the 'administrative' level in terms of the OECD Secretariat. Neither can be studied in isolation from the other. Without member states that actively pay contributions to the €343 million budget and actively contribute delegates and intellectual capital in the day-to-day work in the committees, there would not be an OECD Secretariat at all. In that

(1) Committee for Agriculture (COAG)
  (1.1)   Joint Working Party on Agriculture and Trade
  (1.2)   Joint Working Party on Agriculture and the Environment
  (1.3)   Group on Cereals, Animal Feeds and Sugar
  (1.4)   Group on Meat and Dairy Products
  (1.5)   Working Party on Agricultural Policies and Markets (APM)
  (1.6)   Plenary Meeting of the OECD Scheme for the Application of
          International Standards for Fruit and Vegetables
          (1.6.1) OECD Scheme for the Application of International
                   Standards for Fruit and Vegetables - Meeting of Heads
                   of National Inspection Services
          (1.7)   Annual Meeting of Representatives of the National
                   Designated Authorities for the Implementation of the
                   OECD Schemes for the Varietal Certification of Seed
                   Moving in International Trade
          (1.7.1) Scheme for Grass and Legume Seed
          (1.7.2) Scheme for Crucifer Seed and other Oil or Fiber Species
          (1.7.3) Scheme for Cereals
          (1.7.4) Scheme for Beef
          (1.7.5) Scheme for Maize and Sorghum
          (1.7.6) Scheme for Subterranean Clover and Similar Species
          (1.7.7) Scheme for Vegetables
  (1.8)   Annual Meeting of Representatives of the National Designated
          Authorities for the Implementation of the OECD Standard Codes
          for the Official Testing of Agricultural and Forestry Tractors
  (1.9)   OECD Scheme for the Certification of Forest Reproductive
          Material Moving in International Trade
*(2) Governing Body of the Co-operative Research Programme: Biological
Resource Management for Sustainable Agricultural Systems*
(3) Fisheries Committee (COFI)
(4) Trade Committee
  (4.1)   Working Party of the Trade Committee
  (4.2)   Working Party on Export Credits and Credit Guarantees
  (4.3)   Joint Working Party on Agriculture and Trade
  (4.4)   Joint Working Party on Trade and Environment

Figure 4.3 Committees and other bodies served by the Trade and Agriculture
Directorate

perspective, the OECD is working in the shadow of the member states and
the kinds of interests and preferences that they want to enact through
international co-operation. This clearly limits the possibility for the
OECD Secretariat to unfold its own distinct actorhood. For some, the
OECD can be seen as an agent for the member states – an instrument in
the hands of government leaders. This can be viewed as a natural state of
affairs, or as a problem for the way in which the OECD functions:

  certainly, you have to understand that all these international organisations
  have kind of partly one hand behind their back [...] We don't have freedom

to say what we like, because governments constrain what we do. We try and get a consensus here, though we try and break out of that sometimes. (OECD 19)

In my view, we are far too focused on serving – or placating – the Permanent Delegations. I think that has been a mistake. That has happened particularly the last four/five years. That has increased. (OECD 8)

Another set of interviewees tend to see the OECD Secretariat as an actor in its own right, with a distinct set of values and identity:

We even had people who were seconded to us from their member country governments to work with us for a year or two, and they have so soon become members of the OECD family, if you like, and worked towards our corporate aims in the OECD that you couldn't really tell from what nation they came.
Q: They sort of absorbed the OECD identity?
Very much so. (OECD 11)

According to such a view, there is indeed a set of identifiable corporate aims that go beyond the specific interests and preferences espoused by the member states – to such an extent that it is possible to speak about a distinct OECD identity. In consequence, this latter category would typically explicitly reject the view that national interests play a role in their daily work as an international civil servant:

I mean, in the end, I am just playing the role of another professional. So, depending on who I work for, I represent the OECD which should not be biased by any country. (OECD 15)

I never feel like I am representing any country. If I am representing something, it is the organisation. (OECD 20)

Some do not hesitate to say that they are very proud of working for the OECD, since the organisation makes the world a better place to live in:

And I am proud of the OECD. That is one of the things I like about working at the OECD: I like what the OECD does, it has a positive influence in the world. (OECD 23)

In short, the international bureaucracy and the member states can be seen as mutually constitutive – one cannot be studied without the other. Yet most studies of international organisations have tended to overemphasise the inter-state 'political' dimension of this dual relationship and to underemphasise the nuts and bolts of international bureaucracies. In remedying such a research bias we discover that international bureaucracies are constituted not by one but by several arenas to which identities are attached and on which power battles for resources and influence are fought (see Chapter 10).

The micro-level: an international bureaucracy with its own dynamics

A first overview of the OECD Secretariat will lead us to conclude that horizontal as well as vertical principles of organisations have been applied (Figure 4.4). This is quite natural, and in this sense the OECD Secretariat is no different from any other administrative structure found in other multi-purpose organisations and national central administrations. Among the horizontal structures we find the Executive Directorate that manages the OECD's human, financial and information resources and the General Secretariat which includes the Office of the Secretary-General, a Directorate for Legal Affairs, Programme and Budget Planning and the Secretariat for the Council of Ministers as well as for the Executive Committee.

The vertical principle of organisation – a pillar structure – characterises all the so-called substantive directorates defined by an issue area (Table

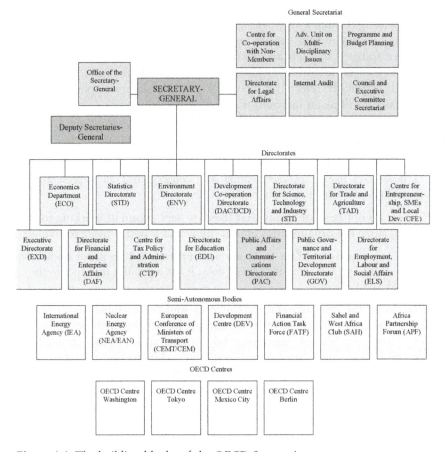

Figure 4.4 The building blocks of the OECD Secretariat

4.3). Among the most expensive directorates in terms of overall costs we find the Economics Department and the Trade and Agriculture Directorate. The costs of directorates depend primarily on the number of employees in the directorate concerned but also, of course, on the activity level in the directorate and its committees.

Table 4.3 A-grade staff by directorate

Directorate/service	A grades
Directorates	
DAF – Directorate for Financial, Fiscal and Enterprise Affairs	86
ECO – Economics Department	84
GOV – Public Governance and Territorial Development	70
TAD – Trade and Agriculture	62
STI – Directorate for Science, Technology and Industry	59
DCD/DAC – Development Co-operation Directorate	59
ELS – Directorate for Employment, Labour and Social Affairs	54
ENV – Environment Directorate	48
EDU – Directorate for Education	46
CTP – Centre for Tax Policy and Administration	34
PAC – Public Affairs and Communications Directorate	31
STD – Statistics Directorate	22
CFE – Centre for Entrepreneurship, SMEs and Local Development	18
Semi-Autonomous Bodies	
IEA – International Energy Agency	95
AEN – Nuclear Energy Agency	40
APF – Africa Partnership Forum	40
DEV – Development Centre	25
CEM – European Conference of Ministers of Transport	14
SAH – Sahel and West Africa Club	14
BOA – Board of Auditors	1
General Secretariat	
SGE – General Secretariat	43
Executive Directorates	
EXD – Executive Directorate	12
EXD/ITN – Information Technology and Network Services	37
EXD/HRM – Human Resource Management	18
EXD/FIN – Finance Service	14
EXD/OPS – Operations Service	10
Other	
ACO – Advisory Committee	9
IOS – Inter-organisations Study Section on Salaries and Prices	7
JPS – Joint Pensions Administrative Section	5
ADP – Staff Association	2
Total	1,026

Source: OECD (2008: 23)

To be in a better position for inter-organisational comparison, we have chosen to focus on the bureaucracies of the trade directorates in the WTO, the Commission and the OECD. The OECD >Trade and Agriculture Directorate (TAD) analyses trade, agriculture, fisheries and food issues and their relations to other areas such as the environment, third world development, economic growth and financial stability. Within the area of trade, TAD applies the OECD method to foster debate, build consensus and promote policy co-ordination, while generally leaving formal trade negotiations to the World Trade Organization (see Chapter 5). In other words, the Directorate undertakes policy analysis of market access and regulatory issues, as well as trade rules and policy links. Recently the former Trade Directorate was merged with food, agriculture and fisheries, making TAD one of the largest directorates in the OECD framework. In these additional areas, the Directorate also undertakes analytical and advisory activities encompassing policy monitoring and evaluation, medium-term outlook scenarios, issues at the interface of domestic and trade policy, and issues in achieving sustainable agriculture and fisheries.

Apart from the first characterisation of the OECD Secretariat in terms of its vertical and horizontal features, a second focus concerns the career and promotion dynamics within the organisation. In this sense, the Trade and Agriculture Directorate is clearly representative of the structure of a typical OECD directorate since it is run by a Director (A7) and a Deputy Director (A6) and is split up into a number of divisions (Figure 4.5). In each division we find a Head of Division (A5), a number of senior analysts (A4) and analysts (A2–A3). Depending on the size of the division, there will be a set of junior analysts (A1) as well as administrative staff involved (B grades). In comparison with the IMF and the World Bank, the OECD cannot compete on salaries, nor can it with jobs in private finance. To avoid too large discrepancies and consequent competition among international organisations for qualified labour, a couple of international organisations have decided to create the so-called 'co-ordinated organisations'. Apart from the OECD itself, the Western European Union, the Council of Europe, the North Atlantic Treaty Organisation, the European Space Agency and the European Centre for Medium-Range Weather Forecasts constitute the co-ordinated organisations. The idea is to define a common system for adjusting the salaries of their staff. The present OECD salary structure does not differ much from those of the WTO and the European Commission.

However, a number of the interviewed civil servants in the Trade and Agriculture Directorate as well as in the Executive Directorate intimated that the OECD salary and incentive structure could be improved. For instance, it is being argued that for people in their early career the OECD can be seen as offering good salary and promotion prospects. However, when moving up the hierarchy there is a marked barrier around the

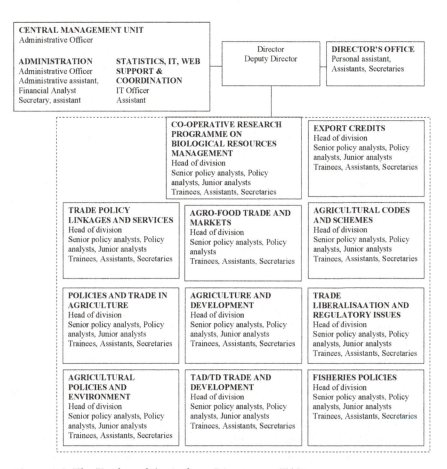

Figure 4.5 The Trade and Agriculture Directorate (TAD)

Grades and job titles: A7, Directors; A6, Deputy Directors; A5, Heads of Divisions; A4, Senior Economists/Senior Policy Analysts; A3, Economists/Policy Analysts; A2, Economists/Policy Analysts; A1, Young Professionals; B6, senior administrative, marketing/communication >and statistical staff; B5, senior administrative, marketing/communication >and statistical staff; B4, personal assistants, administrative assistants, statisticians, junior programmers, documentalists; B3, secretaries/ assistants, accountants, IT technicians; B2, secretaries, safety and reception officers, technical assistants; B1, secretaries, safety and reception officers, technical assistants.

A4–A5 level. If you are skilled and lucky enough to attain an A5 position then you are likely to get no further. This fact alone apparently does not make people leave the organisation:

> The salary levels here, at my level [A4], are good. On average, salary levels at the OECD are good, but it is good from the 30– to 45–year–old level, but not guaranteed between 40 and 50. Early career, definitely a very good

salary. That is, if you are not working in major finance or whatever. Obviously in the financial sector you could do a lot better. Thereafter, I guess, it is still pretty good. There is an expression in the OECD called 'golden handcuffs', which you have probably heard of already. In a sense, it is good salary – it is not going to make you super-rich, but it is a good salary – and it shuts you up. So you tend not to speak up, and that is called golden handcuffs, an expression used around the place. (OECD 13)

The salary scale is divided in grades between A1 (lowest) and A7 (highest). From A3 and upwards the grade is typically linked to a specific job function. Within grades there are a series of salary scales that are applied primarily on the basis of seniority. Following international standards, the basic salary is supplemented with a package of allowances (expatriate, dependent child, household and installation allowances as well as a pension scheme, coverage of travelling and removal expenses, and a medical and social system). In line with international standards, OECD personnel are also exempt from national taxation.

Including staff in all grades and with all kinds of contracts, there were 2,462 officials and temporary staff members serving in the OECD at the end of 2007 (Table 4.4). In line with the marked administrative reforms that have been undertaken since the mid-1990s, the number of regular staff fell drastically between 1997 and 1998 and since then has remained relatively stable at around 1,650. At the same time, the number of project staff has continued to grow, from 142 in 1997 to 542 in 2007. In 1998 the ratio of regular staff to project staff was 10.2:1 whereas in 2007 it stood at 3.0:1. This is reflected in the appointment trend for 2007 – of the 177 A-grade staff recruited, 113 were project staff.

Clearly the 1990s were difficult years for the OECD Secretariat. The number of member states rose from 24 to 30 while the overall staff number remained constant. The majority of the interviewees in the Executive as well as in the Trade and Agriculture Directorates did not hide their feelings that their everyday routines have become extremely pressurised. The turnover of A-grade staff is extremely high and it continues to rise (Table 4.5). Thus, 54 per cent of A-grade staff have worked at the OECD for less than five years.

The A-grade turnover rate has been consistently higher than that of other categories of staff, with a 14 per cent turnover in 2007 for A grades and 7 per cent and 10 per cent for B and C grades respectively. The L- grade turnover rate has increased, from 1.24 per cent in 2003 to 4 per cent in 2007.

Departures among A-grade staff numbered 123 in 2007, higher than in 2003 when there were 115 departures. The two main reasons for A-grade departures are end of contract (66 in 2007) and resignations (35 in 2007). The relatively high number of resignations means that one-third of A-grade departures occur at the initiative of the staff member rather than the OECD.

Table 4.4 Evolution of staff by category

	1990	1991	1992	1993	1994	1995	1996	1997	1998	1999	2000	2001	2002	2003	2004	2005	2006	2007
Regular staff	1,803	1,805	1,860	1,894	1,905	1,934	1,867	1,818	1,696	1,663	1,657	1,663	1,687	1,670	1,674	1,637	1,619	1,638
Project staff	28	43	37	46	68	111	118	142	166	198	254	304	317	307	341	384	475	542
OECD-employed	1,831	1,848	1,897	1,940	1,973	2,045	1,985	1,964	1,862	1,861	1,911	1,967	2,004	1,977	2,015	2,021	2,094	2,180
Consultants	74	70	86	98	100	99	104	88	110[a]	124[a]	116[a]	133[a]	142[a]	143[a]	171[a]	168[a]	161[a]	168[a]
Auxiliaries	107	122	169	191	198	184	173	177	152	145	160	180	157	138	117	99	81	72
Trainees	38	27	41	39	50	52	41	42	17	22	21	32	32	37	29	28	42	42
OECD-paid	2,050	2,067	2,193	2,268	2,321	2,380	2,302	2,269	2,141	2,152	2,208	2,312	2,335	2,295	2,332	2,316	2,378	2,462

Source: OECD (2001: 3), OECD (2008: 9)
[a] Includes 30–40 'seconded consultants'.

Table 4.5 Evolution of A-grade staff

	1960	1969	1991	1992	1993	1994	1995	1996	1997	1998	1999	2000	2001	2002	2003	2004	2005	2006	2007
Total grade A staff	135	205	643	668	705	714	761	747	778	755	773	797	839	874	906	931	934	979	1,045
Average age	–	–	45	45	44	44	45	45	44	44	45	44	44	45	45	45	45	45	45
Average years in grade A	–	–	6	6	5	5	5	5	5	5	4	4	4	4	4	4	4	4	4

Source: OECD (1996: 4), OECD (2001: 16), OECD (2008: 10), Sjöstedt (1973: 198)

Work pressure and the lack of resources are given as typical reasons for dissatisfaction. At every level of the directorates investigated, claims that the workload was higher than the average for international organisations were common, as were claims that the workload has increased considerably over recent years. In combination with the fact that indefinite contracts have been replaced by fixed-term contracts, people feel exposed to considerable stress:

> One of the myths about a place like the OECD is that people sort of sit around and hash on international money and tax breaks and have a good time. However true that might have been in the past, or whether it is just jealousy or whatever, I can tell you – and this is not propaganda – I work very hard. I used to have long nights and I happened to be here at two. And I am not the only one. I'm always amazed at people burning the midnight oil here at the OECD, and working hard. (OECD 13)

> The longer you are here, the harder it gets, I guess. But that is not a safe approach either, because in the last ten years we have seen an awful lot of cuts. Even people that were here many, many years.
> Q: On all levels?
> All levels. I can't think of any level that has escaped. Well, obviously the Secretary-General has not been chopped. The Deputy Secretary-General has not been chopped. And I don't think any A7s, but that is not to say that [...] everybody is under pressure. (OECD 13)

In addition to the quite considerable workload undertaken by OECD civil servants, it is often claimed that the lack of resources has become critical. It has never been the case that the OECD staff had access to unlimited resources but the situation at present, although not as bad as during the 1990s, is that important areas of interests are not being analysed:

> We have, really, stagnant resources, and I don't cry about that because I know that my member governments have exactly the same – if not worse here and there. I know about a lot of countries that they are down-sizing; so are we. But the point is that we really do get more and more and more work. I am not even speaking about the future member countries which will be added. Nobody knows how much additional staff will help us to cope with that. That is a problem. (OECD 7)

> I don't think we have the resources to answer some of the important questions we need to be looking at. (OECD 17)

> Oh, we are always resource-constrained. That is a given. [...] Sometimes I see windows of opportunity that we are not able to exploit because we don't have the resources. (OECD 23)

Well over half of the A-grade population are on fixed-term contracts (62 per cent in 2007). The distribution within the A grades shows that more than 80 per cent of staff at A7 and A6 are on fixed-term contracts, reflecting the adoption in 1999 of a policy stating that staff at these levels are not eligible for open-ended contracts (Table 4.6). In other words, staff hired at A6 and A7 are not eligible to have their contracts converted to open-ended appointments, and A5s promoted to A6 or above must abandon their open-ended contracts. Sixty-six per cent of A3 staff and 90 per cent of A2 staff are on fixed-term contracts, while the proportions of fixed-term contracts at grades A4 and A5 are somewhat lower at 49 per cent and 37 per cent respectively. All A1 grades are on fixed-term contracts.

Table 4.6 Breakdown of A grades by type of appointment, 2007

Grade	Fixed-term contracts	Indefinite contracts	Total	Per cent of fixed term
A7	20	5	25	80
A6	23	4	27	85
A5	44	75	119	37
A4	172	179	351	49
A3	240	123	363	66
A2	100	11	111	90
A1	49	–	49	100
Total	648	397	1,045	62

Source: OECD (2008: 16)

The number of appointments to A grades rose from 99 in 2003 to 177 in 2007. In 2007 there were 533 appointments of temporary staff. For the average OECD civil servant this development means that job security has decreased:

> When I came here, no one had short-term contracts. You had long-term contracts; that was it. And there were very few temporary staff, whereas now you have people coming and going the whole time. So people just don't have the same commitment anymore. That is a pity. (OECD 19)

> Security in terms of losing a job – that's something which is eroding away. (OECD 6)

OECD staff are drawn from all 30 member states with some exceptions allowed by staff rules and regulations. The largest population in the A grade is French with the next two most common nationalities being British and American. At A5 and above (171 posts all in all) the highest proportions among the 22 countries represented were from the UK (36 posts), France (30 posts) and the US (26 posts). This is seen as a problem by some of the interviewees. For some, staff diversity in terms of country of origin can be seen as a clear advantage for a 'reflexive organisation' such as the OECD. In this perspective, a narrow composition of staff will lead to a less innovative organisation. For others, the problem is rather that the criteria for promotion and recruitment are elusive and not explicitly and solely based on merit. If certain countries are favoured over others this could contribute to undermining morale and trust within the organisation:

> For the moment the Secretary-General is under a lot of pressure from different nationalities, who are, basically, asking us to recruit – or promote – people who are not the best candidates.
> Q: Is that lack of diversity something that is particular for your directorate, or does it go for the entire organisation?
> At senior level, I think it's across the entire organisation. I think it's particularly bad in EXD [the Executive Directorate]. When I look at the Heads of Services in EXD, they are universally white male and predominantly British, American and French [...] Japan is the second largest contributor [...] and it's massively under-represented. (OECD 8)

Formally, there is no direct relationship between budgetary contributions from the member states and the national proportion of staff in the OECD. In principle, the OECD is an organisation that hires people on the basis of merit. However, according to the OECD civil servants interviewed, the country shares do indeed play a role. On numerous occasions the fact that applicants from some member states are prioritised over others was brought up for discussion. Comparing the nationality of staff with the budget contributions of the member states, the country with the lowest percentage of nationals among A-grade staff in relation to the size of its budgetary contribution is Japan (Table 4.7). The country with the highest percentage of staff compared to the size of its budget contribution is France. Among directorates with more than 50 staff, the highest geographical mixes are in the Economics Department (138 staff members) and the International Energy Agency (172 staff members) with 26 nationalities each. The Trade and Agriculture Directorate (99 staff from 23 nationalities) and the Directorate for Science, Technology and Industry (95 staff from 22 nationalities) are also among the very diverse directorates in terms of nationalities employed. In contrast, the Executive Directorate with 164 staff from 11 nationalities (115 from France alone) is one of the largest directorates with the lowest geographical mix.

Out of a total of 177 A-grade staff recruited in 2007, 20 were Japanese, 20 were French, 16 were Australian, 15 were British, 15 were American, 14 were German and 14 were Italian, with the remainder being drawn from a range of other countries. The host country, France, continues to account for a large proportion of the applications received in 2007 (8,219 applications) followed by Italy (5,570 applications), the United States (3,062 applications) and Mexico (2,465 applications).

International bureaucracies

Table 4.7 Geographical distribution of A-grade staff and contribution to part 1 of the OECD budget (percentages)[a]

Country	A-grade staff					Members' contribution	Members' contribution (part 1)
	1991	1995	2000	2005	2008	1964	2008
Australia	3.86	4.34	4.77	4.67	4.56	–	2.067
Austria	1.40	1.45	1.00	1.30	1.05	1.16	1.151
Belgium	3.11	1.84	2.01	1.52	1.62	2.23	1.402
Canada	6.07	8.15	7.03	6.08	5.70	6.95	3.364
Czech Rep.	–	–	0.38	0.43	0.29	–	0.479
Denmark	1.24	1.84	2.01	1.41	1.33	1.21	0.965
Finland	0.62	0.92	1.38	0.98	1.24	–	0.783
France	22.55	20.37	19.70	23.45	20.82	11.61	6.756
Germany	7.15	7.23	5.65	5.32	6.08	13.78	9.265
Greece	2.02	1.45	0.88	0.76	0.86	0.51	0.838
Hungary	–	–	0.38	0.54	0.86	–	0.424
Iceland	0.16	0.79	0.50	0.33	0.29	0.10	0.172
Ireland	2.64	1.71	1.88	2.39	2.19	0.32	0.669
Italy	4.20	3.68	5.40	6.41	5.99	5.88	5.595
Japan	5.75	5.12	5.65	5.65	6.37	7.20	16.656
Korea	–	–	1.00	2.39	2.09	–	2.297
Luxembourg	0.16	0.13	0.13	0.22	0.29	0.10	0.216
Mexico		0.53	0.50	0.65	2.09	–	2.09
Netherlands	3.11	2.63	2.26	1.95	2.38	2.25	2.096
New Zealand	0.93	1.18	1.00	1.09	1.52	–	0.442
Norway	0.16	0.66	1.00	0.98	0.76	0.91	1.088
Poland	–	–	0.63	0.54	1.14	–	0.892
Portugal	0.47	0.79	0.75	0.65	0.67	0.31	0.709
Slovak Rep.	–	–	–	0.33	0.19	–	0.253
Spain	0.47	0.79	2.13	2.17	2.66	1.71	3.466
Sweden	2.64	1.97	2.38	2.28	1.81	2.52	1.303
Switzerland	1.71	1.45	1.25	0.54	0.48	1.91	1.5
Turkey	1.09	1.05	1.13	0.76	0.95	0.44	0.851
UK	12.44	12.09	11.29	11.40	11.69	13.90	7.236
USA	15.86	17.87	15.93	12.70	11.60	25.00	24.975
	100.00	100.00	100.00	100.00	100.00	100.00	100.00

Source: OECD (1996: 13), OECD (2001: 22, 26), OECD (2008: 18)

[a] The OECD budget is divided into two parts: general expenses (part 1) and additional expenses (part 2).

Overstretched and in search of a role

The development of an international society overcrowded with regulatory actors that apply all sorts of regulatory instruments in an increasing range of areas has led some people to talk about a veritable regulatory explosion on a global scale (Marcussen 2004b). Regulators that span borders do not inherit a natural legitimacy, as do the public authorities in nation-states. On the global scene regulators engage in tough competition for attention and authority. This competition has intensified since the end of the Cold War.

These developments have completely altered the rules of the game for the OECD and other organisations created from the 1940s until the 1960s. Over the years, the OECD has managed to place itself centrally in global debates about employment, development, the environment, regulatory reform and education. There are many success stories to be told about the OECD. Despite these many and undisputed successes, the OECD can no longer take support from its member states for granted, and its role as an international regulator and its relative position in the regulated global society need to be constantly protected. As discussed above, the OECD has tried to reinvent itself by turning an introvert rich-countries' club into a global player with global responsibility. In OECD parlance, this takes two forms – outreach and enlargement. Today, the OECD is working on a regular basis on a large range of issues with almost all countries in the world. So far the number of member states has increased to 30 but over the coming years we will most likely witness a further 10 member states being adopted into the 'OECD family'.

It does not make it easier for the OECD that its impact, however important, is elusive. Soft governance is by its nature less visible in terms of its causes and effects, and tends to work much more slowly than hard forms of regulation – not to mention the distribution of funds and loans, which are some of the instruments applied by the WTO and the EU. For example, OECD reviewing has a different impact in different member states, which adds to the complexity when the usefulness of the OECD work is evaluated (Marcussen 2004c). The global evaluation trend, which to a large extent is promoted by the OECD itself, has hit the OECD like a boomerang. It is simply incredibly difficult to measure the quality of OECD work in purely quantitative terms. What the OECD can do, and what it has done, to meet the requirements of its complex political environment is to talk more directly to the national media and listen to the needs of the present and future members.

Today, the situation is that the OECD suffers from a serious degree of organisational overstretch, which takes various forms. One element concerns the future of the so-called OECD method of decision making. Today, most inter-state organisations apply the soft-governance instruments that were essentially developed by the OECD. In the European Union this is typically referred to as the Open Method of Co-ordination, and in the WTO it is referred to as conflict resolution. Therefore, it is a paradox that past and future enlargements may undermine the functioning of the OECD method. By reaching out to more member states and more partners of co-operation, the OECD inevitably becomes more diverse in its profile. This is in contrast to the very homogenous profile that used to characterise the 'OECD club'. Since a basic element of the OECD method is a certain minimum level of mutual trust, it will require hard work in the future to catalyse processes of depoliticised learning and socialisation. Critics would argue that the consensus culture will evaporate as a result of consecutive enlargements, and that the neutrality of the OECD arena will be replaced by classical geo-political power battles. Supporters would argue that by reaching out the OECD has a historic chance of consolidating democracy and capitalism at a global level.

Another element of organisational overstretch relates to the financial underpinnings of the OECD. It is widely known and often repeated by the interviewed civil servants within the OECD Secretariat that the OECD is required to do more, on many more issue areas and with ever higher frequency. The OECD's budget has essentially not seen any considerable increases over the last decade, at least not if the increasing number of member states is taken into account; if anything, the budget has remained the same size. At the same time, the share of fixed contributions (part 1 of the OECD budget) from the member states is falling in relation to the voluntary contributions (part 2 of the OECD budget). In practice this means that the OECD to an ever larger extent is acting as a consultant for the member states – one that can be paid to do research and analysis that it may or may not have done anyway. Critics would argue that the OECD is about to lose its independence, and therefore also some of its reliability and authority in global regulation. Supporters will argue that the OECD is just paying attention to the needs of the member states, trying to deal actively with real world problems rather than elusive basic research.

A third element of the overstretch problem relates to the scope and intensity of its activities. As mentioned earlier, the OECD is a multi-purpose organisation that is trying to cover the same kind of areas as much larger multi-purpose organisations. New issues are continuously being added to the already very long list of OECD activities. This is partly due to the fact that member states, as mentioned, can commission the OECD to carry through projects if they contribute financially to the organisation. It is also due to the fact that the OECD is increasingly expected to react rapidly to media demands for news stories. The current rate at which the OECD produces output in terms of reports, analysis and data is supposed to match the accelerated demands of the modern press. To combine thorough comparative analysis with constant media demands for headlines and 'easy to digest solutions' is no easy job. Critics would argue that the depth and innovativeness of OECD work have vanished over recent years. Supporters would argue that the OECD is moving away from being a Babylonic tower of knowledge to being a democratic contributor to informed public debate.

As a result of its organisational overstretch and the various ways in which this is being manifested in practice, we would expect further organisational reforms in the years to come. The OECD is a moving target, in which the shadows of the member states increasingly frame the secretarial dynamics. This has radical consequences for the roles and loyalties that are being enacted by OECD civil servants.

Note

1 In 1948 the OEEC consisted of seventeen signatory states: Belgium, Denmark, Great Britain, France, Greece, the Netherlands, Iceland, Ireland, Italy, Luxembourg, Norway, Portugal, Sweden, Switzerland, Turkey, Germany and Austria. When it became the OECD in 1961, three new member countries entered: Spain, Canada and the USA.

5

The WTO Secretariat

The World Trade Organization (WTO)was established as an intergovernmental organisation in 1995 and is the only global organisation to deal with the regulation of world trade. The creation of the WTO was one of the most dramatic advances in multilateralism since the institution-building period of the late 1940s when *inter alia* GATT (General Agreement on Tariffs and Trade), the predecessor to the WTO, was created (WTO 2004: 9). The increased importance of the GATT/WTO system is illustrated by the fact that the number of contracting parties has grown from 23 when GATT came into force in 1948 to the current number of 153. The organisation has also expanded the number of areas covered as well as its rules, framework and scope of activities. Today, the WTO agreements cover, among other things, market access, subsidies, anti-dumping, agriculture, intellectual property rights, trade and environment, and technical trade barriers. Moreover, in addition to the negotiations on the reduction of trade barriers, the organisation deals with technical assistance, capacity-building for developing countries, dispute settlements and more. The WTO also faces large challenges in finding compromises and solutions among the large number of members as well as in ensuring compliance among members with different agreements and rules. In addition to this, the WTO has been exposed to increasing public scrutiny in the years following its creation – highlighted by repeated demonstrations and protests against the organisation at Ministerial Conferences in the 1990s and 2000s. The increased status and central position of the WTO also put strain on the organisation's bureaucratic machinery, i.e. the WTO Secretariat, which is in a key position to ensure that the organisation operates smoothly.

The WTO Secretariat was formally set up in 1995 to support the WTO. The Secretariat was a continuation of the GATT Secretariat, which since the establishment of GATT in 1947 had gradually developed into a fully fledged international bureaucracy. The WTO Secretariat took over the responsibilities from the GATT Secretariat in addition to being given responsibility for a whole range of new areas corresponding to the new expanded agenda of the WTO (Yi-Chong and Weller 2004 and 2008).

In this chapter we present the WTO Secretariat – its organisational characteristics and its functions and roles within the broader framework of the WTO. The chapter is organised as follows. The first section explores the macro-level of the WTO Secretariat, i.e. the core functions and roles of the international organisation it has been set up to support, the WTO, as well as the wider institutional environment within which the WTO and its Secretariat are embedded. The next section unpacks the meso-level, i.e. the formal organisation of the WTO Secretariat as well as its function within the WTO system. The third section focuses on the micro-level, i.e. the composition of the staff, recruitment procedures, years of tenure, nationality and other demographic factors. The general aim of the chapter is to explore the anatomy of the WTO Secretariat as well as the functions and roles of the Secretariat and its officials and the wider context of both the operation of the WTO and the role of international bureaucracies in general.

The macro-level: the institutional environment of the WTO Secretariat

The WTO's history dates back to 1947 and the establishment of GATT. GATT was an agreement without the formal status of an organisation, and was initially intended to be a part of the planned new organisation ITO (International Trade Organization). However, ITO never came to existence and GATT prevailed as a global trade agreement. GATT was supported by a secretariat which was initially financed by loans from the United Nations (Yi-Chong and Weller 2004). Over time, GATT developed its own system of financing through member contributions. Furthermore, GATT developed into what was in practice an international organisation with the agreements as the 'constitutional' framework, and with the Secretariat together with member state representatives in councils and committees as the organisational parts. Several negotiation rounds have gradually expanded both its number of members and its scope of activities (Van den Bossche 2008).

The WTO was established in 1995 following the Uruguay Round of negotiations (1986–93). GATT was thus in practice replaced by a formal international organisation. The GATT Secretariat was expanded and changed its name to the WTO Secretariat. The WTO has considerably more influence than GATT had, both because its scope of activities was expanded and because of the introduction of new dispute settlement procedures which gave the organisation more power to 'force' member states to abide by its rules. The new dispute settlement procedures gave every WTO member the right to initiate a dispute against another member. The WTO has a more politically sensitive policy coverage and a more prominent public profile in world politics than GATT (Shaffer 2005; Veggeland and Borgen 2005). The organisation has changed its way of working from a 'club model', where a small number of countries assisted by civil servants made deals behind 'closed doors', to a more open and fragmented organisation, where a large number of different member groupings have been established and where WTO officials are closely watched by WTO members as well as by society as a whole (Keohane and Nye 2001; Van den Bossche and Alexovicova 2005; Yi-Chong and Weller 2004). The WTO Secretariat thus assists, supports and administers a more powerful and politicised organisation than was the case under GATT. This sensitive position has also raised questions about the need to reform the Secretariat and to give it a more independent role (Cottier 2007; Shaffer 2005; WTO 2004).

The functions and roles of the WTO
The WTO is the only *global* international organisation dealing with the rules of trade between nations. The WTO's overriding objective is to help trade flow smoothly, freely, fairly and predictably.[1] The WTO has 153 members (in 2008) accounting for over 97 per cent of world trade. Approximately 30 other countries are currently negotiating membership. Decisions on new memberships are made by the entire membership and are typically made by consensus. A majority vote is also possible but it has never been used in the WTO, and was extremely rare under the WTO's predecessor, GATT. The WTO's agreements have been ratified in all members' parliaments. The main functions of the WTO can be summarised as the following:[2]

- Administering trade agreements.
- Acting as a forum for trade negotiations.
- Settling trade disputes.
- Reviewing national trade policies.
- Assisting developing countries with trade policy issues through technical assistance and training programmes.
- Co-operating with other international organisations.

What comes out of WTO negotiations is what can be called 'hard law', i.e. a set of mandatory rules that the members are committed to implementing and obeying. Furthermore, the organisation both monitors member-state implementation and has also put in place procedures to sanction those members that break the rules. Thus, the WTO produces a considerable amount of regulatory outputs, including binding agreements and binding decisions by judicial and political bodies. However, it is important to emphasise that the organisation is member-driven, i.e. the responsibilities for agenda setting, drawing up texts, adopting new rules, initiating dispute settlements, implementing sanctions etc. are all in the hands of the members (WTO 2004).

The organisational configuration of the WTO as a whole
The main features that characterise the WTO are the following (see also Figure 5).[3] The WTO's top decision-making body is the Ministerial Conference which meets at least once every two years. The negotiation rounds are concluded at Ministerial Conferences. Decision by consensus is the rule. Below the Ministerial Conference is the General Council (normally ambassadors and heads of delegation in Geneva but sometimes officials sent from members' capitals) which meets several times a year in the Geneva headquarters. The General Council also meets as the Trade Policy Review Body and the Dispute Settlement Body. At the next level, the Goods Council, Services Council and Intellectual Property (TRIPS) Council report to the General Council. Numerous specialised committees, working groups and working parties deal with the individual agreements and other areas such as the environment, development, membership applications and regional trade agreements. It has been estimated that there are over 70 different WTO councils, committees, working parties and other groupings involving over 2,800 meetings each year (Shaffer 2005: 1). These units actively monitor the implementation of the agreements. All these units are supported by officials from the WTO Secretariat but are chaired by representatives of the WTO members.

Regarding the formal organisational structure of the WTO, a distinction can be made between the political level (member-state governments), which consists of the Ministerial Conferences as well as the councils and committees including the chairs (appointed by and among member-state delegates), and the administrative level (the international bureaucracy), which consists of the WTO Secretariat (i.e. international civil servants). It can also be argued that the head of the WTO Secretariat, the Director-General, has *de facto* a political position in addition to his or her administrative function.

The WTO Secretariat's role in the WTO is stated in Article VI of the Agreement Establishing the World Trade Organization (see Annex 5.1). A key element of Article VI is the clear statement that the WTO Secretariat is supposed to be neutral and shall not accept instructions from any government or other authority external to the WTO. The WTO Secretariat thus formally appears as an administrative apparatus clearly separated from member-state governments and other authorities and with a separate legal status. Article VI does not, however, specify in detail the functions and roles of the Secretariat, although the WTO Staff Regulations lay out more detailed principles 'for the guidance of the Director-General in the staffing and administration of the WTO Secretariat' (WTO Staff Regulations: 1). A key mission of the Secretariat is generally to work as a 'guardian of the

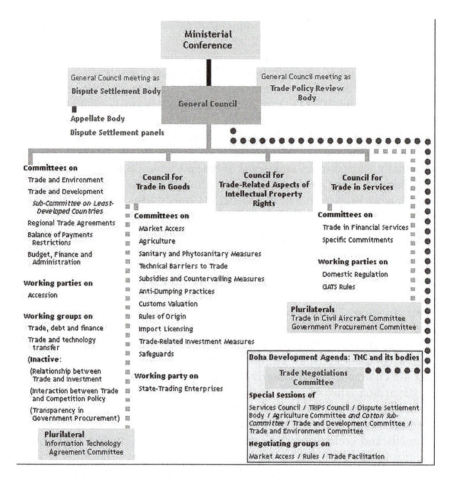

Figure 5.1 The organisational structure of the WTO

treaties' and to assist and support WTO members within the framework of this mission (WTO 2004).

The meso-level: the functions, roles and organisational characteristics of the WTO Secretariat

The WTO Secretariat, based in Geneva, has around 600 staff and is headed by a Director-General. Its annual budget is approximately 160 million Swiss francs.[4] Decisions are taken by the members themselves. The WTO is thus a member-driven organisation, and the Secretariat's role is officially restricted to one of support rather than initiative or decision making (WTO 2004). The Secretariat nevertheless holds an important position within the WTO system as the 'institutional memory' of the organisation, as a key support for WTO members, and as a key provider of expertise on WTO issues and rules (Shaffer 2005; WTO 2004). The Secretariat has been set up to support a relatively narrow agenda (at least compared to, for example, the European Commission), i.e. to develop 'an integrated, more viable and durable multilateral trading system', including efforts at liberalising trade.[5] This agenda is reflected by the fact that all Secretariat officials have tasks that in some way or another are related to trade issues. In this respect, the tasks of the officials are somewhat similar to the tasks of the officials of the European Commission's DG Trade presented in Chapter 3.

Horizontal specialisation: the divisions of the WTO Secretariat
The formal organisational structure of the Secretariat includes a vertical specialisation (a number of hierarchical positions) as well as a horizontal specialisation (a number of divisions). Horizontally, the WTO Secretariat is organised into divisions with functional, information and liaison and support roles respectively. The so-called functional divisions deal with different areas of the substantive work of the organisation. In 2008 there were 16 functional divisions (see below) in addition to a separate secretariat set up to assist the WTO Appellate Body in dispute settlements. There are also divisions which mainly perform support functions (information, interpretation etc.). The functional divisions are:

- Accessions Division;
- Agriculture and Commodities Division;
- Council and Trade Negotiations Committee Division;
- Development Division;
- Doha Development Agenda Special Duties Division;
- Economic Research and Statistics Division;
- Institute for Training and Technical Cooperation;
- Intellectual Property Division;
- Legal Affairs Division;
- Market Access Division;
- Rules Division;
- Technical Cooperation Audit Division;
- Trade and Environment Division;
- Trade and Finance and Trade Facilitation Division;
- Trade in Services Division;
- Trade Policies Review Division.

The information and liaison divisions are:

- External Relations Division;
- Information and Media Relations Division.

The support divisions are:

- External Relations Division;
- Information and Media Relations Division;
- Administration and General Services Division;
- Human Resources Division;
- Informatics Division;
- Language Services and Documentation Division.

The focus in this book is on the functional divisions. Most divisions are organised by purpose (such as the Market Access Division, the Intellectual Property Division and the Agriculture and Commodities Division), and some are organised by process (such as the Accessions Division, the Legal Affairs Division and the Economic Research and Statistics Division). A key task for a functional division is to engage in helping the members to monitor compliance with the existing agreements. The work includes *inter alia* processing notifications from WTO members, and arranging meetings with members. Divisions may also be asked to write papers to help members to assemble information which will be necessary for the review process, i.e. the review of members' implementation of WTO rules.

Vertical specialisation: the hierarchy of the WTO Secretariat
The WTO Secretariat has a relatively flat organisational structure. The top position is the Director-General (DG), a position which is currently (2009) held by Pascal Lamy. The Director- General has a Cabinet to support him which consists of hand-picked civil servants primarily from the Secretariat divisions. In the past, Directors-General 'were sometimes regarded virtually as spiritual leaders of the system' (WTO 2004: 74). The impression today is that Directors-General increasingly see their role as a form of international spokesperson and marketing executive (ibid). This means that much time is spent travelling widely and frequently and having regular contact with political leaders, and their presence and role at WTO headquarters is therefore reduced. The many challenges facing the WTO today, including the issue of leadership, have highlighted the need to clarify the role of the Director-General (WTO 2004: 73).

The level below the DG is the level of Deputy Director-General (DDG). There are currently four DDGs who have been appointed by the WTO Director-General to serve four-year terms. No reason is given as to why there are four DDGs but the prevailing view has been that this number has allowed for some geographical balance at the most senior level of the Secretariat (WTO 2004: 75). The roles and functions that the DDGs have is very much up to the DG. One of the DDGs describes his role and influence as a DDG in the following way:

at the DDG level it is much more at the level of operation, where whatever you do has a systemic kind of influence. So it's the management ... the systemic ... It can be systemic in terms of the house. It can be systemic in terms of the ongoing efforts at the organisation. It can be systemic in terms of what needs to evolve. It can be systemic in terms of links with other organisations. So that's broadly the way that the task is. But when you are doing these systemic things, in order to achieve that task you have to take specific steps. And it may involve just discussion with one key entity – whatever that may be, in house or outside the house. But while doing this one has to keep in mind the trust of the senior management policy, and take things forward. (WTO 14)

Below the DDG level are a number of specialised divisions. Divisions are normally headed up by a Director who reports to a Deputy Director-General or directly to the Director-General. There is no formal hierarchy within the Divisions but there are two main positions below the Director: Economic Affairs Officer and Counsellor. Most of the substantive work is carried out by Economic Affairs Officers and Counsellors while the Director checks on and directs their work. In Figure 5.2 we present a visual illustration of the hierarchical structure of the WTO Secretariat:

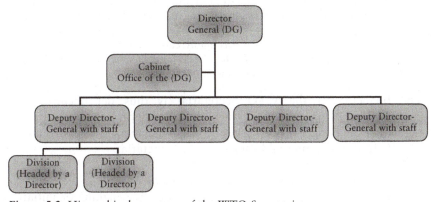

Figure 5.2 Hierarchical structure of the WTO Secretariat

The financing of the WTO Secretariat
The operation of the WTO Secretariat is financed by the members. The provisions regulating the WTO budget and contributions are stated in Article VI of the Agreement Establishing the World Trade Organization. Article VI says *inter alia* that:

the Director-General shall present to the Committee on Budget, Finance and Administration the annual budget estimate and financial statement of the WTO. The Committee on Budget, Finance and Administration shall review the annual budget estimate and the financial statement presented by the Director-General and make recommendations thereon to the General Council. The annual Budget estimate shall be subject to approval by the

General Council [...] The General Council shall adopt the financial
regulations and the annual budget estimate by a two-thirds majority
comprising more than half of the Members of the WTO.

The WTO member-state governments are represented in the Committee
on Budget, Finance and Administration ('Budget Committee'). The
Secretariat submits the budget request to the Budget Committee and needs
to have the budget approved by the members every year, or currently on
a biennial basis because a two-year budget is now submitted. There is also
a mid-term review of the budget in order to adjust it. Through the Budget
Committee, the WTO members are able to intervene in the internal
administration of the Secretariat. A WTO report has pointed out the
tendency towards micro-management by members, in particular through
the Budget Committee (WTO 2004: 74). In our interviews one WTO
official comments on this:

> I mean, do they micro-manage? I think from the Director-General's point of
> view sometimes they micro-manage too much. You know, they
> micro-manage the number of posts we have and that sort of thing. Whereas
> his preference would be 'Well, give us the money and we'll decide how to
> use it'. But no, the Budget Committee is a little bit more interventionist than
> that. But I would say frankly as long as they have confidence in the decisions
> we're making, as long as they don't see a huge misallocation of resources in
> the organisation, then they are reasonably calm [...] But it's a very, very
> time-consuming and pretty difficult process, and then of course collecting
> money from our members is a problem. (WTO 18)

The financing of the WTO Secretariat is thus dependent on the
contributions from the WTO members. Furthermore, the provisions
regulating the budget process give the WTO members the opportunity to
get involved in the internal business of the Secretariat.

The WTO Secretariat's roles and functions in the WTO
The Secretariat does not have autonomous decision-making or initiating
authority. However, the relatively small Secretariat is involved in most of
the work of the WTO and is essential for the functioning of the
organisation. In addition to being member-driven, the WTO is also a
rule-driven organisation. As already indicated, this gives the Secretariat a
central position as a 'guardian of the treaties' (WTO 2004). The
Secretariat possesses considerable expert knowledge regarding the rules of
the WTO agreements, including in particular the application and
understanding of these rules. Thus, although lacking formal decision-
making authority, the Secretariat has the power of knowledge and can
informally influence the decision-making process of the WTO (Yi-Chong
and Weller 2004 and 2008).
     The Secretariat's main duties are to supply technical support for the

various councils and committees and the Ministerial Conferences, to provide technical assistance for developing countries, to analyse world trade and to explain WTO affairs to the public and media (Shaffer 2005). The duty to supply technical support can potentially include more substantial influence on the outcomes, albeit within the limits of the legal framework of the WTO. The Secretariat officials thus personify the WTO, advise individual delegations, provide briefings in technical assistance on the rules of the WTO, and may point out during the Trade Policy Reviews of the members and in other settings what is consistent with WTO rules. The Secretariat's potential for influencing outcomes is enhanced by its legal and economic competence and knowledge, but is also clearly restricted by the formal structure and legal framework of the WTO. However, as argued by Yi-Chong and Weller (2004: 278), within these constraints there is room for action. The Secretariat also provides some forms of legal assistance in the dispute-settlement process and advises governments wishing to become members of the WTO. Here also is the potential to influence the developments of the WTO.

Thus, even though the Secretariat has no formal authority, it can in practice affect the agenda, the outcomes and the interpretation of rules to some extent. This potential for 'invisible governance' (Mathiason 2007) is well formulated by one of the more experienced WTO officials when responding to the question of how much leeway and discretion Secretariat officials have in their work:

> I have quite a bit of discretion, but it's partly because of my recognised expertise in the area. So it's easy enough for me to make reference to what happened during the negotiations, the positions, what were the concerns and what was agreed or not agreed at the time of the negotiations as a background for positions. I think it varies a lot among colleagues depending on their level of expertise or recognised level of expertise, but certainly when you have been working in the area as long as I have, most of our members and delegates, I think, recognise that and they accept that how much freedom really depends on the situation. One feels freer to speak up and express particular views or issues during informal meetings rather than formal meetings of the committee, but it depends in part on who is the chairperson of the committee at the time, and how comfortable they are with the Secretariat taking a more proactive role. [...] I get quite a bit of freedom, I guess. (WTO 15)

The same official argues that even according to the formal role of the Secretariat there is room for influence. During the interview when we suggested that formally there is no role for the Secretariat but that the Secretariat can make a difference informally because of expertise and institutional memory, this official responds:

> Yeah, but I think it actually goes a little further than that because I do think there is even formally a role. As the secretary to the committee there is nothing

that limits the Secretariat to taking the initiative to put out a proposal to the committee or to put out a background document on an issue we think is important to draw attention to. [...] So members can decide to ignore what we put forward, that's their choice, but there is no reason why the Secretariat can't say, you know, 'These transparency provisions are a real problem and here is a proposal of how we could make it better, let's see whether you agree or not' [...] So that's a possibility, and the other of course is that through advising and guiding the chairperson you also have a fair bit of movement, control or ability to influence how things are done, so you can have some countries asking for an issue of [...] and others disagreeing, and the Chairman is asking 'What do you think we want to do?' 'Well, here's a suggestion of how we want to proceed and, you know, maybe in the next meeting ... let's try to downplay it and see what the reaction is'. If they continue to be very insistent, 'Well OK then let's do a special meeting' or, you know, we can have some sense of taking a lead on some of these issues. (WTO 15)

Thus, although the WTO Secretariat is left with very little formal power and discretion within the WTO system, there are WTO officials who perceive that they have quite some leeway in their work within the organisation:

Yeah, I think there is a lot of leeway. You can always put things in terms of these other rules etc., and then one can explain things in terms of different positions from members to cover the whole spectrum of views you might have. And in some context you can always offer your own personal opinion. So I think there is quite a lot of leeway [...] Well, now when I was speaking, I was talking most about our outreach and our technical assistance activities etc. If it's about things that go to the committee, to WTO members as background documents or our own contributions to committee work, then we have to be more careful in terms of first thinking 'What is it that the paper should contribute?' Often what our paper will do different from many of the members' own positions is to summarise the core elements of what everybody is saying; the common denominator, if you so wish, and the history behind it. And then it will, if you have suggested how to move forward, it will always be in terms of options or ideas that have come up ... or possible ways to go forward, so that any debate in the group later is based on alternatives. And it can never be said that we are pushing in one direction or another. (WTO 12)

This quote illustrates that the civil servant perceives that even though he has some leeway, he has to be careful to not be perceived by the members as being too pushy. The same civil servant comments on what the important functions of the Secretariat are, and whether these have any influence when performing the functions:

I think at the end of the day we are facilitators, but I think a bad facilitator can really create big, big problems for any organisation. I think, in the same way as I described my work with the chairman and with delegates, if one does this using a certain level, how should I put this, a very thought-out level of initiative coming from the Secretariat, that is always appreciated even though it might not always be said. But you do want a Secretariat that is moving things forward through its own initiative, otherwise what are we doing here? But it should never look like it is the Secretariat that is doing it. I think that is important, and I think that we are not so bad at that. (WTO 12)

The quote illustrates again very well the image of the 'invisible' international civil servants of the Secretariat (Yi-Chong and Weller 2004: 5). The 'invisible' officials may have an important role 'behind the scenes' in providing input into the WTO processes, while at the same time being careful not to be perceived by the members as initiators or decision makers. Thus, being 'invisible' may enhance the potential for influence. When asked directly about the influence of the WTO Secretariat, a WTO official responds:

I think the Secretariat has a hugely unrecognised influence, because in almost everything that the WTO membership does, the Secretariat is generating the analysis, drafting the documents ... So to the extent that we introduce ideas, we shape existing ideas, so we have influence, but it is totally invisible because it goes out as a committee report or a member tables a paper or a dispute case report of a panel. My perspective is that the Secretariat has quite a bit of influence, but it is probably also not fully using the influence. So there is this constraint by the memberships because the memberships always want to be in control, so there is this tension across how resources are allocated, for example. There is always a question of what members approved. That makes it harder. The Secretariat always has an ownership of the work programme. (WTO 6)

As a 'guardian of the treaties' it is important for the Secretariat to relate its advice and inputs to WTO rules. Nevertheless, one official refers to situations where personal opinions based on legal competence can be relevant to put forward:

Well, you mostly relate it to the rules, but of course it depends on what the question is. For me as a lawyer, most of the questions that I get are legal, so my job is mostly to give them advice on the rules – my framework is the rules. However, sometimes [...] you have to do ... like 'This is my opinion and it doesn't necessarily represent the opinion of the WTO or the Secretariat or the members'. (WTO 4)

Another official comments along the same lines:

I can give my opinion, but I try to still keep it neutral. I just say that 'this is my own personal opinion how I think it would work best'. (WTO 8)

WTO officials constantly have to take into consideration in their work the 'owners' of the WTO, i.e. the member-state governments. At the same time it is important for the civil servants to keep their integrity and to be perceived as neutral by member-state governments. Remaining in a

neutral position is also important in conveying authority when providing
input to the members. When asked what happens if Secretariat officials
are not perceived as neutral and objective, a WTO official responds:

> That is it! Then you are out, you can't play your role. They come to you
> because they trust you. If they don't trust you, or if they feel that you are
> more biased toward one part of the membership and not towards the other,
> it becomes difficult. (WTO 2)

Another official also stresses the need to be careful when expressing
opinions and giving advice:

> So you have to be very, very careful to say ... 'Well, you can do it this way,
> or you can do it that way', without saying 'OK, this is the preferred way'.
> Of course, we all have our opinions, and one can say 'OK you have these
> different options'. [...] So you have to be careful. But you are very much
> bound by what the agreement says [...] It's very sensitive, because people
> can get involved in court cases. Then the worst thing is if they quote
> somebody ... a member of the WTO Secretariat saying certain things that
> just don't hold water. So you have to be careful. (WTO 13)

The WTO Secretariat can thus take on a number of functions and roles in
the WTO – some formal, others informal. The WTO is clearly a
member-driven organisation and the WTO Secretariat officially has no
influence on WTO decision making. Formally, the WTO Secretariat thus
stands out as a neutral facilitator and 'guardian of the treaties' without any
independent influence on the inputs and outputs of the WTO (WTO 2004).
However, in practice, there is room for the Secretariat to make a difference.
The Secretariat's expert knowledge, institutional memory and central
position in WTO bodies put it in a position where potentially it can provide
important input into the WTO's negotiations and decision-making
processes, e.g. in shaping proposals and bringing new ideas to the members.
Hence, the conclusion of Yi-Chong and Weller in their study of the GATT
Secretariat's role under the Uruguay Round of negotiations is also valid for
the WTO Secretariat's role more generally: 'They provide the continuity
and the cement, the credibility and the connections' (2004: 279). Thus,
although lacking formal power and discretion, the WTO Secretariat
nevertheless has the potential to influence WTO activities through its
'invisible governance'. The potential for influence varies, however, among
different civil servants of the Secretariat depending, amongst other things,
on their position, competence and experience. In the next sections we will
explore further the composition of the staff of the Secretariat.

The micro-level: the staff of the WTO Secretariat

In the following sections, we present the composition of the Secretariat
staff including a presentation of the recruitment procedures and statistics

on age, sex, nationality and tenure among the civil servants. The recruitment of Secretariat personnel is based on merit only. There is no formal national quota system. However, on an informal basis nationality may be a factor in recruitment, especially when recruiting to the top positions such as DDGs. The WTO recruitment procedure includes a panel interview, a written functional test based on the qualifications required for the post and a personality test. Vacancies are the subject of open competition and are advertised publicly by means of vacancy notices. Professionals attending the Secretariat are required to possess an advanced university degree in a discipline relevant to a specific area of the WTO's activities. Many of the Secretariat professionals are economists or lawyers specialised in international trade policy.[6] Thus, many WTO officials share a similar educational background and have been through specialised training in trade issues. Age is not a criterion when recruiting new people but some prior experience is required, as indicated in the two tables below. The academic qualifications are often supplemented by experience from national governments, international organisations or other organisations or enterprises dealing with issues of trade policy and international trade relations. Table 5.1 and Table 5.2 include the grading system used for positions in the WTO Secretariat.

Table 5.1 Grading system and required experience and education for professional positions in the Secretariat

Grade	Experience	Education
Director position	A minimum of 15 years' relevant experience	An advanced university degree in a discipline relevant to a specific area of the WTO's activities[a]
Grade 10	A minimum of 10 years' relevant experience	An advanced university degree in a discipline relevant to a specific area of the WTO's activities
Grade 9	A minimum of 8 years' relevant experience	An advanced university degree in a discipline relevant to a specific area of the WTO's activities
Grade 8	A minimum of 5 years' relevant experience	An advanced university degree in a discipline relevant to a specific area of the WTO's activities
Grades 6 and 7	Up to 5 years' relevant experience	An advanced university degree in a discipline relevant to a specific area of the WTO's activities

[a] For example, Law (including studies in international trade law and public international law), Economics, International Relations, Statistics, Computer Science, Human Resources Management, Finance, Accountancy, Business Administration, Translation.

Table 5.2 Grading system and required experience and education for support positions in the Secretariat

Grade	Experience	Education
Grade 7	At least 15 years' relevant experience	Completion of secondary school and/or equivalent technical or commercial school, specialised training in a discipline relevant to the requirements of the position, and proven expertise at a high level.
Grade 6	At least 8 years' relevant experience	Completion of secondary school and/or equivalent technical or commercial school, and specialised training or proven expertise in a discipline relevant to the requirements of the position.
Grade 5	At least 5 years' relevant experience	Completion of secondary school and/or equivalent technical or commercial school.
Grade 4	Three to 4 years' relevant experience	Completion of secondary school and/or equivalent technical or commercial school.
Grade 3	At least 2 years' relevant experience	Completion of secondary school and/or equivalent technical or commercial school.
Grade 2	At least 1 year's relevant experience	Completion of compulsory education.

Personnel are obliged to work for and represent the WTO rather than particular national interests. Article VI of the Agreement establishing the WTO clearly states that the Secretariat shall be neutral and independent of any national or other external interests:

> 4. The responsibilities of the Director-General and of the staff of the Secretariat shall be exclusively international in character. In the discharge of their duties, the Director-General and the staff of the Secretariat shall not seek or accept instructions from any government or any other authority external to the WTO. They shall refrain from any action which might adversely reflect on their position as international officials. The Members of the WTO shall respect the international character of the responsibilities of the Director-General and of the staff of the Secretariat and shall not seek to influence them in the discharge of their duties.

The WTO Staff Regulations state that, 'Staff members shall discharge their duties with the interest and objectives of the WTO in view and, in so doing, shall be subject to the authority of, and responsible to, the Director-General'. The Director-General is thus given a clear hierarchical authority within the Secretariat. The WTO Staff Regulations furthermore state that on taking up their duties, staff members shall make and sign the following declaration:

> I solemnly undertake to exercise in all loyalty, discretion and conscience the functions entrusted to me as an international civil servant of the World Trade Organization, to discharge these functions and regulate my conduct with the interests of the WTO only in view, and not to seek or accept instructions in regard to the performance of my duties from any government or other authority external to the Organization, or to accept remuneration there from with respect to my service with the WTO either prior to, during or after such service.

The WTO Staff Regulations thus clearly underline that the civil servants must be loyal to the WTO and that they must be committed to serving the interests of the organisation in their work. The number of employees in the WTO Secretariat has grown over time, from 530 in 2000 to 632 in 2007. This growth is also evident when we look at the number of staff in the operational divisions of the WTO (Figure 5.3).

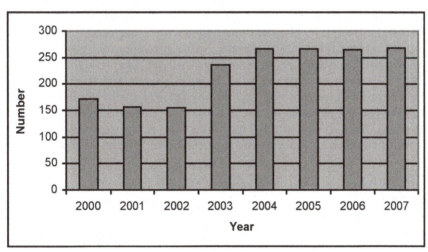

Figure 5.3 WTO staff in operational divisions 2000–2007[a]
[a]The operational (or functional) divisions are as follows: Council and TNC Division, DDA Special Duties Division, Accessions Division, Economic Research and Statistics Division, Legal Affairs Division, Rules Division, Development Division, Institute for Training and Technical Co-operation, Technical Co-operation Audit Division, Trade and Finance and Trade Facilitation Division, Agriculture and Commodities Division, Trade and Environment Division, Trade in Services Division, Intellectual Property Division, Market Access Division, Trade Policies Review Division.

In 2008, 68 nationalities were represented in the WTO Secretariat.[7] The ten most represented countries were: France (181), the United Kingdom (72), Spain (46), Switzerland (44), the United States (30), Canada (23), Germany (16), Italy (13), India (12) and Ireland (11). A total of 382 women and 247 men were employed in the Secretariat. Thus, a large variety of nationalities are represented in the Secretariat but the dominating working language is nevertheless English. Furthermore, as we can see from Table 5.3, the Secretariat has many employees who have worked in the organisation for a long time.

Table 5.3 Distribution of years of service of WTO staff 2000–2007 (percentage of staff)

Years of service	2000	2001	2002	2003	2004	2005	2006	2007
0–5	33	28	26	27	26	26	23	24
5–15	39	43	43	42	33	43	45	38
15–25	17	17	17	16	17	19	20	18
25–35	10	11	13	12	11	10	9	7
Over 35	0	0	0	0	0	0	1	1

From 2000 to 2007 the proportion of staff with more than five years of service actually increased (Table 5.3). It seems that the WTO Secretariat has relatively many employees with a long tenure compared to other international bureaucracies where temporary positions and short-term contracts are more widely used (see Chapters 3 and 4). The level of relatively experienced staff may indicate that there is a high socialisation potential within the Secretariat, where many of the employees are exposed to the WTO's culture, norms, ideas and social pressure over a long time. The impression of an experienced staff is confirmed when considering the age of the civil servants (Table 5.4).

Table 5.4 Distribution of age ranges of WTO staff 2000–2007 (percentage of staff)

Age ranges of WTO staff	2000	2001	2002	2003	2004	2005	2006	2007
21–25	10	7	7	6	6	4	4	5
26–35	28	30	30	32	34	35	34	32
36–45	34	33	30	31	30	30	30	32
46–55	33	34	31	33	32	33	32	32
56–62	10	11	11	12	13	12	13	12

Table 5.4 does not give the impression that the WTO Secretariat is dominated by young people who use the WTO as a career opportunity to move on into even more attractive jobs, which is more the case in other international organisations such as the OECD. On the contrary, the WTO staff are distributed among all age ranges. It is also worth noticing the relatively large proportion of people with long experience – close to 50 per cent of the staff were more than 45 years old in the years 2000–2007. It is also noticeable that only a small proportion of the WTO staff are actually involved in the substantive work of the WTO (Figure 5.4).

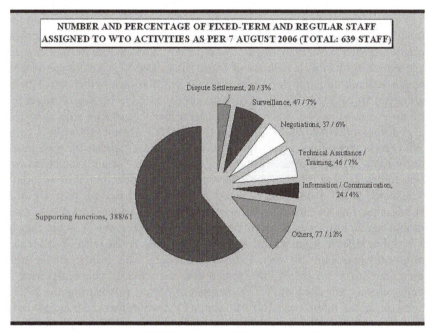

NUMBER AND PERCENTAGE OF FIXED-TERM AND REGULAR STAFF ASSIGNED TO WTO ACTIVITIES AS PER 7 AUGUST 2006 (TOTAL: 639 STAFF)

Dispute Settlement, 20 / 3%

Surveillance, 47 / 7%

Negotiations, 37 / 6%

Technical Assistance / Training, 46 / 7%

Information / Communication, 24 / 4%

Others, 77 / 12%

Supporting functions, 388/61

Figure 5.4 Distribution of WTO staff on WTO activities, 2006

Figure 5.4 shows the distribution of Secretariat staff on different WTO activities (in 2006). We see that 388 persons – 61 per cent of the staff – are involved in support functions whereas 251 persons – 39 per cent of the staff – are assigned to a variety of operational activities. The numbers illustrate that the WTO Secretariat is a small bureaucracy and that the operation of the substantive WTO work is actually handled by a very small number of civil servants. A large part of the staff is involved in support functions, which is understandable considering that the Secretariat has to serve more than 150 members with different needs, levels, infrastructures, administrative capacities, languages etc. The small size of the staff also illustrates that the Secretariat is not in its present form in a position to appear as a powerful autonomous bureaucracy. It is small and has few formal powers and resources but, as illustrated in this chapter, it nevertheless has the potential to make a difference in the operations of the WTO.

The WTO Secretariat: an invisible bureaucracy with potential influence

The WTO has a key role in negotiating trade rules and providing a comprehensive rule-based framework for the regulation of world trade. The new dispute-settlement mechanism, which was established in 1995, has given the WTO more power to settle trade disputes between its members. Currently, in 2009, the WTO is facing great challenges in the ongoing Doha Round of negotiations in which members are seeking to agree on establishing a new set of trade rules. The WTO has experienced many setbacks during the Doha Round negotiations, which have been going on since 2001, and therefore negotiations have been prolonged for many years. However, such setbacks have been more the rule than the exception in the history of GATT and the WTO. Despite its setbacks the WTO has grown into a truly global international organisation with more authority, power and influence than most other international organisations, and it has never received more attention than it does today. Thus, the WTO Secretariat is faced with the challenge of assisting and supporting one of the most powerful international organisations with global reach. However, as pointed out in this chapter, the WTO is clearly a member-driven organisation and the Secretariat is left with little formal autonomy and hardly any formal influence. The politicisation and increased focus on the WTO implies that the work of the Secretariat is being closely watched by WTO members. Within this setting the WTO Secretariat has many roles to fulfil and, as shown in this chapter, actually has the potential to make a difference in the decision-making processes of the WTO.

The WTO Secretariat appears in many ways as a traditional bureaucratic organisation based on neutrality, the rule of law, a hierarchic organisation and a vertical specialisation and with a merit-based recruitment system. However, the WTO Secretariat lacks two important features that characterise national government administrations. Firstly, the Secretariat is subordinated to a multilateral environment consisting of 153 members (in 2008). This creates a fragmented environment where the Secretariat must 'tread a careful path' when giving advice, assisting members and making propositions based on WTO members' inputs. The Secretariat thus lacks a clear and unitary political leadership. Secondly, the Secretariat lacks decision-making and initiating authority and power. Thus, its influence is more based on the civil servants' positions in the system, their expert knowledge and institutional memory, and their potential for informally providing inputs into the system. With its many civil servants with long tenure and broad experience, the Secretariat is in a good position to make a difference in the WTO. However, WTO officials have to be careful not to lose credit among WTO members. Thus, WTO officials have many roles and functions to fulfil within the system: as 'guardians of the treaties', as facilitators, as advisers, as trade and legal experts and as servants of the members. It can be a delicate balance for the Secretariat to live up to all these roles and functions, not least because of the multilateral environment in which they are placed. The need to not lose credit among members could be expected to lead WTO officials to place emphasis on their roles as professional experts (epistemic role) and as neutral and dedicated WTO civil servants (departmental and supranational dynamics). The focused trade agenda of the WTO and the emphasis on recruiting people who are trained in trade issues may also enhance the epistemic dynamic. The WTO officials' long tenure and work experience within the Secretariat may enhance a departmental as well as a supranational dynamic. We will look more closely at the different dynamics in the following chapters.

The WTO has been placed at the centre of world politics, and its significance and outreach in global governance has never been greater. However, the massive critique against the organisation from interest groups and governments all over the world, and the many setbacks in the ongoing negotiations of the Doha Round, have led some observers to state that the organisation is in a crisis, that the WTO is in a situation of 'live or let die'. However, the impression of an organisation in crisis is not shared by the WTO officials we interviewed. On the contrary, they see crisis maximisation, setbacks and delays as 'business as usual' – as phases that a multilateral organisation such as the WTO has to go through in order to find durable compromises and solutions. The officials realise that the work must be done step by step and that such processes may take time. This confirms the impression of the WTO Secretariat as a stabilising element in the operation of the WTO.

Annex 5.1 Marrakesh Agreement Establishing the World Trade Organization

Article VI

The Secretariat

1. There shall be a Secretariat of the WTO (hereinafter referred to as 'the Secretariat') headed by a Director-General.
2. The Ministerial Conference shall appoint the Director-General and adopt regulations setting out the powers, duties, conditions of service and term of office of the Director-General.
3. The Director-General shall appoint the members of the staff of the Secretariat and determine their duties and conditions of service in accordance with regulations adopted by the Ministerial Conference.
4. The responsibilities of the Director-General and of the staff of the Secretariat shall be exclusively international in character. In the discharge of their duties, the Director-General and the staff of the Secretariat shall not seek or accept instructions from any government or any other authority external to the WTO. They shall refrain from any action which might adversely reflect on their position as international officials. The Members of the WTO shall respect the international character of the responsibilities of the Director-General and of the staff of the Secretariat and shall not seek to influence them in the discharge of their duties.

Notes

1 See homepage of the WTO: www.wto.org/.
2 See homepage of the WTO: www.wto.org/.
3 See homepage of the WTO: www.wto.org/.
4 See homepage of the WTO: www.wto.org/.
5 Cf. the chapter of the agreement establishing the WTO.
6 See homepage of the WTO: www.wto.org/.
7 See homepage of the WTO: www.wto.org/

Part III

The dynamics of compound bureaucracies

6

Departmental dynamics in international bureaucracies

This chapter demonstrates the existence of a foundational departmental dynamic within all the international bureaucracies studied – both with respect to contact, co-ordination and conflict patterns and to the identity and role perceptions among the personnel. International bureaucracies seem to have enduring impacts on the officials embedded within them. This strongly signifies that the organisational structures of international bureaucracies influence the staff. These observations are similar among both seconded part-time employed officials and permanent officials with lifelong positions. Consequently, the departmental dynamic is indeed fostered more by international bureaucracies and less by external institutions such as domestic ministries and agencies.

A *departmental* behavioural dynamic predicts officials in international bureaucracies to be 'neutral, intelligent, generalist professionals who advise ministers' (Richards and Smith 2004: 779). In short, officials demonstrating a departmental dynamic tend to evoke an inward-looking behavioural pattern geared towards their 'own' organisation. Officials are expected to evoke the classical Weberian civil servant virtues of being party-politically neutral, attaching identity towards their unit and division, and abiding by the administrative rules and proper procedures of their international bureaucracy. This is the Whitehall model that sees officials as neutral, permanent and loyal to the international bureaucracy. We thus expect officials of international bureaucracies to be guided by the formal rules, routines and procedures of the international bureaucracy in which they are employed. Their role perceptions and loyalties are expected to be primarily directed towards their international bureaucracy, and the officials tend to perceive themselves principally as representatives of their portfolio and/or unit.

How do we recognise the departmental dynamic when we come across it? We anticipate officials to:

- have a primary and undivided loyalty towards their own portfolio/ dossier;
- be formally or informally mandated and co-ordinated by department and unit rules, being guided and driven by internal administrative rules and procedures;
- be guided by preferences and concerns for their department and unit;
- have contact patterns and co-ordination behaviour that are strongly guided by the organisational boundaries, units and departments of the international bureaucracy (both horizontally and vertically);
- have patterns of co-operation and conflict that follow organisational boundaries inside the international bureaucracy.

This chapter is organised as follows: the first section makes a short review of previous studies on international bureaucracy that focus on the departmental behavioural dynamic, and the next section gives data from this study on the departmental behavioural dynamics inside the Commission, the OECD Secretariat and the WTO Secretariat. The chapter is organised according to the proxies suggested above. Within each sub-section of this chapter the departmental dynamics in the Commission, the OECD Secretariat and the WTO Secretariat are compared. The chapter concludes by comparing our main empirical observations across the three cases.

What does literature say about departmental dynamics?

The portfolio logic has long dominated decision making in the Commission. Even in the early days of the High Authority the routinisation of Commission work began to be put in place, resulting in 'a comic incompatibility of humour between Monnet and routine administration' (Duchêne 1994: 240). Recent empirical studies have also indicated the existence of departmental dynamics in international bureaucracies, notably in the Commission. In a case study of the defence industry and the equipment policy of the Commission, Morth (2000) shows that the organisational structure of the Commission accompanies 'frame competition' between different DGs. This competition legitimates different issues, actors, knowledge and decisions, and ultimately defines and re-defines the distribution of power and resources among the Commission DGs. Such frame competition indeed reflects the horizontal specialisation of the Commission services. Other studies have focused on the existence of parallel formal and informal hierarchies within the Commission. One notable observation is the recent increase in the formalisation and strengthening of the formal hierarchy inside the Commission, particularly related to the performance appraisals (Kurpas et al. 2008). According to one veteran Commission official, 'These people arrived from "Planet Audit" and started to use PowerPoint to tell everyone how things should be. Kinnock tried. There was a lot of management speak about "performance management", "audit", "transparency" and "targets". It has notably made the Commission more bureaucratic' (Shore 2007: 202; Ellinas and Suleiman 2008).

Rule-guided behaviour dominates the interaction in the Commission (Böhling 2007). The behaviour of Commission officials is described as being formatted in procedures and regulations. Anthropological studies of the Commission by Maryon McDonald (1997: 51) also illustrate that 'the DGs offer important units of identification'. Similarly, Commission officials tend to identify with the DG rather than with the Commission as a whole (Cini 1997). In our vocabulary, previous studies indicate that departmental identities are stronger than supranational identities among Commission staff. The departmental dynamic is shown to be stronger than both supranational and partisan dynamics at the very top of the Commission within the College of Commissioners (Egeberg 2006). Hooghe (1997: 89) also gives evidence of a departmental dynamic within the 'house with different views'. However, Hooghe's 1997 observation somewhat contradicts her main observations in a more recent publication (Hooghe 2005) where Commission dynamics are primarily explained by external (domestic) socialisation processes. Previously, Hooghe (1997: 105) has argued that 'DGs send ambivalent signals to Commission officials', rendering their decision-making behaviour constrained and biased by the organisational structures within the Commission. Previous studies have demonstrated that the contact patterns of Commission officials are strongly departmentalised. Hooghe (2005: 63) reveals that Commission officials have more frequent contact inside their 'own' DG than horizontally with other DGs or vertically with the College of Commissioners. Whereas Hooghe's research focuses only on top Commission officials, recent research on Commission officials from all ranks at the AD level reveals that informal behaviour in everyday decision making is strongly guided by the formal structure of the Commission services (Suvarierol 2007). The organisational embedment of Commission officials thus seems important for understanding their departmental perceptions. This chapter presents fresh empirical data on the departmental dynamics in the Commission, the OECD Secretariat and the WTO Secretariat.

Departmental dynamics in international bureaucracies

The data presented in this chapter illuminate the existence of a departmentalised behavioural dynamic among Commission, OECD and WTO officials. This chapter transcends existing research by documenting the departmental dynamic within several international administrations.

The chapter also adds an important extension to previous research by documenting similar degrees of departmental behavioural dynamics among permanent and temporary officials. By comparing permanent and contracted Commission officials, our data confirm that the formal organisation of international bureaucracies indeed impacts on the departmental dynamics within international bureaucracies. Although a majority of OECD officials have time-limited contracts and thus often a fairly short tenure, this chapter demonstrates that the OECD Secretariat is indeed characterised by a departmental dynamic. A departmental behavioural dynamic is also observed in the WTO Secretariat, partly reflecting the fairly low turnover and the corresponding long tenure among the staff. Finally, this chapter demonstrates that the formal hierarchy of international bureaucracies is supplemented with informal hierarchies in the everyday behaviour of international civil servants. Formal hierarchical structures are sometimes fairly broad, ambiguous and general-normative frames that provide room for informal structures within units and divisions.

Formal hierarchies, rules and procedures

During our interviews at the Commission, several officials made known their views on the Commission hierarchy. One notable characteristic commented on by most interviewees is that the formal hierarchy of the Commission has become strengthened during the post-Kinnock reform period (2000 to the present day), and that the formal hierarchy of command is constantly supplemented by informal hierarchies that partly criss-cross and supplement the formal hierarchy. As shown in Chapter 2, the new promotion system (CDR) has accompanied the increased bureaucratisation of the services. This reform has not only contributed to NPM-related measures but has also clearly contributed to strengthening bureaucratic elements in the services through an expanded body of control and verification procedures. These observations are supported by the elite survey of Ellinas and Suleiman (2008), who report that a vast majority of top Commission officials consider the Commission as 'too bound by rules'. 'According to some officials, the Kinnock reforms have brought about an "administrative overdrive" that has led to a "proliferation of controllers" and has put officials on guard to protect themselves' (Ellinas and Suleiman 2008: 719). Our own interviewees largely supported these observations. Several seconded officials interviewed for this book describe the Commission as 'a hierarchy of fear' – with particular reference to the CDR system.

The Commission has been pictured as being 'run by men in Armani suits, with a strict hierarchy and an equally strict method of working' (Eppink 2007: 33). The importance attached to the formal rules of decision making in the Commission has been described in the following way: 'In the absence of a common administrative culture, these procedures have acquired the status of a sacred rite' (Eppink 2007: 218). The backcloth of the increased formalisation of the Commission is the legacy of the Delors Presidency which created a parallel *informal* organisation inside the formal Commission apparatus. The formal structures of organisations often provide ambiguous cues for action among the personnel. Under these conditions, the informal structures may complement and supplement the formal rules with informal norms of action. A parallel informal administration was created by Commission President Delors to push forward projects and policy proposals deemed difficult to put on the agenda and implement through the formal Commission hierarchy (Suvarierol 2007: 28). Furthermore, under the Presidency of Barosso, the increased informality within the Commission – both at an administrative level within the DGs and also inside the College – has 'generally strengthened the position of the President, as it gives him the possibility to work with a restricted number of Commissioners outside the College and "on demand". It grants him privileged access to all major dossiers, while regular Commissioners are normally fully involved only on matters that somehow concern their respective portfolio' (Kurpas et al. 2008: 41). When asked about the current Commission machinery (2007), one of our interviewees replies:

> I think it is a pretty heavy machine right now. It really takes time here. We are applying the rules which are existing for six years and, OK, there was a huge progress but it has been six years and there are still places where the light has not really got through. (Commission 1)

> With the after-effects of the Santer Commission, I think, the whole Commission, including this DG, has become more process oriented, more procedural; some would say more bureaucratic, more cumbersome. The amount of resources that are now being used internally for purely administrative tasks has grown as a result of the various reforms that have been introduced. I think the scope for [informal processes] has become much less. The procedures have become more formalised. (Commission 9)

> With the Kinnock Reform things have become a bit more formal. You have much more formal planning now, much more benchmarking, indication of objectives and testing the results with the objectives – that has become more formal. (Commission 24)

Interviews with the Commission officials substantiate that the horizontal specialisation of the Commission services does indeed affect the behaviour and thinking of Commission officials. Notably, the co-ordinating role of the GS is described by several respondents as increasingly presidential. The increased importance of the GS was mentioned by most of our GS interviewees as becoming an executive power base of the President. Most officials at the GS argue that the power of both the President and the GS Secretary-General seem augmented. Concerning the GS:

> EU diplomats have characterised the style of current Commission President, Jose Manuel Barroso, as 'presidential', with Mr. Barroso personally steering Brussels' most important policy dossiers such as energy and the EU Constitution. The presidential system doesn't mean the President is making all the decisions, it means that there is a strong role of the Commission Secretariat. (EUobserver 2007)

A previous member of the Cabinet also reported that 'over the years, the President's role has evolved from a position of "first among equals" to become more truly presidential in style' (Eppink 2007: 221). Currently one of the most salient organisational issues in the GS is the ambition to presidentialise the Commission as a whole – making the GS into a separate DG for the President. The increased presidentialisation of the GS seems to be partly caused by the increased administrative capacities of the GS to steer and co-ordinate the Commission services and partly by the personal ambitions of President Barosso (see Chapter 2). A recent report on the Commission also supports our observation about the increased presidentialisation of the Commission writ large and the GS in particular (Kurpas et al. 2008: 32). According to this report, President Barosso is 'determined to provide this "political guidance" to the institution. He gets more directly involved and takes responsibility for a large number of dossiers' (Kurpas et al. 2008: 32). Comparing the number of proposals prepared under the direct responsibility of Presidents Prodi and Barosso, Kurpas et al. (2008: 33) report that President Barosso has been over-whelmingly more active.

Our interviewees in the Commission GS claim that one organisational strategy that has recently been launched to augment GS control over the sector DGs is to horizontally specialise the GS according to the DG structure. If such a horizontal-sector specialisation was installed within the GS, this structure would in fact mirror the DG structure and would ease mutual relations between the GS and the respective DGs. Organisational duplication of this kind would augment the potential for the GS to control the DGs, but would also provide an opportunity for the DGs to impact on the GS more directly. In summary, such an organisational solution within the GS would make the horizontal principle of purpose apply all the way from the top to the bottom of the Commission. One recent study of the decision-making dynamics within the College of Commissioners also indicates that the departmental portfolio logic seems ever more prevalent among Commissioners. Partly due to the increased size of the College, Commissioners have become more focused on their own portfolio and more rarely engaged in cross-portfolio questions (Kurpas et al. 2008: 38).

The challenge ahead of the GS with respect to the presidentialisation of the Commission and the co-ordination of the Commission services vertically and horizontally is reflected in the following quote:

> The Secretariat General remains the guarantor of collegiality, at the service of the President. I consider that the biggest challenge for the GS today is that of policy integration, bringing together different policy strands at the earliest possible stage of preparation to ensure that when proposals arrive at the College for decision they are coherent with the overall policy goals. (O'Sullivan 2006: 101)

As observed in the Commission, several interviewees in the OECD Secretariat also report that the formal hierarchy of the OECD Secretariat is constantly supplemented by different informal hierarchies that partly criss-cross the formal hierarchy. In the OECD Secretariat the departmental dynamic also seems to be closely connected to the formal organisation of the Secretariat – both the horizontal and the vertical specialisations of the administrative apparatus. The hierarchy is clearly visible in everyday encounters at the office. One A4 OECD official reports that:

> You've got a very vertical hierarchical structure. That is a model of management of the 19th century. (OECD 19)

One Head of Unit makes the claim that:

> That is one of the problems of international organisations as a whole: the system is so heavy. (OECD 20)

Another OECD official reports that:

> Here there is a sort of huge bureaucratic structure you have to learn to live with. (OECD 24)

The hierarchy in the OECD Secretariat is even felt outside the office:

> There is a little bit of grade snobbery in this organisation. I play football for example. In the beginning a colleague said to me 'You're playing football, are you? That's the B grades and C grades, isn't it?' It never occurred to me that I should consider football in those terms. (OECD 13)

The importance of the vertical hierarchy in the OECD Secretariat is supplemented with a strong horizontal specialisation of the services:

> [The OECD is very] decentralised, and each directorate is more or less independent. It makes it difficult to manage big cross-directorate projects. (OECD 4)

> The way in which the different directorates are organised and carried out can be quite heterogeneous. So we talk about different OECDs here. So from this point of view, people who move from one directorate to another can from time to time find very big differences. It depends on the culture of

that particular directorate, the style that the Director gives to the whole directorate and so on. (OECD 28)

Also, recruitment of seconded officials is decentralised to the directorates; the recruitment is entirely decentralized. This is done entirely by directorates. (OECD 10)

This decentralisation of the directorates easily leads to organisational idiosyncrasies and different levels of hierarchy in different directorates. The formal hierarchy is, however, supplemented by considerable room for manoeuvre for the officials in their everyday decision-making processes. One Director reports that:

Within the OECD we have a rather liberal regime as far as the direct day-to-day supervision of the work of the individual Directors by our top management – the Secretary-General and his Deputies – is concerned. They leave the individual Directors a lot of freedom and liberty to run their own affairs. They expect results. They expect that we impress our member countries by the quality of work and services that we provide but how precisely we do that is very much left to us. (OECD 11)

In addition to the strong element of the horizontal and vertical specialisations of the Secretariat, the OECD Secretariat is dominated by a team organisation that often tends to criss-cross the directorate structure. According to one official:

I think our team is exceptional in the way everybody gets on and in the way everyone is encouraged to express their opinions. It is a team that functions extremely well, and on this floor, everybody wants to work on our team if there is an opportunity. (OECD 2)

As in most OECD countries, the OECD Secretariat has itself also implemented performance management systems. However, as we observed in the Commission (Chapter 2), criticism of this system is also explicit among several OECD officials:

I have a clear-cut job work description. I could tell you with a certain degree of accuracy what I will be doing at a certain month in a year. Performance evaluations are not very well tied to mobility within the organisation – either up or down or sideways. So the only place that people take them quite seriously is if they have a fear that, at some point, they might be in danger of losing their job. In places that change slower, perhaps it's easier to have this performance review. I am not sure that the performance evaluations reflect what people expect them to be reflecting, but I think they should either be changed to some extent; they don't receive very much weight, at least not here ... You are trying to put too much weight on something that doesn't necessarily reflect reality. (OECD 6)

There is a frequent use of temporary contracts in the OECD Secretariat. The ratio of temporary to permanent officials is much higher in the OECD

Secretariat than in the Commission. In contrast to the Commission, however, officials on temporary contracts are found at almost all levels in the OECD hierarchy. Hence, the distinction between permanent and temporary officials is blurred and seems less relevant in the OECD Secretariat. According to one official:

> I don't really see any distinction there. I haven't yet come across one case where somebody has tried to defend his or her own country's political interests here in the organisation. It doesn't really matter what the nature of the contract is. (OECD 11)

The importance of the vertical hierarchy of the WTO Secretariat is substantiated by the fact that several interviewees reflected on the power of the WTO Secretariat. The power of the Secretariat with respect to influencing the final WTO 'deliverables' is clearly lower than in national ministries and the Commission. However, whereas some ascribe the WTO Secretariat an important role, others claim that the power of the WTO Secretariat is fairly limited – particularly when compared to domestic governments and to the Commission. Some officials claim that the power of the WTO Secretariat is noticeable partly due to its expertise and partly due to its co-ordination role among the member states. However, the power of the WTO Secretariat may be invisible or at least difficult to disentangle (Mathiason 2007). The behind-the-scenes power of the WTO Secretariat was illustrated in the Doha Round where the WTO Secretariat provided the negotiators with much-needed notes, drafts and advice. However, the limitation of the WTO Secretariat was also demonstrated when the principal states remained far apart (Yi-Chong and Weller 2008: 45). According to one top official, the WTO Secretariat:

> is the conductor of an orchestra. You can have a quartet without a director, but you can not have 150 musicians play by themselves. It is the facilitator; it is the midwife as it says. (WTO 9)

Another official claims:

> I think the Secretariat provides institutional knowledge. And the Secretariat provides individuals with substance background to help the chairman sort through the issues. And the secretary individuals have institutional and historical knowledge, and expert knowledge on a specific agreement. (WTO 10)

Finally, one official says:

> You do want a secretariat that is moving things forward through its own initiative. But it should never look like it is the Secretariat that is doing it. (WTO 12)

However, the ambiguity of the powers of the WTO Secretariat is also reported in our interviews. Some officials claim that the WTO

Secretariat is much less omnipotent and that it is severely member-state driven:

> We have more responsibility for less power. In a national bureaucracy you are a part of a ministry; whereas here, you have a lot of responsibility but it seems that you do not take decisions. (WTO 9)

> Compared to the Commission President, the WTO Director-General has very, very limited powers. I mean his real power is as a sort of arbitrator, broker and steward for the members' interests. Moreover, a Deputy Director-General doesn't have a very defined role here. I mean the Director-General kind of knows what his role is ... The Directors know what their roles are ... to sort of fill gaps in between ... (WTO 18)

As we have seen in the Commission, an increased bureaucratisation and more rule-based procedures are also reported within the WTO Secretariat. One reason given for this is the increased size of the Secretariat. With the increased size comes a greater formalisation of procedures:

> It has become more formalistic. But it's also become much larger, so that's part of it. (WTO 15)

> When I joined GATT we were something like between 200 and 300 staff members, now we are 700 or maybe even more. I think basically we work more or less in the same way but [it has become] more formalised. (WTO 16)

The WTO Secretariat is a fairly small international administration particularly when compared to the Commission. One consequence of this seems to be that the WTO Secretariat is seen as less formalistic and hierarchical than the Commission. There are far fewer hierarchical layers in the WTO Secretariat than in the Commission. Moreover, in contrast to the increased presidentialisation of the Commission, we see less of this trend in the WTO Secretariat. Interviewees report that the WTO Director-General clearly is powerful, and that the Deputy Director-General has indeed *formal* powers but that s/he is only modestly involved in everyday activities inside the Secretariat. The Director level is also described as having fairly little direct hierarchical control and as giving few direct instructions to WTO officials in their everyday work. In effect, officials get fairly large room for manoeuvre.

Departmental contact, co-ordination and conflict patterns
Contact and co-ordination processes among Commission officials are clearly patterned by the vertical hierarchy inside the services. Contacts among Commission officials are structured by the unit and DG structure, and officials report having fairly clear chains of command which they follow. However, the formal hierarchy of Heads of Unit, Directors, Directors-General and Commissioners is supplemented by several informal

hierarchies. The following quotes from the GS reflect hierarchical contact and co-ordination patterns inside the Commission:

> We are not really working a lot with the other units or directorates within the Secretariat General. We have our hierarchical path to adopt a decision ... Our usual circuit is within the Secretariat General just up to Catherine Day ... Contacts go by hierarchy, clearly. If I do not manage to find a solution which would be satisfactory for us and the DGs concerned [I go through hierarchy], which happens from time to time ... If I do find such a solution, I go through Legal Services. I discuss each of the files within my team and with my direct supervisor, sometimes on daily basis, sometimes on weekly basis – it depends on how big the file. But then, once I have prepared the file, it is a decision for the hierarchy, and it goes through myself, the Deputy Head of Unit, the Head of Unit, the Director, the assistant to Catherine Day ... and then back down to the Secretariat. It takes a few days usually. (Commission 1)

Despite the fact that the Commission supplements the formal unit structure with teams, it was seen from the interviews that officials attach more energy and attention towards their *primary* unit structures than towards the *secondary* team structures. This observation supports recent research showing that the majority of the informal contact of Commission officials is clustered within their DGs (Suvarierol 2007: 118). These observations also show that Commission officials are clearly rule-driven. With respect to the logic of hierarchy, the interviewees claim that desk officials may have contact directly up to Director level or even Director-General level – largely bypassing more than one hierarchical level. Often, such direct contact up the hierarchical ladder is caused by the 'hierarchical lifting' of the officials' files. The interviews revealed that direct contact from desk officers to the Director or Director-General level may also be due to the politicisation of particular dossiers when the dossiers are subject to public debate or due to personal interest in particular files from Directors and Directors-General.

Clear differences can be seen between the GS and DG Trade with respect to the overall view on horizontal co-ordination versus sectoral fragmentation inside the Commission. Whereas most officials in the GS agree that they adopt a so-called 'helicopter view' of the whole Commission's work, officials in DG Trade mostly emphasise their 'silo thinking' and focus on trade issues in isolation from other issue areas. From the interviews it seems plausible that this difference is associated with the formal organisation of the GS as a horizontal *process-organised* DG on top of the Commission apparatus, while DG Trade represents a classical *purpose-organised* DG with a strong sector focus. The following GS official makes a thorough reflection on the co-ordination role of the GS and the 'helicopter logic' among GS officials:

I am a policy co-ordinator in internal policy making. I follow up the work of a number of DGs. We try to ensure that there is coherent decision making internally and in-house. Normally our role is in co-ordination. Basically, what that entails is that we get in touch with our DGs very early on, we get to know what they plan in terms of initiatives, sometimes a year ahead or more. Sometimes it is also arbitration, because it is not only bringing the experience from other DGs to the table but also the different policy perspectives. We also prepare the inter-service consultation. So this expression of collegiality is actually what we try to bring in practice, namely to ensure that every department has been informed, has been able to express itself, has been able to put forward its experience, its knowledge. And in some cases when they are not interested, force them to put the experience on the table. So, if you like, from very early on, we try to ensure coherence and co-ordination, translate a bit what happens at the political level for the use of the services in their proposals, and run through the whole internal decision-making process. It's certainly true that we are moving more into a formal approach, simply because DGs set up inter-service steering groups and there is a formal invitation. Since that process has been more formalised within the services as well, we take part in the more formalised process. (Commission 3)

However, the co-ordination ambitions of the GS sometimes exceed their co-ordination abilities. The horizontal interlocking function of the GS often collides with the sectoral decision-making processes of the sector DGs in everyday decision making. An official in the GS makes this point:

There is tremendous power in the departments because of what they know about their policy areas, and their decades of managing and developing policy. There is a large level of experience and knowledge of their areas. And we are inevitably skating on the surface. The most likely role that we will play is to sit down at the table together and squeeze them all to give a bit of ground that they already know. So the departments are very strong. But they can be pulled, of course, into a compromise by each other as much as by us. Proposals from other DGs are far more frequently adjusted and adapted by us rather than blocked or fundamentally changed. We delay people. We tell them their file is not ready because there has to be further discussion, further preparation. They want to run it straight up, get it up for a decision. And we won't necessarily let that happen. One of our instructions in the larger Commission has been to resolve more issues earlier so that the Commission doesn't have to occupy its time so much with things which don't really involve a major policy decision. (Commission 4)

Officials in DG Trade largely confirm this view. DG Trade officials also confirm the presidential ambitions within the GS to co-ordinate the Commission services more firmly. However, officials in DG Trade tend to co-ordinate within their own portfolios to a greater extent than across portfolios. This observation can be predicted from the portfolio organisation of much of the services:

> Even the President says we are thinking in silos and we have a lot of turf fighting. That is, I think, well known and even acknowledged by the President. Barosso says we should now stop with this silo thinking and start working together. (Commission 7)

> The Lisbon setting is where the President has tried to overcome the turf fighting between the DGs and to create first of all a better link between DGs concerned, but also tried to implement a more presidential style of Commission policy making in giving a lot of tasks and responsibilities to the Secretariat General.
> Q: Has he succeeded in that respect?
> Yes and no. But the problem is that it is a new process. That is a difficult balance to strike because we have to change our way of working away from the collegiality of all 27 Commissioners to a more presidential style. They need to strengthen the Secretariat General. They try. Partly they do well, but it certainly is not settled yet.
> Q: One point is to reduce 'silo thinking'. Has it been reduced?
> I think it has been reduced. (Commission 23)

Silo thinking is organisationally vested within the Commission services, mainly due to the horizontal specialisation of the services. The stronghold of silo logic is reported by the following official: 'Don't come close to our territory, we deal with taxation, you don't!' (Commission 22). From our interviews it appears that 'silo logic' reflects the portfolio organisation of the Commission. Historically, the portfolio organisation of the Commission seems to contribute to a departmental logic among the Commissioners:

> In 1967, when the executives were merged, Émile Noël realised that, unlike the High Authority, decisions in the EEC were not prepared by the full Commission, but each Commissioner had a specific sphere of competence and was responsible solely for drawing up the proposals to be submitted in that sphere. (Bitsch 2007b: 192)

The interviews in the GS and DG Trade confirm that the presidentialisation of the Commission and the co-ordination ambitions of the GS are largely driven by the horizontal specialisation of the DGs involved. Notably, the issue of the presidentialisation of the Commission was commented on by all our interviewees in the GS but by none of our interviewees in DG Trade. The fact that the presidentialisation of the Commission is mostly commented on by GS officials and not by officials in DG Trade may be explained by their different organisational embedment within the Commission services. Hence, the statements referred to above reflect the formal organisation of the Commission as well as the organisational embedment of the interviewees. The co-ordination behaviour referred to by interviewees in the GS may be explained by the formal organisation of the GS by the principle of *process*. Consequently, the organisational roles of the GS are to co-ordinate and integrate the sector portfolios of the sector DGs.

Our interviews in DG Trade also confirm that their contact patterns are strongly departmentalised, both vertically and horizontally. Their contact is clearly more frequently directed within rather than across units and DGs. Most officials also report on the complementary roles played by the formal and informal hierarchies in the Commission. Similar to the findings of Ed Page (2008), the formal hierarchy is sometimes relaxed in the everyday operation of the Commission, notably with respect to information circulation in the drafting phase of decision making. However, when the decision-drafting phase translates into a more formal decision-making phase, the formal hierarchy and levels of command tend to come into play. The logic of hierarchy is reflected upon by a Head of Unit as follows:

> We are still very hierarchical. All official notes and signatures go through me. People have contacts with the Director, but this very much depends on the personality of the Directors. I personally do not care as long as they inform me about what they are doing. (Commission 1)

Other Commission officials comment further on how the hierarchy system works in practice:

> You do most of the work yourself, but then, if there's something that is going to commit the Commission, that has to go outside of the house, you'll then put it in the terms of the hierarchy. (Commission 16)

> Q: But you can have direct contact with other DGs?
> At the right level. I am not supposed to have contacts normally with Directors at other DGs, but with Heads of Unit it is no problem at all. Direct contacts with the Cabinet are a rare thing. I don't see a major shift there. (Commission 8)

> From time to time, formal processes can look very formal, but then for practical purposes we have very easy and direct access throughout the organisation. Even though you have this very formal and very elaborate organisation, from time to time you can have very flat and very quick decision moves. I think the informal hierarchy plays very much for information exchange, for the preparation of decisions, whereas the formal hierarchy is the real decision-making hierarchy. You will have nobody taking decisions outside this formal system. (Commission 11)

The interviewees were asked to assess which person in the Commission they viewed as the key figure in the Commission decision-making machinery. The vast majority of the respondents report that the Heads of Unit and the Directors are of the most importance. Hence, leaders that are located *within* their own unit and directorates are considered most influential. This observation clearly reflects the formal structure of the Commission. However, most officials also testify that priorities set at the level of the Secretary-General and the Commissioners also trickle all the way down the hierarchy and are felt in everyday practice among the officials:

> We see a great difference in terms of how the Commissioners work. I mean, Lamy and Mandelson, they are much more hands-on than previous Commissioners. And they watch not just the technical aspects of the case, but they watch all of it.
>
> Q: Who is most important to you?
>
> In my everyday life and everyday work it is the Head of Unit. The hierarchy here in the Commission is a very French one. It is very vertical. Definitely. I felt that already in DG Competition. And you have to be very careful about how to pass on messages, and please don't bypass anybody because they will feel maybe a little bit frustrated or ignored. (Commission 19)
>
> I think that the style of the Commissioner does affect all the way down, and the personality of the DG is influenced by the Director-General. I think the Director is the big player in policy making, but obviously there are ambitious Heads of Unit who are going to become Directors. (Commission 16)

The above interviewees clearly testify that the vertical hierarchy of the Commission guides the everyday behaviour of the officials. Notably, Heads of Unit and Directors seem essential in the uploading of files inside DGs. The above observations also illustrate that the DGs are not loosely coupled organisations but are fairly strongly co-ordinated and steered by hierarchy. The priorities and visions set by the College of Commissioners are often felt at the level of desk officers. Another way of measuring the impact of the hierarchy is to ask whether changes in Directors profoundly affect officials' everyday life at the office. Most of our interviewees confirm that changes of Heads of Unit, Directors, Directors-General and even Commissioners have a significant impact on their decision-making behaviour:

> I don't feel that the general Commission reforms have impacted very much on how I work, but changes in personnel – new Director-General, new Head of Unit – in different ways affected how we operate to a significant extent. (Commission 21)

Patterns of co-operation and conflict inside the Commission are also strongly associated with the formal organisational boundaries of the services. The following quotes illustrate the organisational dimension of co-operation and conflict:

> I can imagine all sorts of conflicts and levels. I mean, now we are in a very tense period of negotiations, so there is a lot of stress all around and there are tensions between geographical units from different DGs. So that is leading to a lot of conflicts starting with desk officers. If it gets bigger, it reaches the Head of Unit, and might even go higher. (Commission 7)

> Generally, I think there is a lot of conflict really, between our Director and other directorates. I can think of a couple of cases where my Director has conflict with another Director, and that affects my relationship with my counterpart in that unit. (Commission 22)

Within the OECD Secretariat the departmental patterns of contact, co-ordination and conflict are closely associated with the vertical and horizontal specialisations of the administrative apparatus. The organisation of the Secretariat into directorates, teams and individual dossiers is reflected in the perceptions reported by most interviewees. The OECD Secretariat combines horizontal specialisation into separate 'silos' with organisational structures that safeguard co-ordination and co-operation across directorates (see Chapter 3). In order to safeguard inter-service co-operation, the OECD Secretariat is largely organised into teams that tend to build bridges across directorates. However, the main organisational principle inside the OECD Secretariat is that of individual dossiers. The portfolio organisation of the work is reflected in the following quotes:

> You have teams, but people also tend to work alone. I'm always amazed at people burning the midnight oil here at the OECD, and they work hard. The main reason for this is that tasks tend to be apportioned to individual people. And you do not necessarily have a team to take up the baton if you are sick or on holiday. You have to get your work done. There are people, I think, who eventually feel quite depressed because of the loneliness of tasks, because of the isolation and the fact that each one is on a hard task. (OECD 13)

> I personally do not interact with people outside the division. The trade export credit division is quite autonomous. There is no co-ordination with the other divisions. (OECD 15)

The portfolio organisation means officials have contact with other directorates and teams who work on issues that relate to their own dossiers:

> Despite horizontal specialisation into separate directorates, there is a lot of contact and partnership between the directorates. All directorates are a bit dependent upon each other. Any directorate that feels independent very soon learns that it isn't, because it needs resources, needs communication. In the end, everything comes back together. (OECD 13)

> A lot of work in the OECD is cross-cutting the directorate divisions; most work at the OECD is done across directorates. And depending on what the nature of the issue is, it happens either directly among the analysts or, where more fundamental issues or strategic matters are involved, it also then happens at the level of Heads of Division or Directors. (OECD 11)

In addition to organisation by purpose (portfolio/dossier), the OECD Secretariat also has process-organised units. Such units have a horizontal function within the whole Secretariat by providing services of different kinds, such as computer services, legal services etc. As in the Commission, we also see that officials in units organised by process evoke a 'helicopter view' of the Secretariat:

> Because I am working in the central service, most of our projects have an impact on all the organisation's substantive directorates, so you have to always communicate with the administrative officers and people working in the directorate to not only get their approval but also feedback on what they think we should do. (OECD 26)

As the above quotes demonstrate, the horizontal specialisation of the OECD Secretariat indeed mobilises biases in the contact patterns among the staff. Similarly, the vertical hierarchy in the OECD Secretariat receives most attention among the majority of OECD officials in their everyday work. As we observed in the Commission, many OECD officials view the Director as a key figure in the hierarchy. Most officials have direct contact with and report directly to the Director. The Secretary-General and the Deputy Secretary-General seem to be less important in the everyday running of the directorates and teams:

> People tend to have most contact within their team – horizontally – and upwards towards their Director. I've got five people working for me, and the Director is very closely involved in this as well. There's no one higher than the Director. (OECD 3)

As we have seen in the Commission, contacts inside the OECD Secretariat also tend to follow the vertical hierarchy. These vertical contact patterns are commented on by many of our interviewees. According to one Head of Division:

> The most important contacts for a Head of Division are the Executive Directorate, the Executive Director, the Secretary-General's office, and the Directors. (OECD 9)

According to one Deputy Executive Director:

> The Deputy Executive Director in the Executive Directorate has intensive contacts with the heads and deputy heads of services, directors, Secretary-General, and heads of programme. (OECD 8)

A senior economist (A4) also reports on the importance of the vertical hierarchy in the OECD Secretariat:

> In this directorate at least, we normally get comments on what we do, not just from other colleagues in each division and colleagues in our own division, but usually you get comments from the Director or Deputy Director as well. (OECD 17)

Finally, patterns of co-operation and conflict inside the OECD Secretariat are also strongly associated with the formal organisational boundaries of the services. Many of our OECD interviewees report how the formal structuring of the OECD Secretariat guides patterns of co-operation and conflict among the personnel. The following quote illustrates the vertical organisational dimension of co-operation and conflict:

> Conflicts, I think, are more about levels. If you are talking as a leader who's good and reasonable, it's good. If it is a belligerent policy line, that is frustrating. Also, I think people – because of the hierarchical systems – take it out on their own level or the level below. There is so much 'yes' going upwards in the echelon and hierarchy. You say 'Yes, yes, yes' even though you don't want to do it, and you take it out on the staff, and you might take it out on your juniors. (OECD 13)

However, our interviewees also testify that patterns of co-operation are also associated with the horizontal portfolio organisation of the OECD Secretariat. Due to the strong compartmentalisation of the services, conflicts can be reduced if there is a sufficient match between dossiers and organisational structures.

The horizontal and vertical specialisations in the WTO Secretariat also accompany departmental contact patterns, co-ordination behaviour and cleavages of conflict among personnel. As a reflection of the horizontal specialisation of the Secretariat, most of our interviewed officials report being primarily oriented towards their own unit and portfolio. The portfolio organisation of the Secretariat is reflected in most of our interviews throughout the WTO Secretariat. Although the WTO Secretariat is internally specialised according to purpose, some divisions are also process organised (see Chapter 4). Our interviewees show that horizontal specialisation by *process* accompanies much inter-service contact across units, whereas organisation by *purpose* leads to more intra-service contact. The following quote is from an official in a purpose-organised unit:

> Because of the organisational specialisation, [officials] are notorious for the fact that they become super-specialised like mules with eye flaps – they lose total sight of the bigger picture. So you have very super-specialised people, but they can't sort of get the bigger picture. They are sort of very comfortable in their own little empires. And nobody should come close to them, it is just not tolerated. If you read different panel reports you will see that there is a big difference in approach between us in the [...] Division and the [...] Division. (WTO 13)

Even at the level of Deputy Director-General, issues seldom cross-cut the organisational boundaries:

> If there is an issue which cuts across more than one of the Deputy Directors-General, then we just say 'Let's meet and discuss this.' Normally it's not cutting across. (WTO 14)

Q: Were you surprised when you started working for the Secretariat at how it works?
I knew it quite well. I was surprised how easy a few things were in terms of administration, how smooth things were, how small it was, very small, you know, like a family ... and at the same time I was surprised at how selfish and individualist some are. People live in their own little cocoons. There are very lonely lives in the Secretariat. (WTO 9)

Our interviewees demonstrate that the departmental dynamic among WTO officials is associated with the horizontal specialisation of the WTO Secretariat. Horizontal specialisation allows more intra-unit contact and co-ordination processes than inter-unit patterns of collaboration. As in the Commission, the purpose specialisation of the WTO Secretariat fosters 'silo logic' among the personnel. One official compares his division to a law firm:

Lawyers work pretty much independently serving the interests of their clients. That's in many ways how we operate here. We've got a bunch of lawyers who have their individual clients that they are working for day in and day out. And so they're working more for their clients than they are with each other. (WTO 10)

People say we work in silos. You know, there is not a lot of working across divisions. (WTO 6)

One pretty much stays in one's niche which you build up. (WTO 13)

In addition to the horizontal specialisation of the WTO into divisions, the formal structure is supplemented with teams and projects. According to one official, the team organisation:

has worked to find incentives to break down the barriers to collaborating across divisions, but because a lot of our work is really focused on services of particular committees, it is not always clear that even passing over divisions necessarily adds value all the time. I think we are in the stage where people recognise that it would be good to not be totally in these isolated silos of divisions. But you don't necessarily want an organisation where everyone is trying to collaborate with everyone at any moment. It's like a tipping point about how much interaction there should be. (WTO 6)

The portfolio logic is also revealed when officials in different units interact. Officials who share similar substantive dossiers tend to engage in cross-unit co-operation more frequently than officials with incompatible dossiers:

There is regular interaction on areas where competences are shared. So, the example of biofuel like here before is also very relevant to agriculture and food security. (WTO 12)

In addition to being horizontally specialised into portfolios, the WTO

Secretariat is vertically specialised into a hierarchy. Despite having fewer hierarchical layers than the Commission, the vertical specialisation of the WTO Secretariat is clearly reflected in the behavioural perceptions of the officials. In our interviews most officials report having close contact with their Director but not directly with the Director-General or his deputies. However, many officials report interacting with the Cabinets of the Director-General and their deputies:

> Normally the request for the DG is channelled through our Director.
> Q: So it kind of goes through the hierarchy?
> Yes, it is a certain question of management, so that also the Director knows what the staff are up to. (WTO 7)

> I work independently, but our Director wants to stay very involved. I mean, it is personal, I think, depending on the Director. But I do feel like I work independently, but under supervision. (WTO 8)

> It depends a lot on your Director. In this division I think we are quite lucky because the Director is sort of a powerful Director within the WTO, so it's a Director that is respected. I'm still surprised at how important sometimes the Directors are. (WTO 17)

As we have seen in the Commission and the OECD Secretariat, the vertical ranks of the interviewees in the WTO Secretariat are clearly reflected in their statements throughout the interviews. One top-ranking WTO official reports that: 'I speak to the Deputy Directors several times a day.' This top-ranking official also says:

> I have basically two hats. I have my administrative hat, and I have my more substantive negotiations hat [...] In my administrative hat it is very much the people internal in the Secretariat, administration and human resources, and the Deputy Directors-General. Being a top official also implies that the top priorities of the Director-General are felt at his desk. It is very political. Where does Lamy want to take the WTO? I have to sell his ideas. No Director-General has had so much [brand] like Lamy has. So it is a very political thing. But at the same time, he doesn't have the power. He has a soft power, not a hard power. (WTO 9)

Similar to the Commission and in the OECD Secretariat, the importance of the formal hierarchy is also highlighted by our WTO interviewees. The logic of hierarchy is particularly shown when Directors come and go, as illustrated by this interviewee:

> We changed Director one year ago and certain things have changed, clearly, in the division, the way we focus to our attention. (WTO 7)

Notwithstanding our observations that the formal WTO hierarchy affects the behavioural patterns of the officials, the fairly small size of the WTO Secretariat also allows room for more informal patterns of behaviour. After all, with respect to staff size the WTO Secretariat is small even when compared to DG Trade. The small size of this Secretariat renders it easy to communicate fairly informally among staff horizontally across organisational borders and vertically across hierarchical layers:

> The sheer size of the organisation seems to foster flexibility and autonomy among the officials. (WTO 15)

Departmental role and identity perceptions

Most of the permanent officials interviewed in the Commission attach strong identity to the Commission services. However, the vast majority report that their main Commission identity is attached to the DG and that only secondary identification is directed to the unit and the Commission as a whole. One explanation for the DG identification is that for most officials the personnel rotation system accompanies fairly short tenure within each unit although a more enduring tenure within the DG as a whole. Whereas previous research underlines the importance of loyalty towards the Commission as a whole (Suvarierol 2007: 122), this book underlines the fact of the sub-systemic DG loyalties, identities and roles:

> I don't identify just with the unit, because I have been here three years and I have done so many other units before. So for me it is one step up in the DG. I have done so many things in this DG, so my identification with the DG is stronger, I would say. (Commission 8)

> I would say [I attach more identification towards] the DG than the Commission. I feel an attachment to the DG Trade, rather than to the Commission as a whole. It is a certain team spirit – the DG Trade – a hard working DG. (Commission 16)

> There is an *esprit de corps* at the level of the directorate. I think it is the culture of this work that is already here. It is something that you cannot see, but you have it there. And it has been probably introduced years ago in order to ensure that the 25 different nationalities end up producing the same thing, irrespective of the fact that I am Greek and somebody else is German or French. (Commission 24)

These observations clearly reveal that the formal organisational structures of the Commission indeed impact on the role and identity perceptions of the permanent staff. A crucial test of the 'Commission effect' on the identities of Commission officials is the extent to which temporary officials (SNEs) also adopt departmental roles and identities inside the Commission. Being hired by the Commission for a maximum of only four years and having an ambiguous organisational affiliation to the Commission during the contract period, the emergence of departmental roles and identity perceptions among SNEs would serve as a critical test of the existence of a departmental dynamic among Commission officials more broadly. Table 6.1 reveals the distribution of loyalties emphasised by both current and former Commission SNEs.

Table 6.1 'To whom do you feel loyal in your current function?' (percentage)[a]

Departmental loyalty patterns:	Current Nordic SNEs	Current Dutch SNEs	Former Dutch SNEs
Towards the Unit they are working in	84	98	90
Towards the DG they are (current SNEs)/ were (former SNEs) working in	84	96	48
Towards the Ministry they are (current SNEs)/were (former SNEs) working in	–	73	77
Mean N	100 (66)	100 (46)	100 (41)

[a] The percentages listed are a sum of officials who have *very strong or fairly strong* loyalty to the entities. This dichotomy stems from the following five-point scale: very strong (value 5), fairly strong (value 4), average (value 3), fairly weak (value 2) and very weak (value 1).

Table 6.1 demonstrates that seconded officials have multiple departmental loyalties, notably towards their *primary* institutions (the Commission DGs and units) and their secondary institutions (their parent ministry at the domestic level). Table 6.1 indicates that seconded officials manage to live with multiple loyalties. The strong departmental loyalties among secondees clearly reflect the *horizontal* specialisation of the Commission services as well as the departmentalised *recruitment procedure* of secondees through the 'submarine procedure'. The strong departmental loyalties also clearly reflect the fact that seconded officials have the Commission – and the unit in which they consume most of their time and energy – as their *primary* organisational affiliation. According to one current Dutch secondee:

> As a secondee you always have a complicated dual position. But I for one, and the people that I know, found a good middle course between on the one hand loyalty to the Commission and on the other hand loyalty to their home country. (Commission 19)

Another Dutch secondee claims that:

> As a secondee you are loyal to the Commission. But one's salary is paid by the Netherlands. I had no problems functioning in that dual position. (Commission 24)

As expected, greatest loyalty is attached towards the immediate organisational environments, i.e. the unit and DG levels in the Commission. However, a great deal of loyalty is also attached towards the corresponding domestic ministry.

This section has illuminated two clear tendencies. Firstly, Commission officials evoke departmental identity and role perceptions, particularly at the DG level. Secondly, only minor variation is discerned between permanent and temporary Commission officials with respect to the departmental dynamic. Seconded officials seem to be strongly affected by the Commission organisation quite quickly upon arrival in Brussels, viewing themselves as 'ordinary' Commission officials. This conclusion is valid both with respect to contact patterns and patterns of co-operation and conflict as well as to patterns of role and identity perceptions (see Trondal, van den Berg and Suvarierol 2008). The following quote sums up these observations:

> It's probably more about the difference between DG Fish and DG Trade than it is about the difference between being seconded and not being seconded. (Commission 22)

Most of the officials interviewed in the OECD Secretariat attach quite strong identities towards semi-autonomous directorates. The vast majority of our interviewees report that their main OECD identity is attached towards the sub-systemic level, and that secondary identification is directed towards the OECD as a whole. Similar to the Commission, the departmental role and identity perceptions among OECD personnel reflect the formal organisation of the administration. Due to the formal embedment of the officials within the OECD organisation writ large as well as within the directorates and teams, we find role and identity perceptions attached to all these levels in the Secretariat.

Firstly, we observe fairly strong OECD-level identities among several interviewees. These identities are clearly multiple – being directed both towards the OECD Secretariat as a whole and towards sub-units inside the Secretariat. As such, part of these observations may illuminate a departmental identification and partly also a supranational logic (see Chapter 6). The following quotes reflect OECD-level roles and identity perceptions:

> My role is to be here for the OECD, not to be a British civil servant at all. We are not here to represent our own countries in any way. I work as an international civil servant in the OECD. I am just surprised about your questions regarding the nationality and representation, because for me it should be clear for anybody working for the OECD that you are not representing your country, you are working for the OECD as a whole. (OECD 2)

> I think [the *esprit de corps*] is quite strong in the OECD. And within the unit or division, of course, the personality of the manager is very important in developing the *esprit de corps* and common purpose. In the OECD I would say that each directorate has its own personality, and that there is a very strong *esprit de corps* in the individual directorates. There is an OECD culture, but the subculture varies from one directorate to the next. (OECD 9)

As already indicated by the official above, the personal attachment at the directorate level is fairly strong in the OECD Secretariat:

> My division has a strong *esprit de corps* ... The organisation is kept largely because of the Head Office – the Secretary-General's office – and that it's a loose confederation of directorates. (OECD 6)

> I think all directorates have an *esprit de corps*.
> Q: Would you say there is also an overall OECD *esprit de corps*?
> Not enough, and for such reasons I said ... I think it is a sort of 'hub and spokes', you know. The 'hub' is, if you like, the Secretary-General's Private Office ... and then you have the spokes, which are the individual directorates, which link out to the ministries.' (OECD 13)

Finally, some officials also attach supplementary identities towards the teams they are affiliated to within the OECD Secretariat. The development of departmental identities – particularly those directed towards the level of unit and division – can be caused by socialisation processes among officials with long tenure inside their units as well as those who interact intensively face-to-face with fellow colleagues in their unit. The following quote signifies that socialisation into the *esprit de corps* can be caused by tenure and intensity of interaction:

> We have a very well-functioning unit with a very high degree of corporate responsibility and understanding of the corporate viewpoints.
> Q: What is this due to?
> This is due to the number of years you have been here. I think that with time you tend to move away from being an egoist to being much more interested in the survival of the group, the company or organisation in this particular case ... I think that being an international civil servant and the more years you do that type of job, the more you tend to represent the organisation rather than individual or division or whatever. (OECD 16)

However, some officials also report a lack of departmental identification in the OECD Secretariat. This lack of 'corporate identity' is associated with the time-limited contracts of the officials that contribute to a general short tenure among a majority of the officials. Similar to the Commission, the rotation of officials inside the OECD Secretariat is reported to hamper the development of group identities at the unit levels. One official reports that:

> I think one of the problems of the OECD is the short-term contracts that make people move a lot from one unit to another. That creates a lack of continuity in the work. This I think prevents having a real own group, own identity. (OECD 22)

Finally, the horizontal specialisation of the WTO Secretariat also plays out with respect to the role and identity perceptions reported by WTO staff. Most officials seem to attach an institutional allegiance towards their unit and teams, towards the WTO Secretariat as a whole and towards the whole WTO organisation. Similar to the Commission and the OECD Secretariat, most WTO officials evoke multiple departmental allegiances. To some extent, these identities may be seen as concentric circles where identification towards the unit level requires some degree of identification towards the Secretariat as a whole. Hence, unit identities may be seen as foundational for the subsequent emergence of higher-level identifications. Consequently, sub-unit allegiances towards units and teams would require allegiances towards the WTO Secretariat in the first place.

Similar to cutting-edge identity research (e.g. Herrman et al. 2004) and parallel to our observations in the Commission and the OECD Secretariat, officials in the WTO Secretariat tend to evoke multiple roles:

> I think I sort of walk the line between being a WTO representative and needing to be impartial. (WTO 6)

The latter official clearly has to strike a balance between supranational, intergovernmental and departmental roles (see also Chapters 6 and 8). As predicted by the organisational approach outlined in Chapter 1, roles tend to shift when officials change organisational affiliations:

> It is obvious that when we are operating outside the WTO, in other intergovernmental organisations, then we are representing the WTO as an institution, and we have to be aware of that. It might be that in some contexts, you know, if you are at an academic conference, you could try to pretend that you are speaking in a personal capacity. (WTO 1)

The fairly small size of the WTO Secretariat and the fairly low turnover of personnel accompany elements of an overarching Secretariat identity. Our interviewees report that WTO officials attach fairly strong identities towards their specialised portfolios. In addition, officials in the WTO Secretariat seem to have a 'corporate' identity towards the Secretariat as a whole, and this identity is attached to the neutrality of being an international civil servant:

> People talk about 'in the house' – this place like a house. I think it reflects a little bit a group feeling. (WTO 5)

As we have seen in Chapter 4, the WTO Secretariat is a strongly horizontally specialised bureaucracy. Our interviewees testify that this horizontal specialisation of the Secretariat leads to strong divisional identities. Hence:

> This co-operative culture doesn't exist in this organisation. (WTO 9)

> I have a loyalty to the [...] division. It is absolutely fatal for people to stay too long in one single division. It's absolutely fatal. And I see it around me

every day. And that's something that needs to be addressed. Why? There is too much comfort, and you fall into a comfort zone if you are dealing with the same issue all the time. (WTO 13)

As shown in the OECD Secretariat, the development of a WTO identity may also reflect the in-house socialisation of the officials. However, processes of pre-socialisation outside the Secretariat also seem to be at play, both through an international family background and as a consequence of the international education of WTO personnel prior to entering the Secretariat. However, we do not observe socialisation processes related to a departmental dynamic in the WTO Secretariat. It is more likely that processes of socialisation may activate epistemic and supranational dynamics (see Chapters 6 and 7). Moreover, when WTO officials represent the WTO externally, all interviewees report that they represent the WTO Secretariat. This representational role seems one most officials play because it is seen as the appropriate thing to do. In addition, there are formal rules of procedure that supplement these perceptions that guide the officials when they represent the WTO externally. These formal rules are referred to as the 'WTO book':

> First, the rule is the WTO book, that's the rule. Now of course, if you read it you will see that it's not so unambiguous, to say the least, and therefore a lot has to do with the way you read the rules. I think we may have written rules but I think they are very broad ... There is of course staff regulations which tell you that you have to always behave as an international civil servant serving the organisation and not the members, and what have you. (WTO 16)

Summing up: the foundational status of the departmental dynamic

This chapter demonstrates the existence of a foundational departmental dynamic within all the international bureaucracies studied – both with respect to contact, co-ordination and conflict patterns and to the identity and role perceptions among the personnel. International bureaucracies seem to have enduring impacts on the officials embedded within them. This observation strongly signifies how the organisational structures of international bureaucracies influence the staff. These observations are similar among both seconded part-time employed officials and permanent officials with lifelong positions. Consequently, the departmental dynamic is indeed fostered more by the international bureaucracy and less by external institutions such as domestic ministries and agencies.

This chapter observes strong perceptional effects of the horizontal specialisation of international bureaucracies. This effect is most clearly seen in the Commission between the GS and DG Trade. However, we also see this organisational effect in the directorates of the OECD Secretariat and the teams there. Hence, different principles of horizontal specialisation accompany different behavioural and role perceptions among the staff of international bureaucracies. The principle of *purpose* seems primarily to foster 'silo logic' among the personnel. The purpose principle accompanies officials that are strongly geared towards their portfolios and the units they are embedded into. The principle of *process* seems to accompany a 'helicopter view', which implies that the officials have more cross-unit contact and co-ordination and that they feel a stronger allegiance towards the international administration as a whole. This latter observation is most clearly reported in the Commission GS. Because the WTO Secretariat is mainly specialised by the purpose principle, this Secretariat offers no clear observations on the process principle.

This chapter also reports some observations of pre-socialisation outside international bureaucracies as well as processes of socialisation inside these apparatuses. In the Commission, international family background as well as educational experience from international universities (e.g. Bruges) may pre-socialise officials to become 'departmentally minded' even before entering formal positions. In the Commission, however, in-house socialisation processes are also seen to occur at the unit and DG levels – accompanied by the length of tenure in these sub-units and also due to intensive face-to-face encounters in everyday work. In the WTO Secretariat we see that long tenure and low turnover accompany a slow socialisation of officials into becoming 'departmentally minded'. However, since few WTO officials have previous experience from national governments, we see only some indications of pre-socialisation of WTO officials through domestic governments.

Finally, this chapter has illuminated that the departmental dynamic is profoundly associated with the vertical hierarchy of international bureaucracies. Officials at the top of the Commission – within the GS – share the view that co-ordination of the Commission as a whole is important, whereas desk officials in DG Trade are more concerned with sectoral co-ordination inside that DG. Officials in top positions in all cases also possess more cross-sectoral preferences, identities and cross-portfolio thinking than officials in low- or medium-level positions. Hence, the departmental dynamic is indeed contingent on the formal organisation of international bureaucracies. Being an international civil servant is thus centred on playing formal roles inside bureaucratic organisations, where the room for manoeuvre and discretion is systematically contingent on formal rules and roles. Notwithstanding the fact that formal organisations are flexible arrangement that allow for choice among incumbents, these formal structures impact on the choices being made in a systematic way.

7

Supranational dynamics in international bureaucracies

Exploring supranational dynamics

In this chapter we will investigate how supranational dynamics are played out among civil servants working in the bureaucracies of the WTO, the OECD and the Commission. In order to do this, we need to have a clear understanding of what 'supranational dynamics' are. What do we mean by 'supranationalism' and what is a 'supranational mode of governance'? What does it mean to act and behave according to a supranational role? What separates supranational dynamics from other types of dynamics?

Supranationalism has been studied for a long time, particularly in connection with the establishment and development of the institutions of the EC/EU (Checkel 2005; Eilstrup-Sangiovanni 2006; Nelsen and Stubb 2003; Rosamond 2000; Sandholtz and Stone Sweet 1998; Somek 2001). A stripped-down definition of supranationalism is presented in Rosamond (2000: 204): 'the development of authoritative institutions of governance and networks of policy-making activity above the nation-state'. An international organisation can thus be denoted 'supranational' when it constitutes an entity distinct from national governments and has a 'separate identity and loyalty and exercises some measure of genuine autonomous power' (Slaughter 2004: 22). A supranational mode of governance can furthermore be defined as a mode of governance in which centralised governmental structures – those organisations constituted at the supranational level – possess jurisdiction over specific policy domains within the territory comprised by the member states (Stone Sweet and Sandholtz 1998: 8). These definitions of supranationalism relate to the systemic level, i.e. to institutions above the nation-state which have a real authority and a meaningful capacity to make decisions. The locus of supranational dynamics is thus institutions at the international level which have some sort of autonomy and status separate from the nation-state.

However, the focus of our study is not on the systemic level but on the individual level, i.e. on the roles of individual civil servants serving in the bureaucracies of international organisations. When we turn our attention to these individuals, what do we then mean by 'supranational'? And what does it mean to enact a supranational role? In classical theories of European integration – such as neo-functionalism – we find the assumption that one of the key driving forces of integration is the shift of individual loyalties from the national to the international level (Eilstrup-Sangiovanni 2006; Rosamond 2000). Within this logic, international institutions are assumed to have a capacity to create a sense of community and belonging beyond the nation-state, i.e. they could socialise (Checkel 2005; Deutsch et al. 1957; Haas 1958). The enactment of a supranational role may thus imply that individuals show loyalty to and feel a sense of belonging to an international organisation, and share and act according to the norms, ideas, beliefs and goals of the organisation.

Thus, in this chapter the study of the supranational dynamic is focused on the individual civil servants' orientation towards the international organisation in which they are serving, and on international institutions' capacity for shaping and changing individual loyalties, identities, beliefs and behaviours. In line with Hooghe (2005: 63), an important question thus becomes: do civil servants who work within international organisations share the norms of the organisation in question, and if so, what are the causal mechanisms? The adoption of the norms of the organisation is thus a key element in the definition of supranational dynamics used in this book. A more specified definition is presented in the next sections.

The supranational dynamic and international bureaucracies

Before further exploring civil servants' enactment of supranational roles in international bureaucracies, it is useful to relate the supranational dynamic to classical models of bureaucracies: the models of *representative bureaucracy* and *Weberian bureaucracy*. These models are based on a set of different assumptions as to the mechanisms involved in shaping the norms and behaviours of civil servants. The models can thus help us to identify factors that are useful in analysing civil servants' role behaviour in international bureaucracies.

The model of the *representative bureaucracy* assumes that the 'baggage' that civil servants bring with them into a bureaucracy affects their role behaviour, and furthermore that organisations perform better if their workforces reflect the characteristics of their constituent populations (Andrews et al. 2005; Selden 1998). The civil servants' former institutional affiliations, their educational backgrounds, their geographical origins etc. are assumed to affect the way they behave as bureaucrats. The bureaucracy will thus change its performance according to the composition of its staff. This is the picture of the 'living' bureaucracy. This model is particularly relevant for the intergovernmental and epistemic dynamics presented elsewhere in this book. These two dynamics presuppose that national and professional backgrounds are key factors that affect the role behaviour of international civil servants. The model can also be relevant for the supranational dynamic. As indicated by Hooghe in her study of the Commission, civil servants may share the international norms of an international organisation because of mechanisms in operation prior to the civil servants entering the organisation (Hooghe 2005). Thus, pre-socialisation can imply that people who choose to work in an international organisation are assumed to be generally favourably disposed to the organisation's norms. Hooghe concludes that more important than socialisation to international norms within the Commission is socialisation outside (2005: 88), and she even states that 'several roads lead to Commission norms, but few run through international socialization' (2005: 64). Thus, the claims of Hooghe are a good illustration of a view which corresponds with the model of the representative bureaucracy, i.e. that what the civil servants bring with them into the organisation is of great importance.

A *Weberian bureaucracy* model assumes that bureaucracies have a strong capacity to shape the people who are employed through a set of different mechanisms, e.g. socialisation (inclusion in an established bureaucratic culture), discipline (incentive structures) and control (hierarchical control and supervision) (Page 1992; Weber 1983; Yi-Chong and Weller 2004). These mechanisms ensure that bureaucracies perform their tasks in a standardised way more or less independently of the individuals who are employed. Much emphasis is thus put on the hierarchy and internal structures of the bureaucracies. The Weberian bureaucracy model provides a picture of the 'bureaucratic machine' as a stabilising element in politics. According to this model, bureaucracies develop their own rationale consistent with a set of goals and formal, hierarchical structures. As seen in Chapter 6, this model implies that civil servants mainly act upon roles that are shaped by the type of organisation and bureaucracy they are placed in and by their specific location within the bureaucratic structure. Thus, the formal structures, bureaucratic culture and goals of the organisation are all factors that are assumed to shape civil servants' behaviour and role conceptions.

The Weberian model is thus particularly relevant for the departmental dynamic which is presented in Chapter 6, and also for the supranational dynamic which is the topic of this chapter. Hooghe suggests that one weakness of international socialisation is that international organisations lack control over their members' life chances (Hooghe 2005: 87). She partly bases this claim on the observation that international organisations are generally thought to be more prone to having employees working for a shorter time period, many on short-term contracts. If a lack of control over the member's life chances was a salient characteristic of an international bureaucracy, it would undermine one of the key elements of the Weberian bureaucracy – namely the idea of stability through bureaucrats' lifelong careers. Hooghe thus assumes that an international organisation has limited capacity for shaping the roles, norms and behaviour of its civil servants, precisely because of the weakness of the key elements suggested by the Weberian model. We challenge this as a general claim regarding international bureaucracies' lack of socialisation and transformation potential, and claim that Hooghe exaggerates the differences between a national and an international bureaucracy in this respect. We generally argue that even international bureaucracies may possess considerable institutional 'power' to socialise and shape their employees.

The supranational dynamic is relevant for the Weberian bureaucracy model in several ways. Firstly, working in an international bureaucracy means that the civil servants must 'leave their passports at the door', i.e. they are obliged to work for and represent the international organisation and not particular national interests. Thus, both the civil servants' prior commitment and dedication to the international organisation in question, including the goals and the vision and mission of the organisation, and the capacity of the international bureaucracy to shape the people who enter, become important factors. The international organisations themselves have been established and designed to work for specific common goals and objectives. If a conflict arises, these common goals and objectives are supposed to override particular member-state interests. Therefore, depending on the international organisation's capacity to shape the attitudes, norms and behaviours of its employees, civil servants may act upon a supranational role working to defend and promote the objectives of the international organisation they work in.

Civil servants are thus supposed to serve the interests of and be loyal to the international organisation only. The agreement establishing the WTO (Article VI) refers to this as the 'international character of the responsibilities'. The WTO agreement even states that the responsibilities of the staff of the organisation should be 'exclusively' international in character (ibid.). This reference is a good illustration of supranational dynamics at the individual level in international bureaucracies, i.e. dynamics which assume that in their work civil servants are exclusively loyal to the international organisation in which they serve. According to the supranational dynamic as defined in this book, civil servants are assumed to be dedicated to the overarching mission of an international organisation. Furthermore, the presence of this dynamic assumes some sort of autonomy for the international bureaucracy in question. The international bureaucracy is not merely pictured as a powerless tool in the hands of national governments, but it is also assumed to have its own 'organisational personality' which is played out within the overarching framework and goals of the wider international organisation (Trondal 2007b).

Thus, as indicated in Chapter 1, the appearance of supranational dynamics denotes actors' feelings of loyalty and allegiance towards the supranational or international level, i.e. in our context the international organisation as a whole. The appearance of supranational dynamics at the actor level presupposes that individual feelings of loyalty and allegiance shift towards the supranational/international level (Deutsch et al. 1957: 5–6; Haas 1958: 16; Herrmann and Brewer 2004: 6). The adoption of international norms is expected to be fostered primarily by the mechanisms of internalisation and socialisation. The adoption of norms may also be contingent on control and discipline mechanisms, i.e. that individuals view the enactment of a supranational role as mandatory, necessary and/or 'appropriate' in that particular institutional context (March and Olsen 1989). Incentives and rewards can thus enhance the individual's adoption of international norms.

Supranational dynamics can thus appear in international bureaucracies in several ways. They can appear through pre-socialised commitments to the organisation within which the civil servants start to work. This implies that there is a self-reinforcing mechanism involved in the recruitment of officials who are already susceptible to supranational dynamics. Supranational dynamics can also appear through transformation and socialisation within the bureaucracy. This implies that internal factors such as organisational characteristics, culture, contact patterns and mechanisms such as socialisation, discipline and control enhance the enactment of supranational roles.

The next section presents an operational framework for the study of how supranational roles are enacted in international organisations: how can we demonstrate that supranational roles are played out in the WTO Secretariat, the OECD Secretariat and the Commission? The following sections will present how supranational behavioural dynamics are played out among officials in the three bureaucracies. The chapter concludes by summing up and analysing the empirical observations with respect to the occurrence of supranational dynamics.

Supranational dynamics: an operational framework

In this chapter, we explore how the supranational dynamic is actually played out in the WTO Secretariat, the OECD Secretariat and the Commission. There may be several reasons why international civil servants enact supranational roles: before entering an international organisation civil servants can be pre-socialised into sharing the goals, ideas and norms of the organisation. They can also share these goals, ideas and norms through socialisation within the organisation. Their loyalty to the goals, ideas and norms can be affected by internal control and discipline (performed within the bureaucracy) as well as by external control and discipline (performed by the owners of the organisation, the member-state governments). Thus, on the one hand we make a distinction between supranational dynamics based on the internalisation of norms and role behaviour, and those based on control and discipline of norms and role behaviour. On the other hand, we also make a distinction between an external dimension – socialisation and control and discipline originating from outside the organisation – and an internal dimension – socialisation and control and discipline taking place within the organisation. We thus end up with a two-dimensional model of supranational dynamics which is presented in Table 7.1.

Table 7.1 Forms of supranational dynamics in international bureaucracies

	External dimension	*Internal dimension*
Internalisation of norms and role behaviour	Pre-socialisation	Socialisation within
Control and discipline of norms and role behaviour	Incentives and rewards by member states	Incentives and rewards by the bureaucracy itself

It is important to note that in practice we expect a significant overlap between the four forms of supranational dynamics, i.e. they are not mutually exclusive. On the contrary, in theory they can mutually reinforce or weaken each other. It may be difficult to see socialisation dynamics taking place if the mechanism of control and discipline operates alone. However, in line with Checkel (2005: 10) we expect that both socialisation/internalisation and control and discipline can be part of the socialisation dynamics. As stated by Checkel (ibid.), strategic calculation (e.g. control and discipline) can be expected to play some role in the socialisation process; the mechanisms of incentives and rewards may thus contribute to the adoption of international norms.

Before studying more closely how supranational roles are enacted among civil servants, we need to specify in more detail how to identify supranational dynamics in our data. How do we recognise a civil servant's enactment of a supranational role when we come across it?

One way of approaching supranational roles among civil servants is to look at what the 'international character' of the civil servants' responsibilities means in practice. The international character of responsibilities means that the civil servants follow the internal logic of the international organisation they are employed in (formal structure, position, rules of procedure etc.). In order to follow a supranational logic they should be loyal to the mission and vision of the international organisation and show this loyalty by 'putting up fences' towards attempts, either by member-state governments or other actors, to move the organisation in other directions. The assumption is that supranational dynamics prevail if loyalty to the mission and vision of the international organisation is not transcended by other dynamics such as loyalty to professional networks or to member-state governments. A crucial precondition for supranational roles to be played out is thus that civil servants are decoupled from national mandates and from loyalty towards member-state governments or other entities outside of the international setting. This precondition is in stark contrast to the intergovernmental dynamic which is studied in Chapter 9 of this book.

We nevertheless have to be careful not to overstate the distinctions between the different dynamics. The occurrence of one dynamic does not necessarily exclude the occurrence of another. For example, there is often a clear congruence between the professional expertise of civil servants (an epistemic dynamic) and the 'international character of responsibilities' (a supranational dynamic). Of course, a certain professional expertise is often a precondition for being able to perform the responsibilities in an international organisation, not least in specialised organisations which are highly dependent on a particular expertise. Furthermore, civil servants may be loyal to professional networks (an epistemic dynamic) and to particular administrative units within the organisation (a departmental dynamic) as well as to the organisation as a whole (a supranational dynamic) without any conflict between loyalties necessarily arising. In the data, therefore, we must be aware of possible 'grey zones' where the same findings can be interpreted as indicators of several dynamics (see Chapter 1).

A supranational role perception thus denotes that civil servants are socialised into a shared system of rules, norms, principles and codes of conduct that are inducted, internalised and taken for granted (pre-socialisation or socialisation within the international organisation) (Checkel 2005). Furthermore, the socialisation process can also be enhanced when civil servants strategically adapt to a supranational role because of institutional incentives and rewards (e.g. internal or external control and discipline). Through the socialisation process, the civil servants are expected to become 'defenders of the system' and to acquire collective interests and collective goals which are then promoted. Thus, the civil servants may acquire a distinct 'organisational personality' within the international organisations.

Therefore, when we seek to identify supranational dynamics we should analyse the perceptions, attitudes and beliefs of the civil servants in the light of the norms and goals of the international organisation. We should also analyse what the civil servant would do when confronted with issues where different dynamics are in conflict. Does the civil servant refer to and defend the goals of the organisation in a situation where, for example, a member state puts forward a proposal which runs contrary to the goal and/or the rules of the organisation? Does the civil servant defend the organisation's rules even though s/he would prefer other solutions from a professional point of view? In summary, we assume that the enactment of supranational role conceptions is enhanced when civil servants:

- believe in the mission, goals and ideas of the international organisation;
- feel allegiance, attachment and loyalty to the international organisation;
- emphasise the role of being a representative of the international organisation as a whole when representing it externally;
- put emphasis in their work on considerations related to the goals and rules of the organisation.

Supranational dynamics in the WTO Secretariat, the OECD Secretariat and the Commission: empirical findings

Based on interviews with officials from the WTO, the OECD and the Commission, in the following sections we will present and analyse what we see as indicators of the enactment of supranational roles among civil servants from the three organisations. The presentation is organised around the mechanisms shown in Table 7.1: pre-socialisation, socialisation within, internal control and discipline, and external control and discipline. We have analysed the interviews and selected quotes which we think illustrate the occurrence of different forms of supranational dynamics.

Socialisation to international norms: pre-socialisation and socialisation within

Civil servants may have shared the norms of the international organisation they serve in even before they started working there. These civil servants are therefore predisposed to be loyal to the organisation's vision and mission. Moreover, if such pre-socialisation is salient, there is a potential for a biased (self-)selection of the kind of civil servants who apply for jobs in international organisations. In line with the ideas of a representative bureaucracy, the international bureaucracy will in such cases be representative mainly of the enthusiasts of the organisation. Hooghe (2005: 88) found in her study of the Commission that these pre-socialisation mechanisms were important, and she even concluded that socialisation outside seemed to be more important than socialisation within. Many examples of pre-socialisation mechanisms appear in our data.

Another form of socialisation is linked to the Weberian bureaucracy model presented earlier, i.e. socialisation within the organisation. The assumption here is that international bureaucracies have autonomous transformative power when it comes to shaping the ideas, norms, beliefs and behaviour of civil servants. In the following, we look in particular at how experience from working within an organisation can affect the civil servants' commitment and loyalty to the organisation. We should also point out that pre-socialisation does not exclude the effect of socialisation within: someone who shares the norms of the international organisation before working there may, of course, be still further socialised within the organisation.

To illustrate this, when asked whether he had to believe in the basic idea of the WTO when he joined the Secretariat, one civil servant responds:

> Oh yes, I am convinced. I saw ... as a junior diplomat I participated in the making of this organisation. I saw this organisation being born. I was here in Geneva when the organisation was created, and I was here in Geneva when these agreements were negotiated. So I truly believe in the ideas. (WTO 9)

The WTO official thus relates his beliefs in the organisation to the close contact he had with the WTO in his former job, many years before he started working there. A Commission official also mentions that her commitment to the EU began a long time before she started to work for the EU institutions:

> But I always bore in mind the possibility to work for the institutions, maybe not from 16 years old but certainly from 22 years old.
> Q: So you were conscious about the EU and the Commission?
> Yes, very early.
> Q: So you became rather pre-socialised before you came here? It was actually a wish for you to come here?
> I would say not politically, more as a civilian or a citizen of Belgium; I was very much conscious of the project of building Europe. From 1973, for instance, I experienced the first enlargement. Where was I then? I was 26 and I thought 'Wow, they are enlarging already'. I was born in the year 1957 and I really grew up with Europe, in the very centre, 200 metres from Schumann. And from the very beginning, 14–15 years old, I was conscious of that. I had friends who were children of officials and my sisters did as well ... Italians, Belgians, Germans etc. And I knew about Jean Monnet [...] and I thought 'It's a big project, an important project, and it is a project *qui vient féderer les états*'. It's politically a very difficult project but it is certainly a project I want to work for with my very small means, my very small competencies and capacities.
> Q: Is it easy to follow that vision – your European vision – in your day-to-day work?
> Yes, because the vision is very strong. My vision of what I want to do and of what the Commission wants to do is very coherent. They match one

another. But also that vision is stronger than, let's say, the everyday life and problems I can have. That is my view. Some other people are more concerned with their own career. (Commission 20)

These quotes from this Commission official illustrate how pre-commitment to the vision and mission of an international organisation can enhance the enactment of a supranational role. Thus, some civil servants start working for an international organisation because they truly believe in the organisation. The need to be dedicated to the organisation is also emphasised in the following quotes from two WTO officials:

> We are the guardians of the book. We have to believe in what is in here, because if we don't believe, nobody believes. Then we might as well go home. (WTO 9)

> I think we have to be committed to what the WTO is as an institution, which basically is for trade liberalisation, and so clearly you have to believe in that. Otherwise it could be very difficult, personally, if you don't believe in the goal of your organisation, that the WTO is an institution which basically is a force for good – you know, the goals of the WTO . . . (WTO 3)

An OECD official indicates that he was pre-socialised into being enthusiastic, not about the OECD in particular but about international organisations in general:

> I think there was probably something philosophical in the beginning, because when I finished university, I was very attracted by the international organisations: the values, the mission, things like that. (OECD 27)

Another OECD official indicates that his enthusiasm for the OECD and what it does comes from his prior experience in the private sector:

> I am the treasurer of the OECD, and I have a business card. And I am proud of the OECD. That is one of the things I like about working at the OECD: I like what the OECD does, it has a positive influence in the world. Coming from the private sector as an American, I am very much in favour of a lot of the things the OECD does – like free trade; like intelligent government policy over business, over taxation; having environment regulations that work, that businesses and people can work with. That governments can promote better policies in areas [such] as taxation, thanks to the work that the OECD does, is very positive. (OECD 23)

A WTO official stated that she believed in GATT/WTO before starting to work there, but she emphasises particular aspects of the organisation's mission:

> I believed that market access for products, and how countries become less dependent on money by helping them to sell abroad . . . I believed in that [. . .] but across the border, random trade liberalisation . . . when I came, no

I didn't think ... But the GATT never stood for that either. The GATT was not about free trade, the GATT was about, the WTO is about, breaking down certain barriers and trade-distorted measures so that countries at least have more opportunity to sell abroad ... (WTO 2)

The quotes illustrate that pre-socialisation to the vision and mission of an international organisation can enhance the enactment of a supranational role. At the same time, pre-socialisation can take several forms. One important distinction runs between the 'true believers' – those who believe in the overall mission of the organisation, even as a 'force for good' – and the 'sector enthusiasts' – those who believe in particular issues that the organisation deals with and in the organisation's role in solving and handling these issues. In both cases, pre-socialisation seems to be an important factor in explaining why these civil servants ended up working in the particular international bureaucracy.

However, civil servants also seem to be affected by internal factors, i.e. they are socialised into the norms of the organisation through experience. The following quote from an OECD official illustrates how long tenure in an international bureaucracy can create attachments to the organisation through socialisation:

Fundamentally, my impression is that when people have joined the OECD, and they have worked here for a while, they no longer behave as nationals of any particular member country, but they serve the interests of the organisation. And it doesn't really matter whether they are Canadian, Australian or Belgian – they work towards the common aim of the organisation. (OECD 11)

When asked about his commitment to the goals of the WTO, a WTO official responds:

Yes, I think so. I mean I've spent 30+ years of my life here, so it would be bizarre if I did not. I do feel commitment to the organisation [...] Yes, I feel a commitment. I think it would be difficult if you didn't believe in an open-rules-based trading system, that it was in the basic interest of humanity. (WTO 1)

The following quote from an OECD official is along the same lines:

The real important one [of the questions] is, I think, the last part of it which deals with your feeling about the organisation and representativeness, what is it exactly you represent, whether it is the organisation or not? But, as I said, I think that being an international civil servant and the more years you do that type of job, the more you tend to represent the organisation rather than individuals or divisions or whatever. (OECD 16)

Socialisation into the norms of the organisation can also be illustrated by the following response from a WTO official when asked what kind of advice she could give the members:

Of course it has to be WTO-friendly, and then after a while you get . . . you cannot go against the philosophy of what this institution stands for. (WTO 2)

In response to the question of whether the WTO Secretariat should be the 'guardians of the treaties', a WTO official clearly confirmed that he had taken on the role of a 'guardian'. However, he also includes a more proactive role, i.e. as an agent for improving the system:

I think this is what has been agreed, but I have my views, and I think there are things that should be changed in this agreement to make it fairer, to make it more effective, and I will be happy to defend my views. But I think it has to be changed by negotiation in this organisation. You are not going to change it by destroying the WTO. That is the message. I am the guardian of the book. The book is not perfect. So my task is to convince people that this book should be improved, here. That is the mission. The mission is to make a multilateral trading system which is fair, which is fair to the developing countries, and which is better than what it is now. (WTO 9)

The quote illustrates both a sense of commitment to the organisation while at the same time seeing the Secretariat's role as being more than a facilitator. The WTO official emphasises the role as a defender of the system, but he goes even further than that – he includes in his role the task of pointing out the need for improvements, the need to 'change to preserve'.

Socialisation can also strengthen the civil servants' feeling of being part of a collective, being part of something important, which persists independently of the person who actually leads the organisation:

I'm clearly an official of the Commission and I have loyalty to the institutions, to defend the position it takes, but at the same time I feel I am part of the bigger project. I am not just serving this President, who will leave at a certain point in time, but we are also constructing Europe. And all the time this has taken different strength and intensity. (Commission 6)

Two other Commission officials emphasise that their feeling of belonging is aimed towards the European Union as such and not towards particular EU institutions or member states:

Definition-wise, I am working for the European Commission and, in a broader sense, for the Union. So I wouldn't have any ideological problems working for the Council Secretariat, for example. (Commission 11)

Well, it is the Community interest in the matter which is prime, and this interest of the Community is not necessarily identical with the interests of any single member state – even if you take them all together. (Commission 14)

This last quote indicates that the civil servant sees the Community interest as something more than and even above the member-state collective interests. It is tempting to interpret this as a belief in a separate supranational interest – a collective EU interest distinct from the member states.

Another Commission official seems to have had his beliefs shaped by the organisation, but in his case socialisation seems to have made him *less* dedicated to the 'EU project':

> I am more focused on what I do. I am very happy with the job I have, with the colleagues I have, I couldn't be happier. I have to struggle to remain faithful to Europe. I am still, but when I joined the Commission, I was for a very long time enthusiastic. I mean I was very proud working in the Commission. Not only proud, I thought we were going to take us very far. But today I am much more sceptical. (Commission 24)

This quote illustrates that socialisation within the organisation can also affect the civil servants in a way that make them less enthusiastic about the organisation. Thus, socialisation can create more tension between the beliefs of the individual and the way the organisation works. We can assume that this kind of mechanism is likely to have most impact when the organisation goes through large reforms which move the organisation in new directions – away from the norms to which the civil servants have been socialised (see Chapter 3 on the reforms of the Commission).

Socialisation to international norms: the role of internal and external control and discipline

As stated earlier, we do not think that socialisation to international norms can take place if the mechanisms of internal and external control and discipline operate alone. However, we argue that control and discipline, through incentives and rewards, can contribute to shaping the norms of civil servants and to enhancing the enactment of a supranational role.

One aspect of the supranational role of civil servants is their external representation of the international organisation. The enactment of a supranational role – as a representative of the international organisation as a whole – is evident in the following quote:

> It is obvious that when we are operating outside the WTO, in other intergovernmental organisations, then we are representing the WTO as an institution, and we have to be aware of that. (WTO 1)

The WTO official indicates in this quote that he *has* to be aware of the supranational role; it is considered mandatory to represent the WTO as a whole. In their external representation, it is important for civil servants to be sensitive to the fact that if they say something that is in conflict with the rules of the organisation or that leans towards particular member states' interests, they may be sanctioned by the internal leadership and by member-state governments. When asked about how to behave when representing the WTO externally, a WTO official responds:

> Yes, of course you have to be careful not to say weird things and things that are totally just not acceptable, or contentious. To say things about the

negotiations sort of... on some contentious issues... or to express a strong opinion that you support one view or another – that is dangerous and it is not to be tolerated. But it's not a question of asking permission. Now of course, to speak at conferences you have to get permission, for obvious reasons. But it's not so much that you send your statement to your boss to check. (WTO 13)

When asked about the possible sanctions for going against these norms, the same official says:

You are fired ... or you are called in. (WTO 13)

Another WTO official was asked how to go about preparing, for example, a background paper to a WTO committee:

Q: Even though the assessments are made according to the WTO rules, do you, as a Secretariat official, have to be careful about making formulations such as 'This is the best solution according to what I believe'? Because if that sentence is there, is there a risk that the paper will just be 'shot down' by the member states?
Oh yes, oh yes, there are things you have to be aware of and, you know, sometimes you get caught by surprise. There's a sensitivity that you weren't aware of and somebody reacts very strongly to something and you ... 'Oh, where did that come from?'. (WTO 15)

This quote shows that civil servants have to 'tread a careful path' because of the awareness and control of member states. The following quotes from OECD officials also illustrate this:

As an OECD person, you should be kind of neutral. I'm not working for the French or US government, I am working for the OECD. Period. (OECD 26)

It is quite imperative not to be biased by your nationality. (OECD 15)

So I am aware of the OECD line and agreed position, and I know it is incumbent upon me to reflect that agreed line and the conclusions of the work that we have done. It's not my position to bolster independent opinions on some policy issues that we have not done any research on or where my research hasn't been done as part of an agreed OECD process. (OECD 17)

When asked if they all consider themselves international civil servants, an OECD official responds:

Yes. You have to, in that job; you wouldn't last long otherwise. We are not here to represent our own countries in any way. (OECD 2)

Another OECD official responds as follows to the question of whether it takes discipline to distinguish between being national and supranational:

Exactly! That is the most important thing that I have learned in the OECD. (OECD 15)

Thus, external and internal control and discipline seem to enhance the adoption of the organisation's norms among civil servants. Some officials seem to enact a supranational role in the form of 'guardians of the system'. A quote from a WTO official illustrates this. He was asked whether the WTO agreements amount to a kind of constitution that the civil servants have to relate to all the time:

> Exactly! But I don't really think ... I don't think I will ever come across someone who doesn't really believe in that. But some people have different views about ... you know, some people look at it more from a developing-country perspective and other people from other perspectives. Some of the people might think that some of the rules are more or less equitable. (WTO 1)

This quote illustrates that even though civil servants may become 'guardians of the system' and have to constantly relate to the organisation's rules in their activities, they do not necessarily believe in or agree with all the rules. Internal and external control and discipline may thus foster a supranational role among civil servants in the sense of 'guardians of the system', but the degree to which the norms of the organisation have been internalised may still vary. Some are true believers – for others the defence of the system is more conditional.

Summing up: supranational dynamics in international bureaucracies

We have seen that supranational dynamics are present among civil servants in the WTO Secretariat, the OECD Secretariat and the Commission. Officials of all three bureaucracies enact supranational roles in their work as international civil servants. Importantly, we have seen that supranational dynamics take several forms.

There are cases where civil servants have been pre-socialised into the norms of the organisation which has made them dedicated and committed to the mission and vision of the organisation even before applying for a position. In some cases this seems to be related to their former position, where they either have been in close contact with the particular organisation or have been working on the same policies and issues for which the organisation is responsible. For example, one OECD official states that he became enthusiastic about the OECD when working on many of the same issues in his former job in the private sector; another WTO official became enthusiastic about the WTO when working in his former job as a national WTO diplomat. In other cases, pre-socialisation seems to have taken place through family background. For example, a Commission official became dedicated to the EU project through her upbringing in Brussels, close to the EU institutions. Therefore, both close interaction and family background may foster pre-socialisation into

international norms. These findings coincide with the conclusion that pre-socialisation can make the civil servants favourably disposed to the international organisation's norms (Hooghe 2005). One possible consequence of this is that there may be a bias towards dedicated civil servants in the recruitment into the organisations.

However, we also find cases where socialisation seems to have taken place within the organisation and thus enhanced the civil servants' adoption of the organisation's norms, ideas and beliefs. We argue that this form of socialisation may be enhanced by long tenure, hierarchical structure and active leadership on the one hand and by external control through the multilateral environment on the other. Such internal and external control and discipline make it imperative for the civil servants to 'stick' to the goals and rules of the organisation and to be perceived as neutral by member-state governments. These factors thus foster the internalisation of the organisation's norms as well as the strategic adoption of these norms – it pays to be considered as 'neutral defenders of the system'.

We can furthermore make a distinction between two different supranational roles. Firstly, there are the policy-based supranationalists. These are civil servants who are enthusiastic about the international organisation because of particular issues that the organisation deals with, but they are not necessarily enthusiastic about everything the organisation does. There is obviously a possible overlap between this dynamic and the epistemic dynamic. Dedication is conditioned by the organisation's position on certain policies, and the civil servants' expertise in these policy areas may enhance their dedication to the organisation. Secondly, there are the true believers. These are civil servants who truly believe in the overall goals of the organisation and view the organisation as a force for good. This is the unconditioned dedicated civil servant. Both the policy-based supranational role and the 'true believer' supranational role can supplement epistemic and departmental dynamics, i.e. we find in the data both civil servants who enact epistemic and departmental roles and who are enthusiastic about the goals of the organisation, and civil servants who are not. Thus, supranational dynamics may complement the other dynamics.

Can we then say something about the differences in how the supranational dynamic plays out in the three organisations? We do not have enough systematic data to make any final conclusions on causal relationships. However, we can point to some of the important factors that can be used to explain why supranational dynamics play out the way they do in the three bureaucracies.

Firstly, the recruitment procedures are assumed to be important. All three organisations have a merit-based recruitment system. However, the OECD and the Commission have stronger elements of a national-quota system than the WTO which has no quota system at all. Recruitment procedures thus favour supranational dynamics more in the WTO compared to the other organisations.

Secondly, long tenure is assumed to foster socialisation within the organisations as well as being a way of disciplining the civil servants to only serve the organisation's interests, not least because of career opportunities. In this respect also the WTO is different from the two other organisations. We see that many civil servants in the WTO have had long careers within the bureaucracy. Furthermore, there is very little use of short-term contracts in the WTO compared to the Commission and OECD. Thus, tenure seems also to favour supranational dynamics more in the WTO than in the two other organisations.

Thirdly, prior institutional affiliation may affect the enactment of supranational roles. Affiliation to institutions with norms that possibly conflict with the international organisation is assumed to reduce the potential for socialisation to the international organisation's norms. However, one can argue that people who in their former positions worked in close interaction with the international organisation in question have more potential for being pre-socialised into the international norms than others. It is difficult to say with certainty how the three bureaucracies differ on this point. All three organisations hire newly educated people, people from the private sector and people with experience from member-state governments. Thus, more systematic data is needed.

Fourthly, hierarchical control is assumed to be an important factor regarding the control of civil servants – to ensure that they act according to the rules of the organisation and defend the system. In this respect, the Commission stands out compared to the two other organisations. The Commission has the most specialised vertical structures and thus the most potential for controlling the civil servants.

Fifthly, the size and scope of activities are assumed to be important. The WTO Secretariat is clearly the smallest bureaucracy of the three. Moreover, it is closely watched by member-state governments and operates within a narrower mandate than the Commission and the OECD Secretariat. Thus, it seems easier and more important for WTO officials to identify with the mission and vision of the organisation within which they operate.

Sixthly, the power and autonomy of the three bureaucracies differ considerably. Both the Commission and the WTO produce hard law, i.e. binding rules, whereas the OECD is a soft-law producer, i.e. it makes recommendations, sets benchmarks, standards and guidelines etc. which are voluntary for member states to follow. We assume that this makes it more likely that the control of member-state governments regarding what the bureaucracy does is stronger in the WTO and the Commission than in the OECD. This may again favour supranational dynamics in the WTO

Secretariat and the Commission because civil servants are more strongly made to appear as neutral defenders of the system who do not lean towards particular member-state interests. Furthermore, the Commission has exclusive legal competences within the Commission and thus clearly has the most power and competences of the three bureaucracies studied in this book. Arguably, this increases the probability that the Commission is more closely linked than the two other organisations to supranational interests as distinct from member-state interests.

In this book we have challenged the claim that supranational dynamics in international organisations are mainly caused by domestic pre-socialisation (Hooghe 2005). Although pre-socialisation takes place in all three organisations, our observations show that there is considerable potential for socialisation within all three bureaucracies. More systematic studies are needed, however, in order to shed more light on the causal relationships involved in shaping and re-shaping the norms and roles of civil servants.

8

Epistemic dynamics in international bureaucracies

Science is much more than the mechanical production of data and analysis. Science has become an institution in itself which is loaded with authority and power. Scientific authority bestows its holder with legitimacy and a communicative platform that reaches far beyond the narrow scientific discipline. Scientific power grants access to constituting basic rules for cause and effect, distinguishing right from wrong, categorising social phenomena and advising about good and bad. It is not knowledge in itself which is powerful; knowledge attributes power only if the kind of knowledge and the position of the knowledgeable generally find approval in society. Thus, it is not any kind of knowledge that functions as the key to authority and power: only 'recognised knowledge' matters.

Universities have traditionally been the places with the monopoly on recognised knowledge. For a variety of reasons, this monopoly has been broken (Drori et al. 2003; Drori and Meyer 2006; Ramirez 2006). Some would argue that knowledge production and management have become pluralised and even democratised; others would argue that knowledge production has become the object of marketisation (Djelic 2006). Today, many political actors – public and private, national and international – seek to establish a sort of expert or scientific authority founded on the idea of evidence-based rulemaking. Apart from seeking rational-legal authority based on the idea of impersonal rulemaking, or delegated authority based on the idea of accountable rulemaking, or moral authority based on the idea of normative or principled rulemaking, the role of knowledge seems to have become central in how political actors engage in processes of authority building (Barnett and Finnemore 2004). Science as the basis for authority was central to Max Weber, who considered rationalisation as one of the most important characteristics of the development of Western society and capitalism (Wrong 1970). Other forms of authority – traditional or charismatic authority relying on religion, magic, supernatural phenomena or personal attributes – were seen as irrational because they were essentially based on personal insight, emotions and feelings. Rationality, in contrast, is governed by reason and calculation. The central features of rationality as a concept are: that results can be calculated by adopting assumptions; that actors attempt to find the most efficient means of achieving their objectives; that social action is governed by generic rules and as a result can be predicted with a certain degree of reliability; and that predictability of social action can be enhanced by constantly constructing better technologies, tools and machinery.

Max Weber expected that rationality would take over more and more spheres of society including religion, politics, administration, sports and music. A process of rationalisation would unfold. At the same time, more control over individual action would be increasingly imposed thereby stifling charisma and tradition and allowing for few alternatives for creative human action. Formal rationality in the shape of universally applied rules, laws and regulations would gradually crowd out the unexpected and different.

Thus, rationalisation, i.e. rule by science, is a classical concept in the study of public administration, and empirical evidence for its existence has been found in various studies over the last forty years or so (Couldner 1979; Marcussen 2006 and 2009). However, two clarifications should be made. Firstly, there is no claim in the rationalisation argument that evidence-based decisions are better than decisions based on other kinds of logic. The kind of positivist science Max Weber is talking about is not the only option. Other post-positivist epistemologies exist, either in competition with this particular kind of rationality or as a supplement to it. Thus, what counts as evidence in evidence-based decisions is highly debated. The issue at stake in this discussion is, therefore, not to investigate whether rationalised bureaucracies make better decisions but rather whether they try to enhance their authority by linking themselves to a scientific discourse.

This leads us to the second clarification, which concerns the distinction between *de*politisation versus *a*politisation. Throughout the 1990s, a large number of public authorities obtained legal autonomy from parliamentary supervision (Christensen and Lægreid 2006). The delegation of authority from politically accountable public administrations to legally independent agencies is explained in theory by referring to the shortsightedness of politicians. Politicians will undertake to manipulate public authorities and policies in order to maximise their chances for re-election, as a result of which certain public authorities and agencies, such as central banks, need to be protected from irresponsible politicians. Thus, certain areas of public life are being depoliticised (Flinders and Buller 2006; Hay 2007). *De*politicisation in itself may lead to a situation where politicians censure their own speech acts. To a more or less marked extent they may voluntarily refrain from verbally interfering in an area which has become legally autonomous. This does not mean, however, that politicians are not observing this area of activity with great interest, and it does not mean that they have no intention of interfering in that area altogether. They may use other means of governing a formally autonomous area of public activities. For example, if politicians have delegated power to an agency, they can always rescind that legal authority, typically by a simple majority in parliament. Legally-autonomous agencies, therefore, are dependent on their public support and on a generalised belief that their area of competence needs to be kept out of reach of elected politicians. They know that they are living in the shadow of politicians who are watching their behaviour.

Because of such a potentially unstable situation, where formal authority can be handed over as well as withdrawn quite easily, most autonomous agencies aspire to achieve a different kind of status which brings them out of the shadow of observing politicians. They aspire to transcend the field of politics all together. This is where *a*politicisation comes into the picture. Whereas depoliticisation is about shielding an area of policy making from active politicians, apoliticisation is about bringing the entire area out of the visible field of policy making. An apoliticised area of policy making is simply not present in the consciousness of policy makers. They do not consider an area characterised by scientisation as being an area of politics. By accepting that people and institutions within a scienticised area have epistemic authority, politicians also accept that this area is *de facto* out of reach with regard to intervention. The details of rocket science are not a subject for political debate. Thus, epistemic communities, to the extent that they exist, do not in principle work under the shadow of politicians; they work under the shadow of the rules of the scientific community itself. Members of a scientific community are each other's judges – accountability is turned inwards. Externally, a true epistemic community will have a variety of instruments at its disposal to constitute, alter and institutionalise policy making (Haas 1990; Haas 1992). But policy makers will not even consider actively, directly or indirectly interfering in the work of an epistemic community. Apart from the normative consequences that such a complete isolation and protection from policy makers may entail, it is clear that an agency which has succeeded in obtaining the status of being part of an epistemic community has obtained a considerable power base.

Basic features of scientisation in international bureaucracies

It would be interesting to know whether the international civil servants in the WTO, OECD and EU Commission would identify with a role of 'knowledge builders', 'truth seekers' and 'researchers' because this would in itself be a role distinct from those of the supranationalist cosmopolitan – the classical Weberian civil servant or the intergovernmental civil servant studied in Chapters 6, 7 and 9. But how do we know that a transnational civil servant is enacting epistemic dynamics?

Firstly, we would expect the civil servants interviewed from the OECD, WTO and Commission to explicitly associate knowledge and expertise with power and authority. One WTO civil servant argues that in *external* contexts her personal prestige is greatly enhanced if she mentions that she comes from a knowledge organisation like the WTO. She is automatically, even in prestigious university circles, considered to be an expert authority when it becomes known that she is employed in the WTO:

> And they immediately have a label for you, 'OK, she must be really expert'. (WTO 2)

The technical expertise possessed by an international bureaucracy also greatly contributes to the external authority and freedom of a unit in relation to member states. This is the clear perception of one of the interviewed civil servants from the Commission who argues that:

> For our area there is not much pressure, because these negotiations are pretty technical and the knowledge of the ministries in the capitals is limited. (Commission 14)

Another civil servant adds that in order to enact the kind of power which can be obtained through the possession of knowledge, one is bound to engage in persuasion and deliberation rather than in more direct forms of governance:

> Well, you know, knowledge is power. And sometimes you can very well help to shape the thinking of people about what's a good solution and what's a bad solution. But you have to do that more indirectly than directly. You know, you can't just sort of say 'I'm in charge here, so you have to do it my way'. You have to help shape their thinking and influence. (WTO 18)

Apart from enhancing the personal prestige and authority in relation to external stakeholders, expertise also functions as a means *internally* to enhance one's autonomy. Although there are clear hierarchies in any organisation, this hierarchy can somehow be circumvented if a civil servant possesses recognised knowledge within a field of work which is central to the organisation. Thus, being asked about her leeway in terms of formal procedures, a WTO civil servant answers that:

> I have quite a bit of discretion, but it's partly because of my recognised expertise in the area ... I get quite a bit of freedom I guess. (WTO 15; see also Commission 21, pp. 00–00)

Another civil servant points to the same dynamic when arguing that expertise conveys freedom of action. In this case, however, the expert power is used strategically to prevent too many reforms taking place in his area of competence. Thus, when new leaders enter the organisation, they will be confronted with people who possess invaluable expertise, as a result of which the new Director-General is prevented from interfering in this area of activity:

> We have a lot of freedom because we have a lot of expertise, and therefore when somebody new, when a new director comes, a new team – because you have a new DG and four new DDGs – they may come with new ideas ... So after a while you [the new leader] realise that you cannot do anything drastic overnight. And that's why things change very slowly in the Secretariat. (WTO 16)

It is noteworthy that the perception of good leadership skills is sometimes connected directly to the level of knowledge that the leaders can mobilise. When describing the positive qualities of his Deputy Director-General, one civil servant in the Commission exclusively emphasised this person's substantial knowledge of a field of work:

> So he knows what we do and understands very, very well what we do ... He certainly thinks for himself. (Commission 21)

Similarly, in more general terms, when describing bad leadership, knowledge is once again at stake. For a civil servant who identifies with 'knowledge production', a bad leader is one who interferes in matters that are obviously not understood and who makes decisions based on purely political considerations rather than on detailed technical knowledge:

> It can be less satisfactory when there is a sense that people who do not understand the details and who are taking decisions on very, very broad, political – perhaps unrelated to the case at hand – considerations, are interfering with how you think the case should be run. That is less satisfactory. (Commission 21)

A second indication that an international civil servant is leaning towards an epistemic dynamic is that s/he is largely decoupled from party politics, national mandates, institutional loyalties and internal organisational considerations of a strategic nature. The main point of reference is not any office, organisation or nation but rather a transborder network of professionals whom s/he consults on a regular basis. It is clearly a horizontal network in which all other professionals around the globe who identify with a certain discipline of work are included. It is an inclusive network in the sense that it does not discriminate against nationalities and rank, but it is exclusive in the sense that it requires knowledge of a certain kind to belong to this network. Unlike the departmental role concept where the main points of reference and lines of loyalty are focused on a narrow single vertical or horizontal dimension within the international bureaucracy, and in contrast to the supranational and intergovernmental role concepts where the entire international organisation or the state of origin forms the basis of an international civil servant loyalty, the epistemic dynamic transcends these physical borderlines and unfolds in an imagined community based on a discipline or specific kind of knowledge.

A description of such a border-crossing scientific community is given by a number of the interviewees, in particular at the OECD and the WTO. When asked whether regular interaction with external experts, universities and research institutions plays a role in the everyday duties in the organisation, an OECD civil servant replies:

> Yes. We do what we do with them a lot, including the theme-based and country-specific work. For all the work that I have done in the last several years, I spent a lot of the time working with experts – frequently academic experts [...] most of what we work on we'll have some interaction with experts – often at universities or research institutes. (OECD 17)

A member of the WTO Secretariat even considers such outward-oriented contact with experts to be more frequent and important than inward-oriented contact with colleagues in the same organisation:

> We have more the links with the World Bank, other sort of research institutes, international organisations, UN, ILO, FAO, Inter-American Development Bank. So we are somehow more connected with research centres of other international organisations: OECD also, not the EC but international organisations, then not within the WTO somehow, and also with universities. (WTO 17)

This construction of a transborder, outward-oriented community of experts also means that hierarchies lose some of their importance. In consequence, instructions do not primarily come from a superior. One civil servant claims that at least the operational divisions of the WTO are characterised by a quite unhierarchical mode of governance:

> It is not an organisation where I get most of the instructions from my Deputy Director-General, who is the head of my department, or from the Director-General. (WTO 1)

In general, for an epistemic civil servant, approval is received from colleagues in the research community and not from some parties external to this community:

> Q: So you kind of work like a research team?
> Yes.
> Q: And not like a hierarchy?
> No. [...] it's not that the co-ordinator is the only one with the responsibility of looking at what somebody else has done. Actually, once everybody has done his own research, we switch parts with each other, and so each of us, sort of, somehow checks what somebody else has done. (WTO 17)

A third feature which is central to scientisation has to do with the methods and job functions of the international civil servant. We recognise an epistemic civil servant when it becomes an objective in itself to formulate problems and to imagine hitherto unseen or underemphasised aspects of social life. Through a problem-oriented philosophy, the epistemic civil servant will tend to engage in exploration rather than exploitation (March 1991). Rather than applying existing techniques in an instrumental fashion, the epistemic civil servant will find satisfaction in discovering new ground. This takes time and patience. The benefit materialises very slowly, if at all. In consequence, risks are taken, costly mistakes are made and blind alleys are sometimes followed. This is considered part of the normal routine of work. In addition, new findings are made through transborder deliberation rather than through negotiation. Communication with other people is considered to be part of important and never-ending learning processes with the objective of developing new tools, methods, instruments, arguments and ideas. In order to do this, the epistemic civil servant will typically engage in scholarly debates within his or her own discipline, either at conferences, in journals or as part of research projects. This means that an epistemic civil servant will on a regular basis and in most social contexts employ concepts, theories, expressions and references that are specific to his or her profession.

In all three international bureaucracies investigated in this book, there seems to be an agreement among the interviewed civil servants that the OECD is the most research-minded organisation of the three. One WTO civil servant is of the opinion that the role of the WTO Secretariat may be modest compared to the executive capabilities of the Commission but also compared to the OECD since:

> The OECD Secretariat maybe doesn't have a lot of executive functions, but it has more freedom to express views and influence public opinions, perhaps, than we do. (WTO 1)

Within the Commission, one civil servant is of the opinion that his own administration ought to move more in the direction of the OECD. Whereas the OECD undertakes more academic research, according to this interviewee Commission research is more pragmatic and more policy-driven. It is maybe not realistic to think about the Commission as a research organisation like the OECD, 'but we could do more and we could do better' (Commission 7).

The perception that the OECD is leading in terms of research capacity is also shared in the OECD itself:

> Q: How do you feel that the other organisations benefit from your work?
> We have, in many areas, superior expertise in economics, in statistics; we have more staff with more competence.

Q: Would you also say that you are considered perhaps more independent than some of the other organisations?
Yes, I think that it is probably fair to say that. (OECD 4)

An epistemic civil servant would, of course, first of all identify with his profession and discipline. Although it may be difficult in practice, a number of the interviewees try to keep up with scientific developments in their area, and try to engage actively in the relevant research community. A WTO civil servant emphasises that, despite complications, she is trying to maintain links with the academic world:

> I try to go to conferences, and present papers, and try to do some teaching if I can hook into local or Swiss programmes that are working on trade economics and agricultural economics. I am trying to find ways so that I can do that. We don't do that much of that kind of work here, so you have to be kind of proactive to find the opportunities. (WTO 6)

In the Commission, constraints on purely academic research activities seem to be greater. One civil servant even thinks that in order to survive for many years in a public bureaucracy such as the Commission one needs to spend extra time and effort to keep updated in one's professional discipline. He argues:

> I strongly identify with what I am doing here. I think it's a way of survival as well – in a public administration. (Commission 13)

It is certainly not always easy to keep track of what is going on in universities, but many feel quite uncomfortable with the idea that they could become completely detached from the world of university research:

> We try to keep contact with universities a bit ... we would not like to be a research group of WTO detached from all the rest of, sort of, more independent research, like the research from the university. So this, I think, is a good thing. It's not as strong as we would be if we were the university because we have to also do other things, but I think we're trying, because we think it's important to keep listening. (WTO 17)

A true epistemic civil servant would also consider it a source of personal pride if quality research was carried out by his bureaucracy. One interviewee argues that the motivation behind applying for a job in the WTO was its reputation for carrying out high-quality research:

> So the whole thing was I had a lot of respect for the quality of the work produced by the Secretariat. And after all, it couldn't be a bad thing to work in an institution like the WTO Secretariat. And, of course, the Director-General asked me once, a couple of months ago, what do I think, because I told him the same story, he asked me am I still happy with it, and I said 'Yes' ... I am so pleasantly surprised by the pool of expertise in this house, it's really out of this world, and the commitment and the dedication of the vast majority of my colleagues. (WTO 13)

When moving from the level of aspirations, hopes and visions to the level of actual job content, it is a quite recurrent feature in all three bureaucracies that the research functions have to be undertaken at the same time as administrative, secretarial and more routine functions. In that sense, the job descriptions of the research-minded civil servants in the WTO, OECD and Commission do not differ much from those of ordinary university professors who also only devote a fraction of their time to conducting pure research:

> Somehow it's similar to what you do in universities. The difference is that here sometimes you get, for instance, an urgent request from the DG, like we did two days ago. And therefore anything that you were doing stops and you have this priority, and when this priority is over, you go back to your research [...] Actually we are quite free to do the type of research we want to do ... we have, sort of, our research projects ... We produce some background papers, but also papers that we submit for publication ... I'm working on new papers with some people of the university here in Geneva. (WTO 17)

However, one clear difference between research at international bureaucracies and research at universities is that sometimes civil servants in international bureaucracies will have to take diplomacy into account. There are limits to what can be argued in their research papers:

> I am basically a researcher, I write research reports. So I seek out research material just like I would at university. The only difference is that I have to be nuanced because we write for governments, we don't write under our own name. We don't have that freedom. So I am a researcher. But also what is different than at university, I have to respond to a lot of requests from the public, from people outside who want material that we produce. That basically summarises what I do day to day. (OECD 19)

An international bureaucracy characterised by epistemic dynamics can also be recognised by the kinds of cleavages that are recurrent among the civil servants. We would expect civil servants who fully identify with research and research methods to frequently engage in inter-paradigmatic debates or purely academic struggles based on different ontological or epistemological points of departure or maybe on just disagreements about data. Thus, different academic disciplines have different research traditions, and it is typically an inherent feature of a dynamic research environment that it is an objective in itself not to close academic debates but rather to maintain open-ended research. Such disciplinary frictions and normal academic quarrels are recurrent particularly in the WTO and the OECD:

> In any organisation you do have some differences between people who think of themselves very much as professional economists or professional lawyers ... and this can lead to friction at times. (WTO 1)

> We do quantitative work and people have different ideas about models, and
> so there is some disagreement between people about which model is the best
> and how to go about quantitative research. (OECD 1)

The fact that people come from many different countries and therefore
bring with them many different national traditions is viewed by the large
majority of the interviewed civil servants as being one of the most
important sources of inspiration and virility. Cultural diversity is seen as
a clear asset for international bureaucracies. In that sense, international
bureaucracies are much more lively, innovative and challenging than
national bureaucracies. Yet some civil servants in these international
bureaucracies regret that there is too little disciplinary disagreement in
their units. Thus, one interviewee argues that from a purely academic
point of view one would always wish for more constructive disagreement
that could lead to new insights:

> There are not that many who question the consensus. That is something
> which is a little bit, you know, personally, coming from a university
> background, is a little bit disappointing. (OECD 19)

Furthermore, a recurrent characteristic of an epistemic civil servant relates
to his or her scholarly background. This particular kind of civil servant is
most likely to possess a higher education, and possibly a PhD – or may
express a wish to have obtained a PhD. In addition, some of the civil
servants in the OECD, WTO and Commission who possess these specific
characteristics may also have been teaching in earlier periods of their
career, or at least have been affiliated with university institutions or other
knowledge-producing institutions. Significantly, it is the OECD that
employs the largest number of people with a PhD degree (followed, to a
lesser extent, by the WTO). In the Commission, quite a number of
interviewees mention that in addition to their national degrees they have
taken a Master's degree in public administration, law or economics at the
College of Europe in Bruges, Belgium.

For some, the choice of working in an international bureaucracy is
based on the wish to obtain inside knowledge on a specific area of
research, or simply some additional experience that can somehow
improve their standing in the field of research. The positioning of the
international bureaucracy is not seen as being inconsistent with research
but rather as supplementing research. Insofar as the concerned civil
servant's desire to engage in knowledge production and dissemination is
satisfied, the person will remain employed in the international bureaucracy. However, it is not the international bureaucracy in itself that is
attractive for the epistemic civil servant but rather the work and the
intellectual challenges that the job function contains. A number of
interviewees argue that they could easily move to another international

bureaucracy to perform the same kind of activities. Thus, one interviewee emphasises that the attachment to the job is really based on whether the functions and colleagues are intellectually stimulating:

> I do associate myself closely with the unit, and that is partly, or perhaps mainly, because (a) the work is quite legal so it fits me well, it's something that I can do reasonably well and find intellectually stimulating; and (b) I have fantastic colleagues, absolutely wonderful, intellectually and on a personal level. (Commission 21)

It should be noted that once civil servants who have had quite long careers in academia in the form of research professorships and the like are employed in an international bureaucracy, typically in a leading position, in practice they will not conduct very much actual research. The management responsibilities seem to totally crowd out research activities. The civil servants concerned do not seem to have a problem in adapting to the new situation or in undertaking their management responsibilities, but it seems a paradox that the main criteria for obtaining such a position at this level formally required a background in advanced and recognised research, whereas the actual job functions involve no research whatsoever. In that sense, much has changed in an organisation such as the OECD. In its earlier days, the first Secretary-General, Thorkil Kristensen, was known for his ability to isolate himself from routines and administrative practices for weeks or months in order to personally undertake research in areas which were of interest to him (Marcussen 2002). Today, this is clearly a luxury that is unaffordable in any leading position in an international bureaucracy.

A-scientific tendencies

The Commission is clearly distinct from the WTO and the OECD in the sense that the civil servants interviewed from DG Trade and the General Secretariat identify to only a limited extent with the epistemic features listed above. With a few exceptions, the interviewees did not associate their job content, their working processes and relations or their own visions and aspirations with knowledge production and scientific method. On the contrary, a number of civil servants explicitly rejected many of the features that would define them as researchers.

One civil servant reports that before taking up his post in the Commission he thought it was actually possible to undertake research-like functions in the DGs. He unsuccessfully attempted to become a university professor in his home country. An alternative option was to realise his research ambitions within an international bureaucracy such as the Commission. He was soon proved wrong: it was not possible to combine research with the day-to-day practical functions within a hierarchically

organised international bureaucracy (Commission 5). Two other interviewees had the same experience and explain:

> Of course, the way of working is very different from academia; my duties are very different from academia. I am not working for the same masters. I have political masters to whom I have to report, I have a hierarchy to which I have to report. And therefore the way I work is very different. (Commission 2)

> Coming from academia, where things are thought through quite carefully before anything is written, was quite a surprise. To see people write emails in hardly intelligible English, with typos and other things, very, very fast and off-the-cuff ... and there is perhaps a culture of too fast and too many emails rather than carefully thought-through stuff. (Commission 21)

In addition, it is argued that there is no room in Commission work to engage in deep research simply because service-mindedness in this context is defined as being brief and fast, 'but not lengthy, lengthy research' (Commission 21). Thus, a service organisation that deals with many countries and external actors on a very frequent basis is perceived to be incommensurable with research practices.

A characteristic feature among the interviewees is that European Commission civil servants simply do not identify with their scholarly discipline such as law (Commission 6) or economics (Commission 17). If anything, they refer in very general terms to the fact that they belong to the 'College of Europe Mafia' (several interviews).

To understand why this difference between the Commission, the WTO and the OECD is so marked, it may be useful to also note that many interviewees felt the need to talk about the formal and informal hierarchical structures that form the Commission (see Chapter 6 on the departmental dynamics in international bureaucracies). For instance, when being asked about the conditions under which hierarchies are important, one interviewee does not hesitate to answer:

> Always! The question is how you maintain hierarchy. (Commission 2)

Being asked explicitly about whether it is 'grades or knowledge' that makes people influential in the Commission, another interviewee immediately answers:

> Definitely the grade. Except in very, very few cases. (Commission 20)

Thus, in contrast to an ideal-typical research environment in which formal as well as informal authority is based on recognised knowledge, authority on an everyday level does not necessarily rest on merit but rather on position. Of course, one would assume that these two attributes overlap to a certain extent but there are interviewees who are frankly surprised about how small a role formal merit actually plays in relation to promotion.

One interviewee even argues that a *de facto* requirement for really making it in the Commission is a long time spent in the system, so 'one does not become a manager purely on merit' (Commission 21). This characterisation may be very specific for the Trade Directorate, since in this area we are dealing with an exclusive Commission competence. This allows the Commission more freedom in relation to member states. The member states cannot contest Commission work to any large degree, as a result of which the Commission can afford to pay less attention to precision.

The majority of the interviewees clearly accept the rules of the game of the Commission – and they do not even consider it a possibility that it could be different from the status quo. However, there is a minority among the interviewees who are deeply convinced that the Commission could do better when it comes to moving from rapid and superficial analysis to basic research. Some talk about the need for a 'methodological change' (Commission 21) towards more in-depth and scientifically consistent analysis.

However, as is clear from the chapters that explicitly deal with the departmental (Chapter 6) and the supranational (Chapter 7) dynamics within the Commission, the primary motivation for getting a job in this particular international bureaucracy seems to either rest on purely material factors such as salary and other benefits, or on a desire to serve a large ideal of underpinning co-operation, welfare and stability at a European level. Whereas the WTO and the OECD seem to attract people with extensive experience from previous jobs in the public and private sectors, people with higher levels of education, and people who tend to be academically interested in very specific areas of activity, the Commission generally does not primarily attract this segment. In addition, there seems to be a tendency for the WTO and the OECD not only to allow but also to expect their A-grade civil servants to conduct independent and innovative analysis, whereas such an expectation is not as present in the Commission. With its clear executive responsibilities and in contrast to the WTO and the OECD, the Commission establishes different expectations to the output of its bureaucracy which will be mirrored in its employment profile. However, the Commission, including the Trade Directorate investigated for the purposes of this book, is such a large organisation compared to the WTO and the OECD that one would expect to find small pockets of so-called scientific civil servants. However, compared to the two other organisations, this expectation was not met.

Summing up: a plurality of dynamics

This chapter has highlighted a number of central features that we would expect to characterise a civil servant in an international bureaucracy that

enacts epistemic role dynamics. In particular, examples from the personal interviews at the OECD, WTO and Commission have been given to illustrate the ways in which people identify with the role as a researcher, employ research methods, engage in transborder scientific communities and actually undertake research activities on the job. Overall, it can be concluded that there are marked differences between the OECD and WTO on the one hand and the Commission on the other. In the first two international bureaucracies, science, research and expertise seem to play important roles in peoples' self-perception, background, aspirations, visions, relationships and patterns of interaction. Thus, hierarchies play less of a role in these two organisations than in the Commission, and the awareness of and pride in the authority, power, freedom and autonomy – internally and well as externally – that can be obtained through expertise and knowledge seem to be much more salient.

This finding should not lead us to conclude that a clear and coherent pattern of role conceptions exists in any of the three international bureaucracies investigated. One complication is that inside all three international bureaucracies there are civil servants who tend to lean towards either the supranational dynamic, the intergovernmental dynamic, the departmental dynamic or the epistemic dynamic. No international bureaucracy can be characterised in relation to only one of these dynamics. There are multiple roles to be played on the arenas of international bureaucracies (see Chapter 10). Another complication concerns the fact that each civil servant interviewed seems to enact various dynamics at the same time. Thus, a recurrent phenomenon is that each civil servant seems to play various roles in the course of undertaking his or her duties in the international bureaucracy. A WTO civil servant explains this very clearly. When asked about the plurality of social roles in the course of a working day, he answers:

Well, I think that that is kind of self-evident, you know, I suppose most people find themselves in that type of situation. (WTO 1)

Another explains that:

It depends of course on where you are. It depends on what audience you have. (WTO 2)

This should not come as a surprise when viewed in the light of the vast literature on role theory that suggests that individuals tend to play an array of different roles that can be described as role sets (Biddle 1986). However, as explained in Chapter 1, it is curious that research on identities and roles in international bureaucracies has so far largely tended to ignore the fact that such a complexity exists. It has been taken for granted that an overall, generic identity and vision tend to exist either in different departments of an international bureaucracy or in an international bureaucracy as a whole. A central finding of this book, which is confirmed by this chapter on the epistemic dynamics in international bureaucracies, is therefore that such a unitary and coherent picture of life in international bureaucracies does not pay sufficient tribute to the vibrant life within international bureaucracies across borders defined by units, disciplines and nationality.

9

Intergovernmental dynamics in international bureaucracies

Traditionally, an *intergovernmental* behavioural pattern has been seen as containing two core ingredients. Firstly, an official is guided by intergovernmental dynamics if s/he acts in accordance with formal or informal instructions or mandates issued by his or her member state. The second aspect of intergovernmental dynamics focuses on the self-perceptions of the officials. An official is thus intergovernmental if s/he is guided by loyalty to his or her national government, has a preference for national interests and/or enjoys close contact with his or her home base. However, in this chapter a complementary way of understanding intergovernmental behavioural patterns will also be presented, adding a second dimension to the concept and, to a lesser extent, emphasising the importance of member states as actors in the game.

What this chapter reveals, in contrast to several previous studies regarding the Commission (Kassim and Menon 2004; Spence and Stevens 2006), is the absence of strong indications of intergovernmental behaviour and perceptions among civil servants in international organisations. On the contrary, several mechanisms and methods of neutralising this type of behaviour and attitude are discovered. However, and somewhat surprisingly, in comparing the Commission with the OECD and WTO Secretariats, more intergovernmental sentiments and behavioural patterns were noticed in the Commission than in the other two organisations.

The classic understanding of intergovernmentalism: pressure and presence

Typical civil servants with an intergovernmental perspective are those employed by the Foreign Office, particularly those in the diplomatic corps. In their purest form, intergovernmental dynamics are built on the assumption that bargains between national interests dominate the functioning and internal behavioural dynamics of international organisations. Nation-states have preferences which they are able to transfer into positions on how different issues should be handled and on what policy is to be pursued in different situations. Consequently, civil servants working in international bureaucracies are affected by these preferences, either by direct instructions, by anticipation or through socialisation. Intergovernmental dynamics may therefore be activated among civil servants in international organisations even when they have not received instructions from their government. In particular, civil servants with a long career in a national administration prior to employment in international bureaucracies, and/or civil servants planning to continue a career in national governments, are likely to activate intergovernmental behaviour and attitudes.

However, intergovernmental perceptions and influences also work in more subtle ways, and guidelines given to civil servants may have a more culture-specific content than clear-cut instructions aimed at certain goals (Bàtora 2008). A civil servant from a French-speaking country may have instructions to speak French at the workplace or to promote the French culture or ways of thinking. It may also be the case that national governments are keen on placing 'their' civil servants in international bureaucracies as a means to achieving long-term diffuse effects, knowing that certain persons with specific skills may advocate and promote certain types of policies and solutions even when not having been given instructions or having been in regular contact with their previous employer or 'home administration'.

All in all, the classic understanding of intergovernmentalism is built on the assumption that domestic stakeholders – the member states – try to influence the decision making of an international organisation by pressure and presence.

A complementary understanding of intergovernmentalism

So far, intergovernmentalism has mainly been seen as a means by which national governments influence international organisations. However, as concluded as early as 1974 by Cox and Jacobson (Cox and Jacobson 1973), national governments may be influential when setting up international organisations but have much more difficulty controlling what happens once this process is completed. Therefore, there is perhaps another side of the coin to the concept of intergovernmentalism which makes it less one-dimensional. The leaders and those working in international organisations may have attained their position by their affiliation to national governments. However, they are not necessarily 'slaves under the national anthem'. Moreover, when they become part of an international organisation their ideals and ambitions may become different from what they were when they were domestic officials, and their understanding of what is in the best interest of their own country may differ from that of their own incumbent government. Paradoxically, by applying the logic of intergovernmentalism, such as a fair repre-sentation of different nationalities in international bureaucracies and an open-door policy for the member states to express their opinions, the international organisation can enhance its legitimacy and con-sequently its influence. By organising itself according to what it believes or anticipates to be in the interest of the different member states, even without outside pressure being put on it, the international bureaucracy can generate an image of serving the member states. In reality, however, this form of intergovermentalism is aimed more at countering the external influence of the member states on the international organisation. With this form of 'organisational' intergovernmentalism, the international bureaucracy actually designs the influence of member states through certain organisational solutions. However, since international civil servants are usually educated and trained in their home countries, some basic home-grown attitudes and values are always implanted in their way of thinking and in how they analyse issues presented to them (Hedetoft 2003). The official may not even see himself or herself as a representative of his or her state or government but his or her training and background will inevitably affect the policy and policy making of the international bureaucracy s/he belongs to.

This type of intergovernmental behaviour can, like the classic type, express itself in different ways, where some forms have a more direct effect on the international bureaucracy and other forms a more indirect effect. For example, an informal quota system may be practised in ways that maximise the influence of certain member states. Influence and attention may also be given to member states that are net contributors to the budget of international organisations. In other cases, nationally driven sub-cultures may be allowed to develop in international bureaucracies by allowing officials from the same member states to work together on topics of specific interest to certain stakeholders. Further-more, when compatriots exchange ideas, concepts and understandings of old and new problems, they may have a greater chance of developing joint understandings, compromises and solutions than officials of different national origins.

Intergovernmental behaviour may thus be of importance internally in international bureaucracies, and the image of national stereotypes could be influential in the organising of the daily work. It may be the case, for example, that certain issues or areas are always handled by civil servants from one country, or that project groups are formed to give advantages to certain national interests at the expense of others.

To conclude the previous discussion, the intergovernmental

behavioural dynamics will be analysed along two dimensions – external versus internal pressure, and direct versus indirect impact.

Table 9.1 Different forms of intergovernmental behavioural dynamics

Type Of Pressure	Impact	
	Direct	*Indirect*
External: Outside in	Officials receive instructions from member states	Officials follow national modes of behaviour
Internal: Inside out	Positions and assignments are allocated along national preferences	National administrative sub-cultures and norms are developed

However, it is important to point out that in practice all four forms may exist at the same time in an international bureaucracy and in the distribution of assignments to the officials, and how they interact can be the result of both internal and external pressure.

External pressure and direct impact

Intergovernmental behaviour of this type in its purest form is quite clear and usually officially accepted. Officials ask for and are expected to receive instructions from their member states and are usually in close contact with their governments, sending and receiving information regarding what is going on in their home country as well as information about the work of the international organisation to which they belong. It is worth pointing out that being an 'intermediator' in terms of conveying information between a member state and an international organisation does not always mean that an official is strictly following instructions from his or her government; it also means passing on information in the other direction and trying to persuade the home administration to be more flexible when conflicting interests are expressed. In fact, it is quite common to find that officials working in an international environment disagree with their government on what is in the best interest of their home country on specific issues, but they nevertheless believe they should serve their home country to the best of their ability (Fouilleux et al. 2007).

In the interviews conducted for this book, generally speaking classic intergovernmentalist attitudes and influences are not that prominent in the three international bureaucracies. When references are made to the importance of nationality in the Commission, concerns are often expressed about the recruitment and behaviour of officials at the upper levels in the hierarchy:

> Nationality matters a lot at a very high administrative and political dimension, let's say Directors-General. Those are posts where MS and the

Commissioner need to have some kind of balance in terms of nationality. We even have a rule now where a Commissioner cannot be of the same nationality [as] the Director-General; so at that level, yes, it matters. When at a lower level, it's really down to your capacities. (Commission 10)

It is also observed that recruitment to the top level of international bureaucracies and the perceptions of the top figures of international bureaucracies are biased by classic intergovernmental behavioural dynamics, as indicated by the following quotes:

I mean, Lamy – he had to have contacts with the French government, but he wasn't working for the French; Mandelson [however] is working for the British government. It's amazing. How can you tell? Everything is Britain-related in what he does. (Commission 15)

I do know he is closely linked to the UK, very closely linked. I've been in meetings with him when he had phone calls from Tony [Blair]. My impression is that he would have closer loyalties to the UK than he would have to the College [of Commissioners]. He is a very national Commissioner. You know, some commissioners are very nationalistic. (Commission 22)

A particularly interesting issue is, of course, how and to what extent style and leadership affect the lower levels of an international bureaucracy. One of the officials interviewed expresses the change from Lamy to Mandelson as Commissioner of Trade in the following way:

First change was language, and therefore that influenced power and influence, because it was the people who could write in English more fluently who rose up. And actually, previously the people who were very fluent in French but couldn't do it in English found they were suffering. Secondly, style: they both have very different styles as commissioners. Lamy liked to get into the details, so you could produce a brief of ten pages and he would make a comment on the tenth page; whereas Mandelson has more of a political sense perhaps, but doesn't like the detail. So you should only draw a brief of one page, otherwise he won't read it; there's no point. So you need to condense it, and also make the message a lot more political. And I think we as a DG found it quite hard to move from being bureaucrats – doing really technical detailed briefing – to having something that he could use, which was much simpler but also more nuanced about strategic 'Let's do this, let's do that'. (Commission 22)

However, there are also strong anti-intergovernmental mechanisms at work among the officials in DG Trade, and many of those interviewed in DG Trade expressed a strong awareness of the problem of intergovernmentalism. Interviewees gave several examples about how to handle this problem[1] – for instance, the rule of not allowing the Directors-General to come from the same member state as the Commissioner under which they serve, and the aim to regularly rotate some of the staff. Many of the Commission officials interviewed indicate a rather low degree of identification with their national governments and infrequent contact with their 'home administration':

> I am not German, as you will notice. We have a principle. The Head of Unit should never be of the country they cover. So that is one guarantee. But, of course, you have linguistic constraints and therefore you end up with mainly people of the countries concerned. So you need to have good checks and balances, but officials very rarely feel dependent on their country. They feel quite independent of their country. And a lot of officials have worked very little in their countries. I never worked for my country. I don't feel at all dependent on what they want. (Commission 8)

One interesting question that particularly concerns the Commission is why member states would keep such a watchful eye on it and would sometimes put such efforts into promoting candidates (*concours* training) for positions at lower levels if this has such a limited effect in terms of influence and power inside the Commission (Spence and Stevens 2006).

Officially, the OECD Secretariat allows little room for external member-state pressure and direct member-state impact, but in reality this type of intergovernmental behaviour can be found in terms of both recruitment and contact in this Secretariat:

> For the moment, the Secretary-General is under a lot of pressure from different nationalities who are basically asking us to recruit – or promote – people who are not the best candidates. (OECD 8)

> We don't have to forget that the delegation often contacts the nationals within the Secretariat because they may think that things will be easier, or they will obtain more information than others, or that they will have a privileged treatment – which is not the case – but this, of course, is also [a] question of mentality ... Some of them do it more than others, but they all do it. (OECD 10)

In contrast, few, if any, officials in the WTO Secretariat report direct external pressure of any importance from member states:

> We have as a Secretariat always resisted any pressure to sort of have national quotas and hiring, you know, and concerns too much in terms of the nationality of the people hired. Our current Director-General seems to have some very strong views in terms of which nationalities he will hire and will not hire. As to people who have been recommended as the best for the job apparently because of nationality background, this could change depending on what happens with the administration. Perhaps what helps is that we hire so few people that he doesn't have much opportunity to perhaps change things too much, but I mean, it is something that could come in for a change. (WTO 15)

The influence of the stakeholders is often of a more defensive and informal type – by having a veto – as indicated by the following quote:

> If your country's government says 'No, I don't like this man', that will make it very difficult for that person to work. So member states are important in the system – if they are upset with you then you can't work. So they must have confidence. It doesn't mean that you always have to do what they would like, or you have to agree with them. Because when I interact with people I don't necessarily say 'Yes, whatever you are saying is correct'. I sometimes question things. I sometimes say 'For this reason, this is not such a good idea'. Often I say 'Fine, this is your concern, you must keep in mind this concern also'. It's a larger picture. But if they just refuse to even treat you seriously, then such discussions can't take place. So that way relationships with member states are important. (WTO 14)

However, in the interviews with officials in the OECD and WTO Secretariats, few comments and references were made that indicated a strong presence of intergovernmental behaviour in terms of outside influence with direct impact. In fact, a number of strong comments made it clear that the whole idea of any externally directed influence by the member states on 'their own officials' was rejected and considered inappropriate.

External pressure and indirect impact

Classic intergovernmentalism can take forms other than direct links between a member state and an official. Civil servants from member states are usually trained and educated in national institutions and may therefore analyse issues differently compared to colleagues from other countries, by using member-state perceptions and pursuing national interests at work. In such cases, they may see themselves as national representatives and may behave accordingly, although not working under formal or informal instructions from their governments, by strongly believing that the policy and culture of their nation-state is the best way forward. However, even this form of classic intergovernmentalism received rather weak responses in our interviews. What we primarily found instead in the international bureaucracies studied were fairly strong anti-intergovernmental behaviour and attitudes.

Many of the interviewed officials report frequent and extended contact with member states but strongly played down the importance of contact with their home state or any specific country. In many cases the international civil servants had split national backgrounds with close ties to more than one country, and in some cases they were recruited to the international bureaucracy at an early age and without prior employment in national administrations. However, in some cases external intergovernmental pressure with an indirect impact can be noticed, again predominantly in the Commission:

> I think the British are not ... well, some of them are very good at making networks and contacts, but there is a pretty weak British network within the

European institutions. If I compare it with some colleagues, I know with the French they regularly have some meetings and when they have a seminar on a certain topic, they invite all the French – not just French national experts, but French nationality functionnaires in a certain area to come and join them. Or there is a very strong Dutch network, with cocktails, and so there is a sense you know all the other Dutch people in your DG. I don't think the Brits do that at all. (Commission 22)

The argument that their own government or colleagues from their own country were not as efficient as colleagues from other states in mobilising support for national interests were expressed by officials in all three international bureaucracies. Interestingly, the grass always seemed to be greener on the other side regardless of what country these interviewees originated from.[2]

In the OECD Secretariat, several respondents did indeed indicate the importance and existence of an intergovernmental behavioural dynamic:

The OECD is there to … we work for countries. People are supposed to represent their country [...] I think the international co-operation should not delete the differences between countries. The objective should be the opposite: keep differences. (OECD 14)

However, we also find mechanisms that balance the impact of external member-state pressures, as with the case of external pressure with direct impact:

So I am very conscious NOT to take a British line when we have an internal discussion. And I am very conscious almost not to network with British people, to be seen to be very British. We have two or three very good people who happen to be Brits, who are quite senior in the hierarchy, and I've made a conscious effort not to be particularly friendly so as not to be seen as a British network, but that is probably a mistake. (Commission 22)

In the OECD Secretariat the counter-mechanism against the intergovernmental dynamic seems to be even stronger than in the Commission:

Fundamentally, my impression is that when people have joined the OECD and they have worked here for a while, they no longer behave as nationals of any particular member country but they serve the interests of the organisation. And it doesn't really matter whether they are Canadian, Australian or Belgian – they work towards a common aim of the organisation. It is important to have nationals from different backgrounds because they have a better understanding of the actual policies of their respective home countries and the political perceptions in these countries, but they would not – in all cases that I know of – represent the political position of their country. They have to understand it better, but then they work jointly towards our joint objectives. (OECD 11)

In addition, officials were concerned about the fact that they had little and weak contact with their own governments and about the difficulty of getting their own governments interested in the topics they were in charge of. On the other hand, when there was frequent contact with the 'home country', the quality and the content of the contact with the capital was more complicated and less straightforward in the OECD and WTO Secretariats than in the Commission. There is sometimes the understanding that the communications cannot be totally open – some things cannot be said:

> Of course, she also has very good contacts with the Japanese delegation, with the Japanese community within the OECD, but in terms of daily work it doesn't affect it at all. That can only be as a good sign in terms of information sharing. But, of course, if we are willing to share the information; sometimes you don't want to do that. In my division, we have an Italian girl and a Swedish girl, and sometimes we are also having good input through them because they have sort of privileged contacts with the Italian delegation or Swedish delegation. (OECD 10)

Others had an even more relaxed attitude towards this problem of self-censorship between officials and their home countries:

> In the beginning the ministers didn't quite know where I was coming from. But it very quickly became clear to them that I was still myself, I hadn't changed my language or anything, that I knew they could trust me – there were things that they could tell me, that I would not pass on. There were things that they asked me, and I told them 'I cannot tell you, please respect me'. They knew that it was working both ways. There were limits to what I could do and tell, and I learned that there were limits to what I could ask. Apart from that, it is very smooth, no big deal. And there's a lot of mutual esteem. Some of the older generation find it awkward, very awkward. But otherwise, no big deal. (WTO 9)

In summary, these interviews indicate that, as is the case with direct intergovernmentalism, mechanisms and attitudes work against the behaviour and attitudes of classic intergovernmentalism rather than in favour of it. However, interestingly enough, several of the interviewees in DG Trade and in the OECD Secretariat believed that officials from some countries acted in an intergovernmental way to a greater extent than they did themselves. Consequently, the self-perceptions of international civil servants as being intergovernmental are sometimes less than the perceptions they have of their fellow colleagues as being intergovernmental. This observation may partly reflect the fact that the intergovernmental dynamics are viewed by several officials as inappropriate and are thus downplayed more when assessing themselves than when assessing others.

Nevertheless, there is more to discuss about classic intergovernmental dynamics in international bureaucracies. International bureaucracies are not homogeneous in terms of personnel: some organisations make use of permanent positions while others only offer temporary employment. A special category of temporary employment is the seconded national expert (SNE), who is often seen as having a particularly strong affiliation to his or her 'home country' – sometimes being referred to as a 'national spy'. However, this assumption has rarely been tested. We have therefore included a special study of the seconded experts of the Commission. To obtain robust empirical observations from SNEs we have included three samples – two samples of current SNEs and one sample of SNEs that have left the Commission (see also Chapter 6).

SNEs' contacts and links with their national governments

What the data reveal is that SNEs are much more detached from the member-state governments than is generally believed. The following phrase reflects the autonomy felt by most secondees: 'Out of sight, out of mind' (CLENAD 2003: 26; Statskontoret 2001:17: 11). Seconded officials receive 'very little feedback from capitals [...] and [...] in general they had expected to be in closer contact with their employer' (EFTA Secretariat 2001: 2). Secondees thus view the Commission as their primary organisational affiliation and their member-state government institutions as secondary. Some secondees report a preference for more intensive contact with their member-state ministries than that offered by these ministries. According to one former UK secondee:

> I did find it quite shocking the way the UK government didn't use its national experts, or didn't keep in contact or ask them anything or learn from their experience. (Commission 22)

These observations reflect the *primacy* of the Commission for secondees and the *de facto* autonomy of secondees vis-à-vis their home governments:

> My experience is generally that actually [secondees] remain pretty independent. They get into the culture of the Commission. (Commission 8)

One reason for this lack of contact initiated by the home administration may be the lack of domestic strategy on seconded officials.[3] For example, the Swedish government admits to lacking an overall strategy on seconded officials and having a rather poor central co-ordination regarding how they recruit and utilise Swedish secondees (Statskontoret 2001:17: 9; The Government Office of Sweden 2002: 14). In addition, the Commission, at least DG Trade, has developed certain strategies in order to embed the SNEs into the organisation culture:

> Here, we are very dependent on national experts, simply because of lack of staff. We don't have sufficient officials. We have to rely on national experts. They also bring a lot in, that they really understand the system. So they bring that expertise to us, which is very important when we are talking about co-managing billions of euro. I am responsible for billions of euro,

even though I am not hands-on with it. So it very useful, having these national experts really knowing the system quite well. My experience is generally that actually they remain pretty independent. They get into the culture of the Commission, it takes time. We are also careful, of course, when I have an expert from Nordrhein-Westfalia, I don't give him responsibility for Nordrhein-Westfalia. (Commission 8)

The effect is that SNEs tend to enact a departmental contact pattern while working for the Commission, much like permanent Commission administrators (see Chapter 6). Table 9.2 substantiates the level of intergovernmental contact patterns among current and former Commission SNEs.

Table 9.2 'How frequently do you have *work-related contact and/or meetings* with the following during a typical week in your current function?' (percentage)[a]

Intergovernmental contact patterns:	*Current Nordic SNEs*	*Current Dutch SNEs*	*Former Dutch SNEs*
with ministries in country of origin working within *other* policy areas than current portfolio	5	5	40
with ministries of other members states working within other policy areas than current portfolio	4	2	3
with the EU Permanent Representation of country of origin	–	18	20
with the EU Permanent Representation of other member states	–	7	2
Mean N	100 (67)	100 (44)	100 100

[a] The percentages listed are the sum of the percentage of officials who have daily or weekly contact with the respective actors. This dichotomy builds from the following five-point scale: daily (value 5), weekly (value 4), monthly (value 3), yearly (value 2), and less than once per year (value 1).

Table 9.2 reveals that intergovernmental contact is small and mainly with the government of other countries, not the government of their country of origin (see also Trondal 2006). Moreover, Table 9.2 reveals that former secondees have more intergovernmental contact by far than current secondees. Hence, the level of intergovernmentalism is clearly contingent on the formal organisational affiliation of the officials towards the international bureaucracy. Not surprisingly, international civil servants with international bureaucracies as their primary everyday employer seem to have much less intergovernmental contact than officials without this kind of affiliation. Many returned secondees report that while they were seconded their home organisation did not seek contact with them. Most seconded officials report in their interviews that their home ministry or agency seldom initiates contact. According to one current Norwegian seconded official, 'I have very little contact with my ministry back home, almost nothing' (Commission 6). 'I only get information [from my home administration] if I ask for it' (CLENAD 2003: 21). Most of the contact that is reported between secondees and their home administrations is initiated by the secondees themselves, partly to allow the organisation to benefit from the experience gained and partly in order not to be forgotten and thus hoping to boost their career opportunities upon return. According to one former Dutch seconded official:

> During my secondment I had quite some contact with my colleagues at home at my own initiative. I also sent out a newsletter to my own unit and to my own department, to keep people in The Hague up to date with what I was doing in Brussels. I also went regularly to return-home days in The Hague. Nonetheless, at the senior/management level there was little attention for what I was doing in Brussels. (Commission 41)

Another former Dutch seconded official reports that:

> At one point I knew my boss was going to visit someone at the DG that I was working at. Nonetheless, it did not occur to him to stop by at my room and to enquire what I was doing there and how I was performing. (Commission 32)

Testimony of the cross-national variation on these views is given by the fact that several Dutch secondees claim that France makes significantly more strategic use of its SNEs. Some Scandinavian secondees also report that French secondees tend to have a stronger intergovernmental behavioural dynamic than other seconded officials:

> France uses the French SNEs to the maximum. They are consulted directly by the French Government. (Commission 2)

Similarly, a study by a Swedish government agency indicates that the British government uses its secondees instrumentally in order to influence the Commission (Statskontoret 2001:17). One explanation for the large number of intergovernmental contact patterns among British and French SNEs may be the sheer effect of probability: there are more French and British officials than Dutch and Nordic officials in the Commission, and accordingly a greater likelihood of intergovernmental contact patterns (see also Suvarierol 2007: 112). Secondly, cross-national variation in intergovernmental contact patterns may also be caused by different domestic government policies/strategies. In stark contrast to the non-existing Swedish policy on seconded officials (see above), the British policy on seconded officials is both explicitly stated and highly co-ordinated by the Cabinet Office (Statskontoret 2001:17: 51). Accordingly, some of our observations may reflect the degree to which national governments have developed a policy regarding the co-ordination of the activities of secondees. According to one former Dutch seconded official:

> The Netherlands is a member state that does not make much use of these possibilities. In the Netherlands lobbying is frowned upon. This is in great contrast with the French who very effectively make use of their nationals within the Commission [...] the French, but also the Irish, have a good grip on their functionnaires within the Commission, and thus those states are ensured that their interests within the EU are permanently being served at a variety of different levels. The Netherlands appears to have ethical objections against such a strategy. In my case civil servants of my home department were told to avoid me if they were in Brussels, because otherwise there would be a danger that I would pass on classified information from within the Commission. For ethical reasons people in The Hague choose to remain ignorant about what is happening in Brussels. (Commission 39)

Seconded officials testify that they are highly aware of their dual position – national experts as well as independent outsiders. However, many felt that although the Commission insists on their independence, other Commission staff viewed them as national officials with national preferences. Some secondees report that they have deliberately brought national problems to the table:

> SNEs make no secret about their country of origin. You are clearly fulfilling a dual role, so you are able to bring problems or positions from your member state to the fore. Other functionnaires at the Commission also approach you to have an 'early test' as to whether a specific proposal would be welcomed with enthusiasm in the Netherlands or not. As an SNE you can then say 'This proposal is never going to survive in the Netherlands'. So, by the presence of SNEs, the policy process proceeds more smoothly and quicker because as an SNE you are well informed of the national positions. (Commission 20)

In other words, SNEs are to a much lesser extent instruments of classic intergovernmentalism than is generally believed but there are variations depending on member-state strategies and administrative traditions within different DGs of the Commission as well as on the sheer effect of probability.

Internal pressure and direct impact

Organisations are usually conscious of what the environment demands of them. From an intergovernmental perspective this puts pressure on international organisations to demonstrate that they are not biased towards certain member-state governments but are still able to accommodate member-state concerns. One way of demonstrating the capacity to balance member-state concerns inside international organisations is to allocate the portfolios inside these bureaucracies in accordance with presumed national preferences – creating a representative administration that balances nationality horizontally and vertically in the administrative services. In this type of intergovernmentalism the connections to the member states are less stringent and straightforward, but officials are nevertheless recruited on grounds of nationality – perhaps best described as national representatives in a freer role than when classic intergovernmental behavioural dynamics are at work.

The presence of this type of inside-out intergovernmentalism is of particular interest in the cases of the OECD and WTO Secretariats as the classic form of intergovernmentalism is more acknowledged in the Commission. However the interviews do not give particularly strong support to this type of intergovernmental behavioural dynamic either:

> We debate time and time again, and so far – in the OECD at least – I haven't seen the real answer to that. Clearly, the OECD is not so much ... what other ... the EU, for instance, or also the UN, but particularly the EU where you have a kind of national quota to fulfil. Here, the perception is that some sort of correspondence should be there. For instance it would be inappropriate to have, let's say, two per cent of the OECD staff being of US nationality. So there is some sort of ... but there is much less constraining, I think; we go for the best. Then, of course, you have the issue to tackle: where is that position located? And if you go from, let's say, Australia; and you have already one from Australia, and from New Zealand there is another Division Head, so taking a third Australian wouldn't go through easily. I wouldn't do that. (OECD 7)

In recent years the WTO Secretariat has established a Cabinet around its Secretary-General. The recruitment and composition of the Cabinet has followed intergovernmental principles to the extent that members of the Cabinet are of different national origins. Officially, the WTO does not apply quotas when recruiting new officials. However, in reality the nationality of a new employee may sometimes play a role:

> It is almost a non-issue. I say almost because Lamy, for example, chose people here according to their nationalities, and the DDGs. So to say that it is a complete non-issue is not true. Also, in some divisions, you would be careful not to have the whole staff of the division from the same nationality, or a predominant nationality in one division. The Rules Division is known in the Secretariat as being the American-dominated division. So they are, indeed, three Americans there and another three Europeans. When you recruit in the Rules Division, you would try to diversify but that is always a second consideration. The first consideration is knowledge, merit and

experience in WTO issues. If on the same level on merit you can diversify, then you would choose to diversify.' (WTO 9)

In all three international bureaucracies, however, respondents argue that an important aspect of a diversified recruitment policy had more to do with the need to generate knowledge about specific countries and cultures and the ability to communicate in different languages:

> No, we don't have any quota system. Nationality may be, to some extent, a factor in recruitment in the sense that we try to have some sort of balance within the Secretariat. This is not necessarily a decision at my level, although I am also aware of the importance of some sort of balance within the division. I mean, it is not only for presentational reasons, it is also for operational reasons – you need languages, you need people with contacts in the different parts of the world and so on, to understand what is happening in the different parts of the world. We don't have any fixed quotas, but we do have some sort of awareness of this need to be truly international in our own composition. When it comes to assigning a task to particular officers, it is extremely rare that we would think twice about nationality. (WTO 1)

A special form of intergovernmental mentality was expressed during some of the interviews when officials pointed out that they felt a strong commitment to supporting the position of certain states (especially the states of the developing world) in the internal discussions of the organisation, although they had no ties to these countries.

A similar example of the importance of inside-out intergovernmental dynamics in terms of direct impact (representation) in relation to the stakeholders and the organisational environment, broadly speaking, is when certain positions are never given to certain nationalities:

> In my work, yes, it does make a difference – especially vis-à-vis Russia. If you are Polish or Estonian or Lithuanian you would find it much more difficult to get the trust than if you have the nationality that I have. I have had this experience very often: that in the end you are not this kind of de-nationalised civil servant. You always keep your passport in that sense and that makes a difference. (Commission 11)

In other words, inside-out intergovernmental behaviour and attitudes are also active with regard to forming the organisation. It is not only a matter of the extent to which officials receive or adopt national instructions and attitudes; the mere suspicion or expectation by stakeholders or clients can trigger 'alternative intergovernmental' behaviour:

> We would never staff a panel only with, let's say, two US solicitors if the US is a part. Not at all. And, of course, you also have a counterbalance in the composition of the panellist, because you cannot be a citizen of any of the countries that's involved in the dispute. (WTO 13)

To conclude, these interviews give some support to the hypothesis of the existence of inside-out intergovernmental dynamics in international bureaucracies where the classic type of intergovernmentalism is not officially accepted. On the other hand, the evidence is not particularly strong, and other factors can explain the need to create a representative public administration – such as the quest for knowledge of what is going on in different parts of the world (i.e. in the member states or stake-holders) and the need to know other languages in order to communicate efficiently with different member states.

Internal pressure and indirect impact

It is a well-known fact that administrative cultures are not the same worldwide. In Europe there is quite a difference between countries in how the public administrations are organised and operate, notwithstanding diverse administrative cultures and styles (Page and Wright 1999; Peters 1995). It should therefore not be surprising to find that international civil servants from the same state or administrative culture prefer working together or want to recruit people from the same country or administrative culture. In the history of the Commission, it became evident early on that some DGs and units more or less 'belonged' to certain member states or had specific language regimes (Cini 1996: 126). This type of geographic clustering, where certain nationalities or language regimes monopolise parts of the organisation, is often regarded by the leadership as counterproductive and something that needs to be contained or limited as far as possible, but nevertheless it may be accepted for reasons of legitimacy and tradition. A special type of intergovernmentalism could be based on the existence of national stereotypes, for example that a Frenchman never completely trusts a Briton, or that both of them refuse to communicate in English/French:

> We know there is 'cloning' in some directorates; there is no doubt about it, because you get the people [...] it tends to be a 'roll-over', and you know that if someone comes from, I don't know [...] the Federal Reserve Bank, and when that person leaves, well, 'We might just as well get someone else because it worked out.' (OECD 2)

Some of the interviewed officials argued that this phenomenon of 'flag postings' has gradually become less visible as more states have joined the organisation and as the international bureaucracy has become more mature and institutionalised over time:

> It may have been like that in the past, and it could have been – in certain departments – more visible a case than in the others. You used to have almost like national flags planted on a particular department, but as far as I can see it, all these so-called 'traditional flag postings' have to a large extent disappeared. Since there are more nationalities the dilution has become much greater. (Commission 12)

An answer of particular interest is from one of the interviewed OECD officials who indicates that the degree of informal inside-out intergovernmental dynamics is linked to the size and importance of member states:

> For example, if I recommend an Irish person, they would look suspiciously at that when promoting. No matter how good the person is, no matter how many prizes they have won, whatever the credentials are, 'He is promoting the Irish, isn't he?' While if I had been British, it would have been 'God, sounds good'. And I think there is a bit that the big countries get away with that, and the small countries find it harder to justify it. So you tend to not promote your own because you are afraid of being accused of just promoting your own. (OECD 13)

The existence and the importance of national stereotypes was downplayed in the interviews and numerous examples were given of how appointing on the basis of nationality is not appropriate procedure. However, in some cases nationality may play a part in how work is informally organised at the unit level:

> I guess you tend to be attracted to similar ways of dealing with things like you do yourself. Although no one will say this up front, there will be some type of . . . not discrimination, but some kind of moving towards people that have the same way of dealing with things as you do yourself. And there may be a reflection of culture in there, and nationality. (OECD 16)

Judging by the interviews, however, this type of intergovernmentalism is decreasing in the Commission. In the WTO Secretariat this phenomenon was less visible to begin with; in the OECD Secretariat, where the tension between the French and the British culture was originally quite high, it has turned into a more symbolic battle over flags. On the other hand, both the OECD Secretariat and the WTO Secretariat are being increasingly challenged by new members and non-European members due to their alleged bias towards the Western administrative culture.

Summing up: international civil servants – men without a country?[4]

Today, opinions are somewhat diverging, particularly when it comes to the Commission, on how international bureaucracies' internal work is affected by its legal mandate, by the stakeholders (member states), and by the wider administrative environment. A long-held assumption has been that nationality affects the internal functioning of the Commission. As claimed by Amitai Etzioni (2004: 1), 'The Commission is composed of national representatives'. However, the observations reported above challenge these claims, at least when it comes to the levels below the Directors-General. This chapter concludes that the Commission is certainly not a 'hothouse' for intergovernmentalism. As such, the observations reported here support recent research on Commission decision making (Egeberg 2007; Suvarierol 2007). As seen by a former member of the Cabinet staff of Commissioner Bolkestein, 'The Commission is no longer a mixture of French bureaucracy, the German military and the Italian academy of art, with an occasional British busybody thrown in. The enlargement of the European Union to 27 countries has helped to dilute national identity within the administrative structure' (Eppink 2007: 35). In addition, recent research on the Cabinets of the College of Commissioners suggests that they are largely de-nationalised, and increasingly so (Egeberg and Heskestad 2009).

According to this study, quite strong mechanisms and attitudes counteract and balance intergovernmentalism dynamics, at least in their classic form: the Director-General should not be of the same nationality as the Commissioner; the officials should be rotated on a regular basis; and there is a general belief in the value of mixing different nationalities, of having them working together. Not even the seconded experts in this study report strong links to their home countries. In fact, several expressed surprise and sometimes perhaps disappointment over the lack of ability of the member states to make use of the knowledge of the seconded national experts. Intergovernmental behavioural dynamics in their classic form are without doubt of limited importance in the Commission, at least judging by our data from DG Trade and the General Secretariat.

Nevertheless, when comparing the Commission to the OECD and WTO Secretariats, the Commission quite surprisingly shows most signs of classic intergovernmentalism. It could perhaps have been expected that the other two organisations, which are officially based on an inter-governmental co-operation between states, would show signs of intergovernmental behaviour more clearly played out in their internal power structures and in their daily business. What we found instead in those two international bureaucracies, and more strongly than in the Commission, were quite strong attitudes and mechanisms to counteract the impact of classic intergovernmentalism, even if in some cases ingre-dients of intergovernmentalism were reported. Previous research shows that language matters more than nationality in explaining informal contact patterns among Commission officials (Suvarierol 2007: 97). Our research confirms that this observation also applies to the WTO and OECD Secretariats, and perhaps to even a higher degree than in the Commission.

On the other hand, if the definition of intergovernmentalism is broadened somewhat to include behaviour and reactions of anticipation and proactive behaviour from leaders or from lower levels in the organisation, a slightly different result emerges. The interviews give several examples of inside-out intergovernmentalism, particularly in the OECD Secretariat but also in the WTO Secretariat. In the Commission, markedly fewer examples are given of this type of intergovernmentalism. In fact, the Commission seems prone to strong counter-mechanisms and attitudes in this field. The national earmarking (the flags) that used to characterise different parts of the administration has to a large extent gone, and most of the officials express satisfaction when it comes to working with other nationalities. This is hardly surprising since the Commission is under more pressure from classic intergovernmentalism. In effect, the room for and the need for inside-out intergovernmentalism is not as strong – the Commission cannot improve its efficiency and legitimacy to the same extent as the other two international bureaucracies by increasing intergovernmentalism dynamics. Instead it needs to demonstrate that its house is in order and in its own hands.

By contrast, in both the WTO Secretariat and the OECD Secretariat there is some awareness of the need to create a representative administration in order to generate an impression of neutrality and impartiality. However, in terms of recruitment, the ambition to always select the best candidate cannot hide the fact that geographical concerns are often taken into consideration when a new position is to be filled. However, it should be mentioned that the effort to recruit personnel from different parts of the world is not only due to intergovernmental considerations but also to concerns of administrative efficiency and internal communications.

Notes

1 The discovery of counteracting forces is nothing new; see, for example, Shore (2000).
2 Perhaps with the exception of France.
3 Sometimes secondees are recruited from national agencies without the knowledge of the ministry (Statskontoret 2001:17: 27).
4 After a long and arduous career in one – or several – international organisations, the returning or retiring civil servant may very well find himself in the unenviable position of his infamous predecessor John Lackland, or the rulers in the Bible (Isaiah 34:12), i.e. that he has become 'a man without a country' in every sense.

Part IV

Conclusions

10

Complexity and stability in international bureaucracies

The normalisation of IO studies

What happens when people (including civil servants) enter multi-structural, multi-disciplinary, multi-national and multilingual bureaucracies? The large majority will initially probably be puzzled by the differences, idiosyncrasies and novelty. The routines, procedures, justifications and ways of doing things in international bureaucracies are typically different from national bureaucracies – public or private. In fact, many civil servants entering positions in international bureaucracies report that it is exactly these differences and the associated challenges that are so attractive and that made them apply for a job in the international bureaucracy in the first place. As the years pass, some continue to regard these challenges as valuable sources of innovation and inspiration. Others think that the initial challenges turn out to become problems that are hard to overcome and that can eventually lead to decline and decay for the international organisation in question. Perspectives definitely vary depending on the position and function of the civil servant and, of course, on his or her personal and professional history. It is these challenges, and the perceptions of and reactions to them, that are central to this book.

We analyse international bureaucracies as compound institutions in which multiple role-plays take place among decision makers. International bureaucracies share some important characteristics with national bureaucracies such as the fact that they are vertically specialised and rule-based organisations, cf. the key elements of the Weberian model of bureaucracy. We nevertheless assume that international bureaucracies are in some ways *sui generis* compared to national bureaucracies. These differences concern all the organisational aspects of international bureaucracy – its technologies and procedures, its culture and people, and its vertical and horizontal structures. They particularly concern the political and institutional context of the international bureaucracies.

Firstly, *making decisions* in international organisations is complex. Some international organisations are primarily intergovernmental in the sense that each and every national parliament of the member states must give its assent to the decisions being made. Others are primarily supranational, meaning that decisions are made that bind minorities and that such decisions have a direct impact on the citizens. Supranational bureaucracies have some room for manoeuvre and power to make majority decisions. This book also pictures international bureaucracies as having departmental and epistemic characteristics. In fact, most international organisations carry multiple features of these kinds which are combined in multiple ways, demonstrating the compound nature of international bureaucracies. The complexity is enhanced by the fact that the product of decision making in international organisations takes hard as well as soft forms. Whereas decision-making dynamics in a certain area of policy making are very similar across countries, international bureaucracies demonstrate huge variations from one international organisation to the next. However, this book illuminates systematic variations across international organisations, which are largely conditioned by the way these bureaucracies are formally organised. We argue that decision-making dynamics in international bureaucracies are most affected by the organisational characteristics of the international bureaucracies themselves and less by the type of international organisation in which they are formally embedded. When comparing international bureaucracies, we are able to conclude that the behavioural patterns within them are conditioned by the formal structuring of the bureaucracies themselves.

Secondly, the staffing of international bureaucracies is a distinct challenge in itself. Integrating *people* with many different expectations and backgrounds, cultivating their varied talents and professional skills, and creating the foundation for a common culture that supplements rather than destroys national diversities is a leadership challenge that goes beyond anything that would happen in national bureaucracies. For example, the language regime of an international bureaucracy paradoxically both contributes to and undermines the sense of cohesion inside international organisations. On the one hand, the formal or informal definition of a few or only one language (typically English) to become the most commonly used means of communication ensures fast and safe communication along the decision-making process. On the other hand, the definition of a shared language creates additional cleavages among both those who master the language to perfection and those who will always be disadvantaged by communicating in a foreign language. In addition, common languages do not necessarily overcome the cultural cleavages that exist in complex international bureaucracies.

Thirdly, although international bureaucracies have grown enormously in size, scope and complexity since the end of the Second World War, the multi-dimensional formal *structures* of international bureaucracies endure over time. To talk about multilevel administrative features would not even capture the compound nature of decision making. What used to be understood as separate decision-making layers at local, regional, national, international and global levels are, in the EU context, merged into one polycentric polity in Europe (Bulmer 2008) and one multilevel union administration than spans levels of government (Egeberg 2006). The actual structural features, of course, vary from one issue area to the next, and the informal structures of a bureaucracy are a separate discussion. The differences highlighted here concern the fact that for many national administrations the international dimension is only occasionally present in terms of formal interaction with international organisations, and sometimes the international dimension is entirely absent. In contrast, the global and the national dimensions are always present for the international bureaucracy. Again, in terms of organisational structures, the complexity of international bureaucracies makes them distinct from national bureaucracies.

This leads us directly to the fourth dimension in which international bureaucracies differ from national bureaucracies – the *political context* of international decision making. Formal decision making in international organisations is largely carried out by external constituencies, i.e. the member states represented in the plenary assemblies of the organisations. Moreover, the constituency of international organisations shows great variations between large and small states, between rich and poor states, and between newcomers and founding member states. Member states typically share certain basic features, such as a belief in liberal democracy, human rights and capitalism, but the ways in which these values and principles are interpreted and carried out in practice differ to a large extent. This diversity in its constituency requires the complete attention of the international bureaucracy at any time in order to balance diversity with unity (Olsen 2008). The way in which differences in the constituency are mediated, moderated, communicated and sometimes even exploited is decisive for the political legitimacy, and ultimately the survival, of the international bureaucracy.

Finally, the composite *technical context* of the international bureaucracy exposes it to enormous challenges. The role of international bureaucracies in global governance is seen by some as rooted in knowledge and epistemic communities (Adler and Bernstein 2005). Transborder problems are almost by definition more complex than problems delimited by a national frontier. If 'silo thinking' is still a dominating feature of national bureaucracies and of the way in which they perceive problems and solutions, international bureaucracies will have to transcend disciplinary boundaries and adopt holistic perspectives in order to cope with problems of global scope. As political, economic and cultural globalisation unfolds, the technical environment of international bureaucracies becomes very real. Large parts of national bureaucracies can still decouple their globalisation talk from their globalisation action. International bureaucracies cannot afford that luxury of *de facto* everyday hypocrisy; they are right in the middle of globalisation. In fact, some would argue that international organisations are the essence of and the main powers in global governance, providing rules ('hard law') and standards ('soft law') for the world that both constrain and enable action by their member states (Barnett and Duvall 2005; Barnett and Finnemore 2004; Brunsson and Jacobsson 2000).

For these reasons we believe we can safely assume that international bureaucracy constitutes a distinct and increasingly important feature of public administration studies. With this book we also aspire to take the first steps into a third generation of IO studies. Paradoxically, this entails that the study of international organisations is somehow 'normalised', i.e. that a public administrative 'turn' comes to characterise IO studies (Trondal 2007a). Until now the study of international bureaucracy has been marked by a unitary-actor perspective, most typically illustrated by an assumption that international bureaucracies have interests of their own. We also note that there is a tendency to assume that international bureaucracies are legal entities that can best be understood by reading their formal mandates and legal provisions. This book argues that one of the defining features of international bureaucracies is their compound nature consisting of multiple dynamics, role definitions and identities among the incumbents. This feature of international bureaucracy has so far been largely untouched in relevant literature. Since the study of national core-executive institutions has a long tradition of studying the lives and day-to-day routines of national civil servants, such a perspective, if applied to international bureaucracies, would imply a normalisation of IO studies – a so-called public administrative turn. Despite the obvious differences that exist between national and international bureaucracies, a third generation of IO studies would be based on long and extensive experience and theoretical development within the area of public administration studies. This entails that new questions be asked and new concepts applied to the field of IO research.

When we study international bureaucracies as institutions in which multiple role-plays take place, a variety of identity structures are enacted and numerous values are put into play. It would be interesting to know whether there is a pattern in this. Until now established knowledge has suggested that international organisations are torn by the old struggle between intergovernmental and supranational role dynamics (Niemann 2006). This can hardly be the whole story about the identity constellations within complex social frameworks. The empirical challenge is therefore to study the perceptions of international civil servants about their own roles and identities, and about the past, present and future roles of their international organisations. This entails a frank and confidential dialogue with a high number of the people who are central to this study – the international civil servants. It also requires us to allow for new types of role conceptions to manifest on the basis of this rich interview material. Thus, we do not make *a priori* assumptions about what life in international bureaucracies is like; we let the civil servants themselves tell the story of their life from inside the international bureaucracies. On this basis, we make three empirical conclusions that all have theoretical ramifications.

Conclusion 1: International bureaucracies are stabilisers of global governance

Whether we apply a narrow definition of intergovernmentalism or a broader and more encompassing definition, there is little intergovernmentalism in international bureaucracies. This is an interesting and also unexpected conclusion from our study. We would have expected that the shadow of the member states which constantly looms over the international organisation and to which it has to pay constant attention would be reflected in the in-depth interviews conducted with the civil servants. This would particularly be predicted within international organisations that are typically pictured as intergovernmental, such as the OECD and WTO. In the most radical situation, some of the civil servants could somehow have acted as national Trojan horses within the international bureaucracy. A less obvious instance of intergovernmentalism could be expressed as a normative affinity towards certain member states, whether intended or not. None of this seems to adequately describe how international civil servants think of themselves and their roles.

Occasionally some signs of intergovernmentalism can be noticed but mainly at the organisational helm of international bureaucracies – among the top leaders. Intergovernmentalism at the top level rarely filters down to the lower levels of international bureaucracies – among desk officials. If it is true that international bureaucracies are somehow largely intergovernmental-free zones, this underlines an additional feature of international bureaucracies that distinguishes them from national bureaucracies – stability. When stability is sought in a national context, depoliticisation is typically considered an appropriate answer. The organisational solution to this is augmenting administrative autonomy, safeguarded by organising ministerial departments at arm's length distance from the political leadership as agency-type organisations (Christensen and Lægreid 2006; Egeberg and Trondal 2009; Pollitt et al. 2004). Within the area of monetary policy making, for instance, national central banks have been reformed over the 1990s with a view to exempting them from the supervision of national politicians. Thus, central banks have been given formal autonomy in order to create a zone of stability (Dyson and Marcussen 2009). If this works as intended, politicisation will be directed towards other fields of policy making and away from the area that is thought to be politically sensitive. However, autonomisation and stability at the national level are always relative concepts. Formal independence can be granted by national parliaments and can at any time be withdrawn by national parliamentarians, typically by a simple majority. To continue this line of argument, national central banks are, of course, aware of this situation, as a result of which they have no interest in taking a minority position that risks jeopardising their autonomous status. In the end, national politicians remain in control of their national administrations. This organisational solution to safeguarding stability is not available to the same extent in international organisations. Thus, it is telling that the European Central Bank (ECB) has not only been granted the most autonomous status in the world of central banks, but it is also enshrined in the treaties of the European Union that a unanimously adopted and nationally ratified revision of the basic treaties to amend the status of the ECB be taken.

The inherent problem with multilateral decision making and the provision of public goods by co-ordinated action is that it is very sensitive and vulnerable to the discretion of individual states. In this sense, sovereign states are potential sources of international instability and suboptimal decision making. These tensions characterise the 'political layers' of international organisations – the councils and the committees, for instance – but they seem to be almost absent from the bureaucracies of international organisations. Hence, intergovernmentalism is largely buffered within international bureaucracies. If anything, *the international bureaucracy functions as a stabilising element of inter-state negotiations*. Rather than replicating intergovernmental cleavages, international bureaucracies seem to get a life of their own, undisturbed by struggles in the politicised sphere of international policy making. International civil servants have been given an opportunity to act in isolation from the narrow interests of individual member states, and they seem to exploit that opportunity to the fullest, knowing that, in contrast to autonomised national agencies, their autonomy cannot easily be withdrawn by design. The stabilising element of international bureaucracies is actually enhanced by the multilateral setting in which the bureaucracies are placed. Thus, the neutrality of international bureaucracies is ensured by the checks and controls of the member-state governments.

A couple of notes of caution should be given at this stage. Firstly, in contrast to neo-liberalist scholars of international relations (not to be confused with the neo-liberal economic doctrine), we do not claim that such zones of bureaucratic stability are deliberately created by member states to reduce the transaction costs involved in multilateral relations. Rather, we suspect that international bureaucracies may develop in unintended ways. For instance, those who are personally involved in international bureaucracies have typically witnessed many member states competing to fill management positions with civil servants of their own nationality. The reason for doing so is primarily to try to influence the way in which the international bureaucracy works and to steer it in certain directions or to prevent other countries gaining increased influence. The intention here is not to minimise transaction costs in any way. This kind of parachutage is based on quite discretionary definitions of the public good. Our findings actually indicate that such attempts at injecting a national bias into the international bureaucracy do not, on the whole, actually influence the work of the international bureaucracy. The national Trojan horse seems to 'go native' inside the international bureaucracy. Even temporary officials inside international bureaucracies – as seen among seconded national experts in the Commission – tend to 'go native' and take on the role of an ordinary Commission civil servant.

Secondly, we do not argue that stability is absolute in the sense that member states have no chance of repoliticising the international bureaucracy. Since the end of the Cold War almost all international organisations have been confronted with a requirement to undertake reform. This applies both to universal organisations like the United Nations, the IMF, the World Bank and the WTO, and to specialised and regionally delimited organisations such as the EU and the OECD. Our argument is rather that national agencies can be, and indeed often are, changed overnight. In contrast, international bureaucracies often need to be exposed to constant external pressures over a number of years before a momentum for reform is created. It typically takes institutional shocks, a new Managing Director or Secretary-General, consistent pressure from the largest member states and, importantly, an international normative environment in favour of certain kinds of reform before an international bureaucracy can be expected to reform seriously. Even when these factors are present, the international bureaucracy is able to resist some of the most blatant reform attempts because of its expertise. In the case of the Commission, for example, an institutional shock in 1999 was perhaps needed to kick off the largest internal reforms in its history. Nevertheless, the basic principles of organisation within the Commission are largely unaffected by these reforms (see Chapter 3).

Thirdly, a functionalist interpretation of international bureaucracies would emphasise that autonomy and political stabilisation lead to improved efficiency and quality of decisions within international bureaucracies. According to this argument, the civil servants would be completely absorbed in providing sovereignty-neutral public benefits.

In addition, in contrast to national politicians who have an electorate to cultivate in the short term, the neutral international civil servant can afford to pay attention beyond electoral cycles and can thus adopt a long-term heuristic view on policy making. Thus, a zone protected from political inference will liberate energy that can be applied to improving decision making. However, we cannot confirm such an interpretation of the effects of depoliticisation. When national considerations are removed, other kinds of narrow considerations take their place. The series of interviews demonstrates that many international civil servants are frustrated by the fact that new ideas are hard to develop, that decisions take a long time to be made and that implementation is slow and cumbersome. In addition, many argue that accountability is fairly low in international bureaucracies as there are so many formal and informal veto points that it is difficult to assign responsibility to anyone – both when it comes to rewarding successes and when it comes to reprimanding failures. In other words, depoliticisation and stability may lead to rigidity, suboptimal decision making and organisational stealth. This is a point which is further elaborated upon below.

Conclusion 2: Civil servants in international bureaucracies are rooted in their department but think and act globally

A large majority of the interviewed civil servants express a strong affinity towards the unit, section or department in which they are organisationally embedded. It is to be expected that a departmental logic plays out quite clearly, and the conclusion corresponds to the old dictum 'Where you stand depends on where you sit'. In practice, this means that not only is the international civil servant characterised by a surprising lack of member-state affinities but also that identification with the organisational structures and their substantive dossiers/portfolios is very dominant. In other words, nationality does not play much of a role but it is rather the functions undertaken and the responsibilities assumed that define what it means to be an international civil servant. We observe that many civil servants in international bureaucracies identify with some of the features that we normally attribute to an ideal-typical Weberian civil servant. The idea of a 'bureaucracy' is quite strong in the mindset of the international civil servants, and the basic ideas implied in this organisational principle are directly or indirectly assigned to the international bureaucracy. Thus, in the civil servants' understanding, functions are described in terms of standardised procedure, there is a well-defined division of labour among offices and office holders, there is a merit-based recruitment system leading to stable linear careers, and there is a formal hierarchy spelling out the distribution of authority and status among actors and offices. In addition, the prevalent self-perception of being an impersonal, impartial and free civil servant who performs his or her duty in the service of a higher authority supports the conclusion that the departmental dynamic is strong within international bureaucracies.

Again, a couple of notes of caution have to be made. Firstly, the fact that a Weberian type of civil servant appears to constitute a mirror in which many international civil servants can recognise themselves does not mean that the international civil servants draw the conclusion that we are talking about ideal bureaucracies. Many of the fallacies of bureaucracies that are well covered in the public administration literature are also listed by the interviewees. For instance, there are frequent references to political in-fights aimed at maximising budgets and competences at the cost of other units and sections of the international bureaucracy (particularly in the Commission and the OECD Secretariat). In fact, some interviewees even consider such interdepartmental struggles to be the essence of leadership and consequently the most important task for departmental managers. When resources are scarce, the survival and hopefully the expansion of one unit means proportional cuts elsewhere in the organisation. Our interviews with Commission staff indicated that this world of tugs-of-war is sometimes described as a 'hierarchy of fear'. Among other problems frequently mentioned, in particular by Commission officials, were that in reality competences can be unclear, that individual civil servants are not fully aware of the larger consequences of their actions, that procedures are rigid and decision making slow or even impossible when facing some unusual cases, and that change, evolution and adaptation of old procedures to new circumstances may be delayed or even prevented. In addition, some refer to 'groupthink' when complaining about a worrying lack of critical thinking. Others complain that more and more rules and procedures are being formulated and that their complexity is rising; rather than ruling by common sense, everything is written down in terms of formal procedures that reduce the civil servants to rule followers. Finally, some interviewees argue that it is *de facto* impossible to find out where and by whom the most decisive decisions are made (particularly in the Commission and the OECD Secretariat). A parallel power structure – often described as informal hierarchies that exist in parallel to the formal hierarchy – has developed that grants some officials disproportionate power in an otherwise regulated and rule-driven bureaucracy. Interestingly, the informal organisation mainly seems to exist to compensate and support the formal one, in contrast to national administration where the informal power structure is often used to bypass the formal one.

The formal organisation of international bureaucracies seems to be at least as important as it is in national administration. Part of the explanation as to why international bureaucracies are strongly driven by their formal organisational structures can be found in the need for generating legitimacy in a turbulent environment. It is a well-known fact that internal stability (security) by the creation of an extensive and complex bureaucracy can be used by a public administration to compensate for a limited capacity in problem solving (Warwick 1975). Most of the missions that international organisations are asked to perform where many interests are at stake are extremely difficult to handle, and international bureaucracies therefore have to tread carefully, which is partly secured by building up formal guidelines and bureaucratic procedures.

Secondly, the fact that the departmental dynamic seems to be overwhelmingly present does not mean that other dynamics are absent. Rather, the departmental logic seems to be the basis and maybe even the precondition for two other dynamics to play out – the supranational and the epistemic dynamics. With their feet safely planted in the departmental dynamic, there is nothing that prevents the civil servants from praising the overall objectives and visions of the entire organisation. In addition, affinity towards one's unit does not prevent a civil servant from enacting an epistemic role. In other words, it seems to be the case within international bureaucracies that a loyalty towards one's immediate institutional affiliation – the department, the unit, the section etc. – is the *foundation* for double or even triple loyalties. More often than not, loyalties tend to overlap rather than conflict. On some occasions roles and loyalties may also be difficult to disentangle. The new aspect that this brings to research on the micro-foundations of international bureaucracies concerns the fact that different kinds of civil servant loyalties are related to the same institutional affiliation and that these loyalties complement rather than contradict each other. In previous research, a mention of double loyalties would imply that the international civil servant has one kind of loyalty associated with his or her secondary institutional affiliation – normally his or her nationally based affiliation – and another kind of loyalty associated with his or her primary institutional affiliation – normally the international bureaucracy (Egeberg 2006). This book advocates that various kinds of loyalties can be associated with the same institutional affiliation, in this case the international bureaucracy. This world of multiple loyalties may be seen as organised around concentric circles where *the departmental dynamic serves as the foundational dynamic* at the very centre of bureaucracy. As mentioned earlier, the kinds of loyalties directed back towards individual member states are not particularly prevalent in the three bureaucracies investigated in this volume.

In addition, one branch of neo-institutional scholarship argues that when different kinds of loyalties – or the talk, decisions and actions of organisations – are in conflict with each other, the result is an organisational decoupling (e.g. Brunsson and Jacobsson 2000). It has been assumed that double loyalties would reflect the fact that there are discrepancies between what is said and what is done. Such a decoupling can be the result of strategic thinking on the part of the civil servants or may just be expressions of mild forms of schizophrenia within an international bureaucracy. We argue that decoupling is not necessarily at stake when different roles and loyalties are enacted. Research reported in this book demonstrates that it is much more relevant to talk about complementary role-sets, i.e. dynamic combinations of roles, when describing the lives, visions, justifications, understandings and aspirations of civil servants in international bureaucracies. The interviewees are very explicit and conscious about the different roles they play and how these roles are combined appropriately in different situations – there is nothing schizophrenic in that. Rather, this finding demonstrates that the average international civil servant possesses high levels of social capital, and it documents their professionalism in coping with the kind of complexity which characterises compound international bureaucracies.

Conclusion 3: International bureaucracies are organisationally contingent

Students of international organisations have tended to adopt neo-liberal, realist and principal–agent approaches to understanding the baseline dynamics of international organisations (e.g. Hasenclever, Mayer and Rittberger 1996). This book is influenced by the organisational and neo-institutional theory turn in political science. These approaches see political and administrative life as contextualised and embedded. This turn contributes to introducing organisational and institutional variables to the study of international bureaucracy. We believe that organisational theory is a powerful tool for approaching such organisations. Political processes and political systems cannot be adequately understood or explained without including the organisational dimension(s) of international bureaucracies. The independent variables suggested by this book benefit from these organisational and institutional schools of thought. The book basically demonstrates that the way in which global governance (i.e. the balancing of diverse behavioural dynamics within international bureaucracies) is exercised is conditioned by the formal structuring of international bureaucracy. In short, the politics of global governance operate in the 'shadow of hierarchy' and thus have a strong organisational dimension to them (Sverdrup and Trondal 2008).

Part III of this book shows that the Westphalian intergovernmental dynamic is largely absent in international bureaucracies, although more so in some organisational settings than in others. This book demonstrates that the compound mix of decision-making dynamics evoked by officials of international bureaucracies is *organisationally contingent* and more complex than assumed by international relations (IR) orthodoxy.

Officials of international bureaucracies are expected to perform increasingly complex tasks, and an international bureaucracy is best described as a compound system of public administration that balances a complementary set of decision-making dynamics. Different behavioural dynamics are played out in the Commission, the WTO Secretariat and the OECD Secretariat due to different organisational properties, different recruitment procedures, different organisational affiliations towards external organisations and different demographic characteristics among the personnel. Nevertheless, due to similarities in these variables, international bureaucracies may often share important behavioural dynamics, notwithstanding the wider organisational embedment of the bureaucracy. For example, the lives of trade analysts in the Commission and the WTO Secretariat tend to exhibit more similarities than differences because they have fairly equivalent portfolios that guide them towards similar sets of problems, solutions and consequences.

The empirical observations presented in this volume indicate that supranational dynamics are associated with a long tenure among the officials of international bureaucracies, a high intensity of actor interaction among officials inside international bureaucracies, and the primacy of organisational affiliations towards the international bureaucracy. Supranationally oriented officials are also typically recruited into permanent positions on the basis of merit. The WTO Secretariat also demonstrates that supranational dynamics may emanate from the issue specificity of international bureaucracies. Highly specialised professional civil servants seem to create a particular loyalty that disregards and transcends national borders. In the WTO case, this is illustrated by the appearance of a number of free-trade defenders among WTO officials. Finally, and largely in contrast to Hooghe (2005), this book suggests that the supranational dynamic within international bureaucracies reflects both processes of socialisation within international bureaucracies – associated with intensive face-to-face interaction among civil servants – and organisational properties *inside* bureaucracies. However, the institutional allegiance towards the international bureaucracy writ large, as well as towards the loyalties to the larger mission of the organisation, also seems to be subject to outside pre-socialisation processes. In summary, supranational dynamics may be understood as being caused both by pre-socialisation and by re-socialisation in international bureaucracies.

This book also illuminates how organisational properties are conducive to departmental and epistemic behavioural dynamics among the incumbents. The departmental dynamic is shown to be foundational within the international bureaucracies studied. This empirical observation substantiates that departmental and epistemic dynamics are fostered by the vertical as well as the horizontal specialisation of international bureaucracies. Part III also illustrates that departmental and epistemic dynamics may reflect the meritocratic recruitment procedure – safeguarding bureaucratic autonomy among civil servants as well as securing a high-calibre group of specialists. Epistemic dynamics, however, are also shown to be associated with pre-socialisation through higher education. The recruitment of a highly educated professional staff may safeguard epistemic roles and loyalties among bureaucrats. Moreover, the horizontal specialisation of international bureaucracies may also leave room for the pursuit of expert knowledge and may even nurture an epistemic dynamic.

Finally, this book demonstrates fairly similar behavioural dynamics among permanent and temporary officials – notably within the Commission. This observation clearly reflects the impact of the formal organisation of international bureaucracies as well as the impact of primary organisational affiliations. The fact that seconded officials behave much like ordinary full-time international bureaucrats may help to illustrate the lack of intergovernmentalism within these bureaucracies. If these officials do not uphold the national connection while working within international bureaucracies, we should not expect this to happen among permanent international civil servants.

A note of caution should be mentioned at this point. A sophisticated analysis of the complex causal relationships between the four independent variables and the four decision-making dynamics suggested in Chapters 1 and 2 warrants data that are not yet available. To make satisfactory empirical tests of the relative explanatory power of each variable requires large-N survey data among international bureaucrats. This would at the least require survey data from a large number of civil servants. It would also necessitate that the comparative analysis of international bureaucracy covers a larger group of organisations than those presented in this book. Consequently, the conclusions drawn in this book are merely probability probes that should be tested against larger comparative data sets in future research.

Next steps in the research on international bureaucracy

This book has suggested some first vital elements of a third generation of IO studies. International bureaucracies are seen as complex and multidimensional institutions that stabilise inter-state relations by building organisational capacities for bureaucratic autonomy. International bureaucracies represent continuity and possess institutional memories, both of which are important stabilising elements in international organisations. Compound international bureaucracies cultivate multiple decision-making dynamics among the staff.

Secondly, patterned variations in the compound mix of dynamics are largely explained by formal organisational features. However, far more research needs to be done to fill this new perspective on international bureaucracy with robust empirical tests. We would like to suggest that future research pays more empirical attention to testing the causal relationships between the *management of international bureaucracies* and the role conceptions, loyalties, identities and decision-making behaviour of the incumbents. Thus, more studies should be made of the political and administrative leadership of international bureaucracies. Do hierarchical centres manage to steer administrative behaviour in their own house, foster horizontal and vertical co-ordination of the services, and reduce so-called 'silo thinking' among administrative divisions? How do managers combine the balances of unity and diversity, change and stability, exploration and exploitation within international bureaucracies (March 2008)?

Existing literature on public management and leadership is primarily occupied with studying national bureaucracies. Our knowledge about the circumstances in which the management of people, cultures, technologies, functions and structures and of the political and technical environment takes place in international bureaucracies is almost absent. Until now it has been taken for granted that experiences gained at national level can be transferred directly to international bureaucracies. However, as mentioned previously, international bureaucracies are distinct entities on several dimensions. They differ from their national counterparts on all important dimensions in terms of complexity. Complexity management seems to be what managers in international bureaucracies are faced with on a daily basis. But what works and what does not work? And how can researchers distinguish success from failure? Leadership in international organisations may be about cultivating integrity by developing anti-corruption schemes and allowing for external and internal audits. It may also deal with developing high levels of policy competence regarding the innovation, application and adaptation of ideas. It also probably concerns the building up of administrative capacities in terms of staff, organisational routines and co-ordination, training and accountability systems. Researchers currently have no solid knowledge base from which to assess and guide management in international bureaucracies. How is organisational autonomy fostered, internal and external reliability assured, and crisis management undertaken? These are some of the questions that are in need of answers if we are to understand the compound nature of international bureaucracies.

A second dimension of the third generation of IO studies would also include more focus on the *actual workings of international bureaucracies*. Detailed and process-oriented accounts of agenda setting, decision making, and implementation in and by international bureaucracies are almost non-existent. Studies of life in international bureaucracies need to go beyond simple replications of formal routines and anecdotal accounts of reforms and history-making events. This would require difficult and cumbersome process tracing and a detailed mapping of personal networks. Essentially, such research endeavours should be comparative by carefully incorporating a selection of international bureaucracies on the basis of a coherent research design. The value-added would be that we would be more able to conclude decisively about the causal relationship between the organisational and institutional characteristics of international bureaucracies on the one hand and patterns of behaviour, identities and roles among the incumbents on the other. Recognising that international bureaucracies are complex institutions implies that we need to take decision-making dynamics in these institutions seriously and to develop theory that is directly targeted at understanding the specificity of international bureaucracies. In addition, the comparative study of international bureaucracy is also in critical need of large-N survey data that may provide general overviews of life inside international bureaucracies. Large-N survey data are also strongly needed to critically test the theoretical suggestions outlined in this book. Moreover, a research agenda for the comparative study of international bureaucracy should aim at establishing longitudinal data sets that would support analysing continuity and change. Large-N time series data would confirm whether the observations presented in this book are merely provisional or are enduring patterns of international bureaucracy. The overall research programme is about constituting the study of international bureaucracy as an integral element in public administration studies, i.e. to normalise the study of international bureaucracy within political science.

Appendix

Interview guide to officials at the Commission, the WTO Secretariat, and OECD Secretariat

Background

What is your educational and professional background?

For how long have you worked in current institution/unit/portfolio?

When, why, how and from where were you recruited to this institution?

What are the main differences between working here and in previous positions?

General institutional questions

How would you generally describe your daily work?

Currently, what issues are central in your work?

What is your current position, rank, unit?

Do you have a clear-cut work-description?

Inside your unit/division/portfolio, what issues cause divisions of opinion/conflicts? (Are these large or minor conflicts?)

Behavioural questions

With whom do you regularly interact *at work*?

- Colleagues in your unit/division?
- Other units/divisions/DGs?
- Head of unit?
- The top administrative leadership of your DG/institution?
- Domestic government institutions? – ministries/agencies? (Within your own portfolio or across portfolios?)
- External experts/universities/research institutions?

- Industry/consultancies etc?
- Other international bureaucracies?

With whom do you regularly interact *outside office?*

- Colleagues in your unit/DG?
- Own nationals?
- Other nationals?

In general, what would you consider to be *the most important contacts* in your position?

Personal perceptions

Does your nationality or the nationality of your colleagues 'matter' with respect to your daily work?

Has an *esprit de corps* developed within your unit/division?

To what extent do you identify with or feel a personal attachment towards:

- your unit/portfolio?
- your institution as a whole (the Commission, the OECD Secretariat, the WTO Secretariat)?
- your profession, educational background?
- the member-state central administrations?

What kind of roles do you regularly emphasise at work?

- As representative for the institution as a whole (supranational)?
- As representative for the unit/portfolio (departmental)?
- As representative for your professional expertise (epistemic)?
- As representative for the member states or for your own country of origin (intergovernmental)?

What considerations are vital for you?

- Your institution as a whole?
- Your unit/division?
- Your profession/expertise?
- The member states?
- Your policy sector/portfolio?
- Formal rules and procedures within your institution/unit?

References

Aberbach, J., R.D. Putnam and B.A. Rockman, 1981, *Bureaucrats and Politicians in Western Democracies* (Cambridge: Harvard University Press).

Aberback, J.D., 2003, 'Introduction: Administration in an Era of Change', *Governance*, 16:3, 315–319.

Abrams, D. and G.R. de Moura, 2001, 'Organizational Identification: Psychological Anchorage and Turnover', in M.A. Hogg and D.J. Terry (eds), *Social Identity Processes in Organizational Contexts* (Ann Arbor: Sheridan Books), pp. 131–148.

Acharya, A. and A.I. Johnston (eds), 2007, *Crafting Cooperation: Regional International Institutions in Comparative Perspective* (Cambridge: Cambridge University Press).

Adler, E. and S. Bernstein, 2005, 'Knowledge in Power: The Epistemic Construction of Global Governance', in M. Barnett and R. Duvall (eds), *Power in Global Governance* (Cambridge: Cambridge University Press), pp. 294–318.

Aggestam, L., 1999, 'Role Conceptions and the Politics of Identity in Foreign Policy', ARENA working paper, No. 8.

Alderson, K., 2001, 'Making Sense of State Socialization', *Review of International Studies*, 27:3, 415–433.

Alger, C., 1963, 'United Nations Participation as a Learning Experience', *Public Opinion Quarterly*, Fall, 425–440.

Andersson, J. J., 2002, 'Europeanization and the Transformation of Democratic Polity, 1945–2000', *Journal of Common Market Studies*, 40:5, 793–822.

Andrews, R., G.A. Boyne, K.J. Meier, L.J. O'Toole Jr. and R.M. Walker, 2005, 'Representative Bureaucracy, Organizational Strategy, and Public Service Performance: An Empirical Analysis of English Local Government', *Journal of Public Administration Research and Theory*, 15, 489–504.

Ansell, C.K., 2004, 'Territoriality, Authority and Democracy', in C.K. Ansell and G.D. Palma (eds), *Restructuring Territoriality: Europe and the United States Compared* (Cambridge: Cambridge University Press), pp. 225–245.

Ashford, B.E. and S.A. Johnson, 2001, 'Which Hat to Wear? The Relative Salience of Multiple Identities in Organizational Contexts', in M.A. Hogg and D.J. Terry (eds), *Social Identity Processes in Organizational Contexts* (Ann Arbor: Psychology Press), pp. 31–48.

Bach, M., 1999, *Die Bürokratisierung Europas* (Frankfurt am Main: Campus).

Bache, I. and M. Flinders (eds), 2004, *Multi-level Governance* (Oxford: Oxford University Press).

Ban, C., 2008, 'Performance Appraisal and Promotion in the European Commission: The challenge of Linking Organizational and Individual Accountability', paper presented at the conference 'Accountability and Governance in International Organizations', University of Konstanz, June.

Barnett, M., 1993, 'Institutions, Rules, and Disorder: The Case of the Arab States System', *International Studies Quarterly*, 37, 271–296.

Barnett, M. and R. Duvall (eds), 2005, *Power in Global Governance* (Cambridge: Cambridge University Press).

Barnett, M. and M. Finnemore, 1999, 'The Politics, Power, and Pathologies of International Organizations', *International Organization*, 53:4, 699–733.

Barnett, M. and M. Finnemore, 2004, *Rules for The World: International Organizations in Global Politics* (Ithaca: Cornell University Press).

Bàtora, J., 2008, 'Collusions and Collisions in Organizing Diplomacy in the EU', in U. Sverdrup and J. Trondal (eds), *The Organizational Dimension of Politics* (Bergen: Fagbokforlaget), pp. 234–260.

Bauer, M.W., 2007, 'The Politics of Reforming the European Commission Administration', in M.W. Buaer and C. Knill (eds), *Management Reforms in International Organizations* (Baden-Baden: Nomos), pp. 51–70.

Bauer, M.W. and C. Knill (eds), 2007, *Management Reforms in International Organizations* (Baden-Baden: Nomos).

Bauer, S., 2006, 'Does Bureaucracy Really Matter? The Authority of Intergovernmental Treaty Secretariats in Global Environmental Politics', *Global Environmental Politics*, 6:1, 23–49.

Bekke, H.A.G.M. and F.M. van der Meer (eds), 2000, *Civil Service Systems in Western Europe* (Cheltenham: Edward Elgar).

Bennett, A.L. and J.K. Oliver, 2002, *International Organizations: Principles and Issues*, Seventh Edition (Upper Saddle River: Prentice Hall).

Bevir, M., R.A.W. Rhodes and P. Weller, 2003, 'Traditions of Governance: Interpreting the Changing Role of the Public Sector', *Public Administration*, 81:1, 1–17.

Beyers, J. and J. Trondal, 2004, 'How Nation-States "Hit" Europe – Ambiguity and Representation in the European Union', *West European Politics*, 27:4, 919–942.

Biddle, B.J., 1986, 'Recent Developments in Role Theory', *Annual Review of Sociology*, 12, 67–92.

Biersteker, T.J., 2003, 'State, Sovereignty and Territory', in W. Carlsnaes, T. Risse and B.A. Simmons (eds), *Handbook of International Relations* (London: SAGE), pp. 157–172.

Bitsch, M.-T., 2007a, 'The Hallstein Commission 1958–1967', in M. Dumoulin (ed.), *The European Commission, 1958–72: History and Memories* (Brussels: European Commission), pp. 51–78.

Bitsch, M.-T., 2007b, 'The College of Commissioners: A New Type of Public Authority', in M. Dumoulin (ed.), *The European Commission, 1958–72: History and Memories* (Brussels: European Commission), pp. 181–204.

Böhling, K., 2007, *Opening Up the Black Box: Organizational Learning in the European Commission* (Frankfurt am Main: Peter Lang).

Bossuat, G., 2007, 'Émile Noël, a Loyal Servant of the Community of Europe', in M. Dumoulin (ed.), *The European Commission, 1958–72. History and Memories* (Brussels: European Commission, 2007), pp. 205–218.

Brunsson, N. and B. Jacobsson (eds), 2000, *A World of Standards* (Oxford: Oxford University Press).

Bulmer, S., 2008, 'Building a Multi-level Polity in Europe', in S. Sverdrup and J. Trondal (eds), *The Organizational Dimension of Politics* (Bergen: Fagbokforlaget), pp. 170–185.

Bulmer, S. and M. Burch, 1998, 'Organizing for Europe: Whitehall, The British State and European Union', *Public Administration*, 76, 601–628.

Checkel, J.T., 2003, '"Going Native" in Europe? Theorizing Social Interaction in European Institutions', *Comparative Political Studies*, 36:1–2, 209–231.

Checkel, J.T., 2004, 'Social Mechanisms and the Quality of Cooperation: Are Europe and the EU Really All That Different?', ARENA working paper, 8.

Checkel, J.T., 2005, 'International Institutions and Socialization in Europe: Introduction and Framework', *International Organization* (Special Issue), 59, 801–826.

Chesterman, S. (ed.), 2007, *Secretary or General? The UN Secretary-General in World Politics* (Cambridge: Cambridge University Press).

Christensen, T. and P. Lægreid (eds), 2002, *New Public Management: The Transformation of Ideas and Practices* (Aldershot: Ashgate).

Christensen, T. and P. Lægreid (eds), 2006, *Autonomy and Regulation: Coping with Agencies in the Modern State* (Cheltenham: Edward Elgar).

Christensen, T. and P. Lægreid (eds), 2007, *Transcending New Public Management: The Transformation of Public Sector Reforms* (Aldershot: Ashgate).

Christiansen, T., 1996, 'A Maturing Bureaucracy? The Role of the Commission in the Policy Process', in J. Richardson (ed.), *European Union: Power and Policy-Making* (London: Routledge), pp. 77–95.

Christiansen, T., 1997, 'Tensions of European Governance: Politicized Bureaucracy and Multiple Accountability in the European Commission', *Journal of European Public Policy*, 4:1, 73–90.

Christiansen, T., 2001, 'The Council of Ministers: The Politics of Institutionalised Intergovernmentalism', in J. Richardson (ed.), *European Union: Power and Policy-Making* (London: Routledge), pp. 135–154.

Cini, M., 1996, *The European Commission: Leadership, Organisation and Culture in the EU Administration* (Manchester: Manchester University Press).

Cini, M., 1997, 'Administrative Culture in the European Commission: The Cases of Competition and Environment', in N. Nugent (ed.), *At the Heart of the Union: Studies of the European Commission* (Houndmills: Macmillan Press), pp. 71–88.

Claude, I.L. Jr., 1956, *Swords into Plowshares: The Problems and Progress of International Organization* (New York: Random House).

CLENAD, 2003, *Report of the Working Group 'Life after SNE'* (Brussels).

Coombes, D., 1970, *Politics and Bureaucracy of the European Union* (London: George Allen and Unwin, 1970).

Cortell, A.P. and S. Peterson (eds), 2003, *Altered States: International Relations, Domestic Politics, And Institutional Change* (Lanham: Lexington Books).

Cottier, T., 2007, 'Genetic Engineering, Trade and Human Rights', in F. Francioni (ed.), *Biotechnologies and International Human Rights* (Oxford: Hart Publishing), pp. 275–314.

Couldner, A.W., 1979, *The Future of the Intellectuals and the Rise of the New Class* (New York: The Macmillan Press Ltd).

Coull, J. and C. Lewis, 2003, 'The Impact of Reform of the Staff Regulations in Making the Commission a More Modern and Efficient Organisation: An Insider's Perspective', *EIPASCOPE*, 3.

Cowles, M.G., J. Caporaso and T. Risse (eds), 2001, *Transforming Europe: Europeanization and Domestic Change* (Ithaca: Cornell University Press).

Cox, R.W., 1969, 'The Executive Head: An Essay on Leadership in International Organization', *International Organization*, 23:2, 205–230.

Cox, R.W. and H.K. Jacobson, 1973, *The Anatomy of Influence: Decision Making in International Organizations* (New Haven: Yale University Press).

Curtin, D. and M. Egeberg, 2008, 'Tradition and Innovation: Europe's Accumulated Executive Order', *West European Politics* (Special Issue), 31:4, 639–661.

Deutsch, K., S.A. Burrell and R.A. Kann, 1957, *Political Community and the North Atlantic Area: International Organization in the Light of Historical Experience* (Princeton: Princeton University Press).

Dimitrakopoulos, D.G. and H. Kassim, 2005, 'The European Commission and the Debate on the Future of Europe', paper presented at the CONNEX workshop, 27–28 May, Oslo.

Dinan, D., 2004, *Europe Recast: A History of European Integration* (Houndmills: Palgrave Macmillan).

Djelic, M.-L., 2006, 'Marketization, From Intellectual Agenda to Global Policy-Making', in M.-L. Djelic and K. Sahlin-Andersson (eds), *Transnational Governance: Institutional Dynamics of Regulation* (Cambridge: Cambridge University Press), pp. 53–73.

Drake, H., 2000, *Jacques Delors: Perspectives on a European Leader* (London: Routledge).

Drori, G.S. and J.W. Meyer, 2006, 'Scientization: Making a World Safe for Organizing', in M.-L. Djelic and K. Sahlin-Andersson (eds), *Transnational Governance: Institutional Dynamics of Regulation* (Cambridge: Cambridge University Press), pp. 31–52.

Drori, G.S., J.W. Meyer, F.O. Ramirez and E. Schofer, 2003, *Science in the Modern World Polity: Institutionalization and Globalization* (Stanford: Stanford University Press).

Duchêne, F., 1994, *Jean Monnet: The First Statesman of Interdependence* (New York: W.W. Norton & Company).

Dumoulin, M., 2007a, 'The Administration', in M. Dumoulin (ed.), *The European Commission, 1958–72: History and Memories* (Brussels: European Commission), pp. 219–240.

Dumoulin, M., 2007b, 'Like Strangers in the City? European Officials in Brussels', in M. Dumoulin (ed.), *The European Commission, 1958–72: History and Memories* (Brussels: European Commission), pp. 241–272.

Dyson, K. and M. Marcussen (eds), 2009, *Central Banks in the Age of the Euro: Europeanization, Convergence and Power* (Oxford: Oxford University Press).

Edwards, G. and D. Spence (eds), 1997, *The European Commission*, Second Edition (London: Cartermill Publishing).

EEA, 2002, 'Guidelines for Secondment of EEA EFTA National Experts to the European Commission', 4/00/W/031, 1 Annex (Brussels).

EFTA Secretariat, 2001, *Evaluation of Arrangements with Secondments* (4/FE/W/008, 2 Annexes, Brussels).

Egeberg, M., 1996, 'Organization and Nationality in the European Commission Services', *Public Administration*, 74:4, 721–735.

Egeberg, M., 2003a, 'How Bureaucratic Structure Matters: An Organizational Perspective', in B.G. Peters and J. Pierre (eds), *Handbook of Public Administration* (London: SAGE), pp. 116–126.

Egeberg, M., 2003b, 'The European Commission', in M. Cini (ed.), *European Union Politics* (Oxford: Oxford University Press), pp. 139–153.

Egeberg, M. (ed.), 2006, *Multilevel Union Administration: The Transformation of Executive Politics in Europe* (Houndmills: Palgrave Macmillan).

Egeberg, M., 2007, 'The European Commission', in M. Cini (ed.), *European Union Politics* (Oxford: Oxford University Press), pp. 139–153.

Egeberg, M. and A. Heskestad, forthcoming, 'Denationalisation of the Cabinets in the European Commission: A Research Note', *Journal of Common Market Studies*.

Egeberg, M., G.F. Schaefer and J. Trondal, 2003, 'The Many Faces of EU Committee Governance', *West European Politics*, 26:3, 19–40.

Egeberg, M. and J. Trondal, 1999, 'Differentiated Integration in Europe: The Case of the EEA Country Norway', *Journal of Common Market Studies*, 37:1, 133–142.

Egeberg, M. and J. Trondal, 2009, 'National Agencies in the European Administrative Space: Government Driven, Commission Driven or Networked?', *Public Administration*, 84:4.

Eilstrup-Sangiovanni, M. (ed.), 2006, *Debates on European Integration* (New York: Palgrave Macmillan).

Ellinas, A. and E. Suleiman, 2008, 'Reforming the Commission: Between Modernization and Bureaucratization', *Journal of European Public Policy* (Special Issue), 15:5, 708–725.

Eppink, D.-J., 2007, *Life of a European Mandarin: Inside the Commission* (Tielt: Lannoo).

Eriksen, E.O. and J.E. Fossum (eds), 2000, *Democracy in the European Union: Integration Through Deliberation?* (London: Routledge).

Ernst, M., 1973, 'Attitudes of Diplomats at the United Nations: The Effects of Organizational Participation on the Evaluation of the Organization', *International Organization*, 32:4, 1037–1044.

Etzioni, A., 2004, 'The EU as Test Case of Halfway Supranationality', *EUSA Review*, 17:1, 1–3.

EUobserver, 2006, 'Commission Bureaucrats are Getting Too Powerful, says Verheugen' (5 October).

EUobserver, 2007, 'EU Commission Sees Civil Servants' Power Grow' (23. 02. 2007).

European Commission, 2000, *Towards a European Research Area* (COM (2000)6, Brussels).

European Commission, 2001, *European Governance* (White Paper, COM (2001)428 final, Brussels).

European Commission, 2002, *Communication from the Commission on the Collection and Use of Expertise by the Commission: Principles and Guidelines* (COM (2002)713, Brussels).

European Commission, 2004, *Staff Regulations of Officials of the European Communities* (Brussels).

European Commission, 2007, *Planning & Optimising Commission Human Resources to Serve EU Priorities* (SEC (2007)530, Brussels).

Finnemore, M., 1996, *National Interests in International Society* (Ithaca: Cornell University Press).

Finnemore, M. and K. Sikkink, 1998, 'International Norm Dynamics and Political Change', *International Organization*, 52:4, 887–917.

Flinders, M., and J. Buller, 'Depoliticization: Principles, Tactics and Tools', *British Politics*, 1:1, 1–26.

Flora, P., S. Kuhnle and D. Urwin (eds), 1999, *State Formation, Nation-Building and Mass Politics in Europe: The Theory of Stein Rokkan* (Oxford: Oxford University Press).

Fouilleux, E., J. de Maillard and A. Smith, 2007, 'Council Working Groups: Spaces for Sectorized European Policy Deliberation', in T. Christiansen and T. Larsson (eds), *The Role of Committees in the Policy-process of the European Union: Legislation, Implementation and Deliberation* (Cheltenham: Edward Elgar).

Gehring, T., 2003, 'International Institutions as Decision-making Systems. Lessons from the European Union', paper presented at the 8th Biennial International Conference of the European Studies Association, Nashville, Tennessee, 27–29 March.

Georgakakis, D. and M. de Lassalle, 2007, 'Who are the Directors-General? European Construction and Administrative Careers in the Commission', paper presented at EU–Consent workshop, 21–22 June, Paris.

Geyer, R., 2003, 'European Integration, the Problem of Complexity and the Revision of Theory', *Journal of Common Market Studies*, 41:1, 15–35.

Gornitzka, Å. and U. Sverdrup, 2008, 'Who Consults? The Configuration of Expert Groups in the European Union', *West European Politics* (Special Issue), 31:4, 725–750.

Gould, D.J. and H.C. Kelman, 1970, 'Horizons of Research on the International Civil Service', *Public Administration Review*, 30:3, 244–251.

Gourevitch, P., 2003, 'Domestic Politics and International Relations', in W. Carlsnaes, T. Risse and B.A. Simmons (eds), *Handbook of International Relations* (London: SAGE,), pp. 309–324.

Graziano, P. and M.P. Vink (eds), 2007, *Europeanization: New Research Agendas* (Houndmills: Palgrave Macmillan).

Greenwood, R. and C.R. Hinings, 1996, 'Understanding Radical Organizational Change: Bringing Together the Old and the New Institutionalism', *Academy of Management Review*, 21:4, 1022–1054.

Griffiths, D., 1999, 'The Welsh Office and Welsh Autonomy', *Public Administration*, 77:4, 793–807.

Groenleer, M., 2006, 'The European Commission and Agencies', in D. Spence (ed.), *The European Commission*, Third Edition (London: John Harper Publishing), pp. 156–172.

Gulick, L., 1937, 'Notes on The Theory of Organizations: With Special References to Government in the United States', in L. Gulick and L.F. Urwick (eds), *Papers on the Science of Administration* (New York: Institute of Public Administration, Columbia University), pp. 1–40.

Haas, E., 1958, *The Uniting of Europe* (Stanford: Stanford University Press).

Haas, E.B., 1990, *When Knowledge is Power: Three Models of Change in International Organizations* (Berkeley: University of California Press).

Haas, P., 1992, 'Epistemic Communities and International Policy Coordination', *International Organization*, 46:1, 1–35.

Haftel, Y.Z. and A. Thompson, 2006, 'The Independence of International Organizations', *Journal of Conflict Resolution*, 50:2, 253–275.

Hasenclever, A., P. Mayer and V. Rittberger, 1996, 'Interests, Power, Knowledge: The Study of International Regimes', *Mershon International Studies Review*, 40, 177–228.

Hawkins, D.G., D.A. Lake, D.L. Nielson and M.J. Tierney (eds), 2006, *Delegation and Agency in International Organizations* (Cambridge: Cambridge University Press).

Hay, C., 2007, *Why We Hate Politics* (London: Polity).

Heady, F., 1998, 'Comparative and International Public Administration: Building Intellectual Bridges', *Public Administration Review*, 58:1, 32–39.

Hedetoft, U., 2003 'Culture of States and Informal Governance in the EU: An Exploratory Study of Elites, Power and Identity', in T. Christiansen and S. Piattoni (eds), *Informal Governance in the European Union* (Cheltenham: Edward Elgar), pp. 36–56.

Herrmann, R. and M.B. Brewer, 2004, 'Identities and Institutions: Becoming European in the EU', in R.K. Herrmann, T. Risse and M.B. Brewer (eds), *Transnational Identities: Becoming European in the EU* (Lanham: Rowman & Littlefield), pp. 1–22.

Herrmann, R.K., T. Risse and M.B. Brewer (eds), 2004, *Transnational Identities: Becoming European in the EU* (Lanham: Rowman & Littlefield).

Hix, S., 2008, 'Towards a Partisan Theory of EU Politics', *Journal of European Public Policy*, 15:8, 1254–1265.

Hooghe, L., 1997, 'A House with Differing Views: The European Commission and Cohesion Policy', in N. Nugent (ed.), *At the Heart of the Union: Studies of the European Commission* (Houndmills: Macmillan Press), pp. 89–108.

Hooghe, L., 2001, *The European Commission and the Integration of Europe: Images of Governance* (Cambridge: Cambridge University Press).

Hooghe, L., 2005, 'Several Roads Lead to International Norms, But Few via International Socialization: A Case Study of the European Commission', *International Organization* (Special Issue), 59, 861–898.

Hooghe, L. and N. Nugent, 2006, 'The Commission's Services', in J. Peterson and M. Shackleton (eds), *The Institutions of the European Union*, Second Edition (Oxford: Oxford University Press).

Hurrelmann, A., S. Leibfried, K. Martens and P. Mayer (eds), 2007, *Transforming the Golden-Age Nation State* (Houndmills: Palgrave Macmillan).

Ingraham, P.W., 1995, *The Foundation of Merit: Public Service in American*

Democracy (Baltimore: The Johns Hopkins University Press).

Jacobsen, D.I., 2007, 'The Tragedy of the Councils? A Reputational Approach to Measuring the Power of Local Politicians', unpublished paper (Kristiansand: University of Agder).

Jacobsen, K.D., 1960, 'Lojalitet, nøytralitet og faglig uavhengighet i sentraladministrasjonen', *Tidsskrift for samfunnsforskning*, 1, 231–248.

Johnston, A.I., 2005, 'Conclusions and Extensions: Towards Mid-Range Theorizing and Beyond Europe', *International Organization* (Special Issue), 59, 1013–1044.

Jordan, A. and A. Schout, 2007, *The Coordination of the European Union: Exploring the Capacities of Networked Governance* (Oxford: Oxford University Press, 2007).

Jordan, R.S., 1971, *International Administration: Its Evolution and Contemporary Applications* (New York: Oxford University Press).

Jörgens, H., M.W. Bauer and C. Knill, 2009, 'International Organizations as Formal Organizations: A Framework for Analysis', paper presented at the workshop 'The Transformation of the Executive Branch of Government in the EU', ARENA, University of Oslo, 4–6 June.

Karns, M.P. and K.A. Mingst, 2004, *International Organizations: The Politics and Processes of Global Governance* (London: Lynne Rienner Publishers).

Kassim, H., 2004a, 'The Kinnock Reforms in Perspective: Why Reforming the Commission is an Heroic, but Thankless Task', *Public Policy and Administration*, 19:3, 25–41.

Kassim, H., 2004b, 'The Secretariat General of the European Commission, 1958–2003: A Singular Institution', in A. Smith (ed.), *Politics and the European Commission: Actors, Interdependence, Legitimacy* (London: Routledge), pp. 47–66.

Kassim, H., 2008, '"Mission Impossible", but Mission Accomplished: The Kinnock Reforms and the European Commission', *Journal of European Public Policy* (Special Issue), 15:5, 648–668.

Kassim, H. and A. Menon, 2004, 'EU Member States and the Prodi Commission', in D.G. Dimitrakopoulos (ed.), *The Changing European Commission* (Manchester: Manchester University Press), pp. 89–104.

Kegley, C.W. and G.A. Raymond, 2002, *Exorcising the Ghost of Westphalia: Building World Order in the new Millennium* (Upper Saddle River: Prentice Hall).

Keohane, R. and J.S. Nye, 2001, 'The Club Model of Multilateral Cooperation and Problems of Democratic Legitimacy', in R.B. Porter, P. Sauvé, A. Subramanian and A.B. Zampetti (eds), *Efficiency, Equity, and Legitimacy: The Multilateral Trading System at the Millennium* (Washington: Brookings).

Knight, J., 1970, 'On the Influence of the Secretary-General: Can We Know What It Is?', *International Organization*, 24:3, 594–600.

Knill, C. and T. Balint, 2008, 'Explaining Variation in Organizational Change: The Reform of Human Resource Management in the European Commission and the OECD', *Journal of European Public Policy* (Special Issue), 15:5, 669–690.

Kratochwil, F. and J.G. Ruggie, 1986, 'International Organizations: A State of the Art and an Art of the State', *International Organization*, 40:4, 753–775.

Kurpas, S., C. Grøn and P.M. Kacsynski, 2008, *The European Commission after Enlargement: Does More Add Up to Less?* (Brussels: CEPS Special Report).

Larsson, T., 2003, *Precooking in the European Union: The World of Expert Groups* (Stockholm: Ministry of Finance, Ds 2003:16).

Larsson, T. and J. Trondal, 2006, 'Agenda Setting in the European Commission: How the European Commission Structure and Influence the EU Agenda', in H.C.H. Hofmann and A.H. Turk (eds), *EU Administrative Governance* (Cheltenham: Edward Elgar), pp. 11–43.

League of Nations, 1920, *Official Journal.*

Lemoine, J., 1995, *The International Civil Servant: An Engangered Species* (The Hague: Kluwer Law International).

Lequesne, C., 2000, 'The European Commission: A Balancing Act between Autonomy and Dependence', in K. Neunreither and A. Wiener (eds), *European Integration After Amsterdam: Institutional Dynamics and Prospects for Democracy* (Oxford: Oxford University Press), pp. 36–51.

Lerdell, D. and K. Sahlin-Andersson, 1997, *Att lära över gränser. En studie av OECD:s förvaltningspolitiska samarbete* (Stockholm: SOU, 1997:33).

Lewis, J., 2000, 'The Methods of Community in EU Decision-making and Administrative Rivalry in the Council's Infrastructure', *Journal of European Public Policy*, 7:2, 261–289.

Lewis, J., 2003, 'Informal Integration and the Supranational Construction of the Council', *Journal of European Public Policy* (Special Issue), 10:6, 996–1019.

Loughlin, J., 2001, *Subnational Demoncracy in the European Union: Challenges and Opportunities* (Oxford: Oxford University Press).

MacMullen, A., 1997, 'European Commissioners 1952–1995: National Routes to a European Elite', in N. Nugent (ed.), *At the Heart of the Union: Studies of the European Commission* (Houndmills: Macmillan Press), pp. 27–48.

March, J.G., 1991, 'Exploration and Exploitation in Organizational Learning', *Organization Science*, 2:1, 71–87.

March, J.G., 1994, *A Primer on Decision Making: How Decisions Happen* (New York: The Free Press).

March, J.G., 2008, *Explorations in Organizations* (Stanford: Stanford Business Books).

March, J.G., 2009, 'Public Administration, Organizations and Democracy', in P.G. Roness and H. Saetren (eds), *Change and Continuity in Public Sector Organizations* (Bergen: Fagbokforlaget), pp. 23–44.

March, J.G. and J.P. Olsen, 1984, 'The New Institutionalism: Organizational Factors in Political Life', *American Political Science Review*, 78, 734–749.

March, J.G. and J.P. Olsen, 1989, *Rediscovering Institutions: The Organizational Basis of Politics* (New York: The Free Press).

March, J.G. and J.P. Olsen, 1995, *Democratic Governance* (New York: The Free Press).

March, J.G. and J.P. Olsen, 1998, 'The Institutional Dynamics of International Political Orders', *International Organization*, 52:4, 943–969.

March, J.G. and J.P. Olsen, 2006, 'Elaborating the "New Institutionalism"', in R.A.W. Rhodes, S.A. Binder and B.A. Rockman (eds), *The Oxford Handbook of Political Institutions* (Oxford: Oxford University Press), pp. 3–20.

Marcussen, M., 2002, *OECD og idèspillet: Game Over?* (Copenhagen: Hans Reitzels Forlag).

Marcussen, M., 2004a, 'OECD Governance Through Soft Law', in U. Mörth (ed.), *Soft Law in Governance and Regulation: An Interdisciplinary Analysis* (Cheltenham: Edward Elgar).

Marcussen, M., 2004b, 'The OECD as Ideational Artist and Arbitrator: Reality or Dream?' in B. Reinalda and B. Verbeek (eds), *Decision-Making Within International Organization* (London: Routledge), pp. 90–105.

Marcussen, M., 2004c, 'Multilateral Surveillance and the OECD: Playing the Idea-Game', in K. Armingeon and M. Beyeler (eds), *The OECD and European Welfare States* (Cheltenham: Edward Elgar).

Marcussen, M., 2006, 'Institutional Transformation? The Scientization of Central Banking as Case', in T. Christensen and P. Lægreid (eds), *Autonomy and Regulation: Coping with Agencies in the Modern State* (Cheltenham: Edward Elgar), pp. 81–109.

Marcussen, M., 2009, 'Scientization: A-politization of Central Banking?', in K. Dyson and M. Marcussen (eds), *Central Banks in the Age of the Euro: Europeanization, Convergence and Power* (Oxford: Oxford University Press.

Marcussen, M., forthcoming, 'The OECD as the Nanny of Democratic Governance in Central and Eastern Europe', in T. Flockhart (ed.), *Socialising Democratic Norms: The Role of International Organisations for the Construction of Europe* (London: Palgrave).

Mathiason, J., 2007, *Invisible Governance: International Secretariats in Global Politics* (Bloomfield: Kumarian Press).

Mayntz, R., 1999, 'Organizations, Agents and Representatives', in M. Egeberg and P. Lægreid (eds), *Organizing Political Institutions* (Oslo: Scandinavian University Press).

McDonald, M., 1997, 'Identities in the European Commission', in N. Nugent (ed.), *At the Heart of the Union: Studies of the European Commission* (Houndmills: Macmillan Press), pp. 49–70.

McElroy, G., 2006, 'Legislative Politics', in K.E. Joergensen, M.A. Pollack and B. Rosamond (eds), *Handbook of European Union Politics* (London: SAGE), pp. 175–194.

Michelmann, H.J., 1978, 'Multinational Staffing and Organizational Functioning in the Commission of the European Communities', *International Organization*, 32:2, 477–496.

Moravcsik, A., 1998, *The Choice for Europe: Social Purpose and State Power from Messina to Maastricht* (Ithaca: Cornell University Press).

Morth, U., 2000, 'Competing frames in the European Commission: The Case of the Defence Industry and Equipment Issue', *Journal of European Public Policy*, 7:2, 173–189.

Mouritzen, H., 1990, *The International Civil Service: A Study of Bureaucracy: International Organisations* (Aldershot: Dartmouth).

National Intelligence Council, 2008, *Global Trends 2025: A Transformed World* (Washington DC).

Nelsen, B.F. and A. Stubb (eds), 2003, *The European Union: Readings on the Theory and Practice of European Integration* (London: Lynne Rienner Publishers).

Niemann, A., 2006, *Explaining Decisions in the European Union* (Cambridge: Cambridge University Press).

Nugent, N., 2001, *The European Commission* (Houndmills: Palgrave).

Nugent, N., 2006, *The Government and Politics of the European Union* (Durham: Duke University Press).

Nye, R.O., 1975, 'International Organization and the Crisis of Interdependence', *International Organization*, 29:2, 357–365.

OECD, 1996, *OECD Staff Profile Statistics* (C/WP/SP/WD(96)6, Paris: OECD).

OECD, 2001, *Staff Profile Statistics, 2000* (C(2001)129, Paris: OECD).

OECD, 2008, *OECD Staff Profile Statistics, 2007* (C(2008)56, Paris: OECD).

Olsen, J.P., 2003a, 'The Many Faces of Europeanisation', *Journal of Common Market Studies*, 40:5, 921–952.

Olsen, J.P., 2003b, 'Citizens, Public Administration and the Search for Theoretical Foundations', the 17th Annual John Gaus Lecture, Americal Political Science Association, 29 August, Philadelphia PA.

Olsen, J.P., 2007a, *Europe in Search of Political Order* (Oxford: Oxford University Press).

Olsen, J.P., 2007b, 'The Ups and Downs of Bureaucratic Organization', ARENA working paper, 14.

Olsen, J.P., 2008, 'Institutional Autonomy and Democratic Government', ARENA working paper, 20.

Olsen, J.P. and B.G. Peters, 1996, *Lessons from Experience: Experiential Learning in Administrative Reforms in Eight Democracies* (Oslo: Scandinavian University Press).

O'Sullivan, D., 2006, 'The Secretary General of the Commission: A Personal Comment by David O'Sullivan', in D. Spence and G. Edwards (eds), *The European Commission*, Third Edition (London: John Harper Publishing), pp. 100–102.

Page, E.C., 1992, *Political Authority and Bureaucratic Power: A Comparative Analysis* (New York: Harvester Wheatsheaf).

Page, E.C., 1997, *People Who Run Europe* (Oxford: Clarendon Press).

Page, E.C., 2008, 'Delegation, Detail and Discretion: Bureaucrats and the Construction of Policies', in U. Sverdrup and J. Trondal (eds), *The Organisational Dimension of Politics: Essays in Honor of Morten Egeberg* (Bergen: Fagbokforlaget), pp. 66–80.

Page, E.C. and V. Wright (eds), 1999, *Bureaucratic Élites in Western European States: A Comparative Analysis of Top Officials* (Oxford: Oxford University Press).

Pentland, C., 1973, *International Theory and European Integration* (New York: The Free Press).

Peters, B.G., 1995, *The Politics of Bureaucracy* (New York: Longman).

Poguntke, T. and P. Webb (eds), *The Presidentialization of Politics: A Comparative Study of Modern Democracies* (Oxford: Oxford University Press).

Pollitt, C., C. Talbot, J. Caulfield and A. Smullen, 2004, *Agencies: How Governments Do Things Through Semi-autonomous Organizations* (Houndmills: Palgrave Macmillan).

Ramirez, F.O., 2006, 'The Rationalization of Universities', in M.-L. Djelic and K. Sahlin-Andersson (eds), *Transnational Governance: Institutional Dynamics of Regulation* (Cambridge: Cambridge University Press), pp. 225–244.

Reinalda, B. and B. Verbeek, 2004a, 'The Issue of Decision-making Within International Organizations', in B. Reinalda and B. Verbeek (eds), *Decision Making Within International Organizations* (London: Routledge), pp. 9–41.

Reinalda, B. and B. Verbeek (eds), 2004b, *Decision Making Within International Organizations* (London: Routledge).

Reymond, H. and S. Mailick, 1986, 'The International Civil Service Revisited', *Public Administration Review*, 46:2, 135–141.

Richards, D. and M.J. Smith, 2004, 'Interpreting the World of Political Elites', *Public Administration*, 82:4, 777–800.

Risse, T. and M.L. Maier, 2003, *Europeanization, Collective Identities and Public Discourses* (Draft Final Report of the IDNET Thematic Network submitted to the European Commission. European University Institute and Robert Schuman Centre for Advanced Studies).

Rochester, M.J., 1986, 'The Rise and Fall of International Organization as a Field of Study', *International Organization*, 40:4, 777–813.

Rokkan, S., 1987, *Stat, nasjon, klasse* (Oslo: Universitetsforlaget).

Rosamond, B., 2000, *Theories of European Integration* (New York: Palgrave).

Rosenau, J.N., 1996, 'Pre-Theories and Theories of Foreign Policy', in J.A. Vasquez (ed.), *Classics of International Relations,* Third Edition (Upper Saddle River: Prentice Hall), pp. 179–190.

Rosenau, J.N., 1997, *Along the Domestic–Foreign Frontier: Exploring Governance in a Turbulent World* (Cambridge: Cambridge University Press).

Sahlin-Andersson, K., 2000, 'Arenas as Standardizers', in N. Brunsson, B. Jacobsson et al. (eds), *A World of Standards* (Oxford: Oxford University Press), pp. 101–124.

Sandholtz, W. and A. Stone Sweet, 1998, *European Integration and Supranational Governance* (Oxford: Oxford University Press).

Schemeil, Y., 2004, 'Expertise and Political Competence: Consensus Making Within the Word Trade Organization and the World Meteorological Organization', in B. Reinalda and B. Verbeek (eds), *Decision Making Within International Organizations* (London: Routledge), pp. 77–89.

Schmidt, V.A., 2006, *Democracy in Europe: The EU and National Polities* (Oxford: Oxford University Press).

Schneider, G., 2008, 'Neither Goethe nor Bismarck: On the Link Between Theory and Empirics in Council Decision-Making Studies', in D. Naurin and H. Wallace (eds), *Unveiling the Council of the European Union: Games Governments Play in Brussels* (Houndmills: Palgrave Macmillan), pp. 277–289.

Searing, D.D., 1991, 'Roles, Rules, and Rationality in the New Institutionalism', *American Political Science Review*, 85:4, 1239–1260.

Selden, S.C., 1997, *The Promise of Representative Bureaucracy: Diversity and Responsiveness in a Government Agency* (Armonk, New York: M.E. Sharpe).

Selznick, P., 1957, *Leadership in Administration* (New York: Harper & Son).

Shaffer, G., 2005, 'The Role of the WTO Director-General and Secretariat', *World Trade Review* 4:3, 429–438.

Shore, C., 2000, *Building Europe: The Cultural Politics of European Integration* (London: Routledge).

Shore, C., 2007, 'European Integration in Anthropological Perspective: Studying the "Culture" of the EU Civil Service', in R.A.W. Rhodes, P. t'Hart and M. Noordegraaf (eds), *Observing Government Elites: Up Close and Personal* (Houndmills: Palgrave Macmillan).

Simmons, B.A. and L.L. Martin, 2003, 'International Organizations and Institutions', in W. Carlsnaes, T. Risse and B.A. Simmons (eds), *Handbook of International Relations* (London: SAGE), pp. 192–211.

Simon, H., 1957, *Administrative Behavior*, Second Edition (New York: Macmillan).

Sjöstedt, G., 1973, *OECD-samarbetet: Funktioner och Effekter* (SU, Statsvetenskapliga inst., Stockholm Political Studies 3, Stockholm).

Slaughter, A.M., 2004, *A New World Order* (Princeton: Princeton University Press).

Smith, J., 2001, 'Cultural Aspects of Europeanization: The Case of the Scottish Office', *Public Administration*, 79:1, 147–165.

Smith, K.A., 1973, 'The European Economic Community and National Civil Servants of the Member States – A Comment', *International Organization*, 27, 563–568.

Somek, A., 2001, 'On Supranationality', *European Integration Online Papers*, 5:3: http://eiop.or.at/eiop/texte/2001–003a.htm (accessed October 2009).

Spence, D. (ed.), 2006, *The European Commission* (London: John Harper Publishing).

Spence, D. and A. Stevens, 2006, 'Staff and Personnel Policy in the Commission', in D. Spence (ed.), *The European Commission* (London: John Harper Publishing), pp. 173–208.

Spierenburg, D., 1979, *Proposals for Reform of the Commission of the European Communities and Its Services* (Brussels: European Commission).

Statistical Bulletin of Commission Staff, 2008, (Brussels: The Directorate-General for Personnel and Administration, 04/2008).

Statskontoret, 2001, *Svenska nationalla experter i EU-tjänst* (Stockholm, 2001:17).

Stevens, A. and H. Stevens, 2001, *Brussels Bureaucrats? The Administration of the European Union* (London: Palgrave).

Stone Sweet, A. and W. Sandholtz, 1998, 'Integration, Supranational Governance, and the Institutionalization of the European Polity', in W. Sandholtz and A. Stone Sweet (eds), *European Integration and Supranational Governance* (Oxford: Oxford University Press), pp. 1–26.

Stone Sweet, A., W. Sandholtz and N. Fligstein (eds), 2001, *The Institutionalization of Europe* (Oxford: Oxford University Press).

Suvarierol, S., 2007, *Beyond the Myth of Nationality: A Study of the Networks of European Commission Officials* (PhD Thesis, Utrecht School of Governance, Utrecht University).

Sverdrup, U., 2000, 'Precedents and Present Events in the European Union: An Institutional Perspective on Treaty Reform', in K. Neunreither and A. Wiener (eds), *European Integration After Amsterdam: Institutional Dynamics and Prospects for Democracy* (Oxford: Oxford University Press), pp. 241–265.

Sverdrup, U., 2007, 'Implementation', in P. Graziano and M.P. Vink (eds), *Europeanization: New Research Agendas* (Houndmills: Palgrave Macmillan), pp. 197–211.

References 223

Sverdrup, U. and J. Trondal (eds), 2008, *The Organizational Dimension of Politics* (Bergen: Fagbokforlaget).

Taylor, S., 2001, 'Coping with the Commission at that "Difficult" Age', *European Voice*, 7:6.

The Government Office of Sweden, 2002, *Svenskar i EU.institutionerna: Bakgrund och handlingsprogram* (Stockholm: The Government Office of Sweden).

Thompson, J.D., 1967, *Organizations in Actions* (New York: McGraw Hill).

Trondal, J., 2001, 'Is There any Social Constructivist–Institutionalist Divide? Unpacking Social Mechanisms Affecting Representational Roles among EU Decision-Makers', *Journal of European Public Policy*, 8:1, 1–23.

Trondal, J., 2004a, 'Political Dynamics of the Parallel Administration of the European Commission', in A. Smith (ed.), *Policies and the European Commission: Actors, Interdependences, Legitimacy* (London: Routledge), pp. 67–82.

Trondal, J., 2004b, 'Re-socializing Civil Servants: The Transformative Powers of EU Institutions', *Acta Politica: International Journal of Political Science*, 39:1, 4–30.

Trondal, J., 2006, 'Governing at the Frontier of the European Commission: The Case of Seconded National Experts', *West European Politics*, 29:1, 147–160.

Trondal, J., 2007a, 'The Public Administration Turn in Integration Research', *Journal of European Public Policy*, 14:6, 960–972.

Trondal, J., 2007b, 'Is the European Commission a Hothouse for Supranationalism? Exploring Actor-level Supranationalism', *Journal of Common Market Studies*, 45:5, 1111–1133.

Trondal, J. and L. Jeppesen, 2008, 'Images of Agency Governance in the European Union', *West European Politics*, 31:3, 417–441.

Trondal, J., C. van den Berg and S. Suvarierol, 2008, 'The Compound Machinery of Government: The Case of Seconded Officials in the European Commission', *Governance*, 21:2 , 253–274.

Underdal, A., 2008, 'The Organizational Infrastructure of International Environmental Regimes', in U. Sverdrup and J. Trondal (eds), *The Organizational Dimension of Politics* (Bergen: Fagbokforlaget), pp. 186–205.

Van den Bossche, P., 2008, *The Law and Policy of the World Trade Organization: Text, Cases and Materials*, Second Edition (Cambridge: Cambridge University Press).

Van den Bossche, P. and I. Alexovicova, 2005, 'Effective Global Economic Governance by the World Trade Organization', *Journal of International Economic Law*, 8:3, 667–690.

Van der Harst, J., 2007, 'Sicco Mansholt: Courage and Conviction', in M. Dumoulin (ed.), *The European Commission, 1958–72: History and Memories* (Brussels: European Commission), pp. 156–180.

Van Knippenberg, D. and E. Van Leeuwen, 2001, 'Organizational Identity After a Merger: Sense of Continuity as the Key to Postmerger Identification', in M.A. Hogg and D.J. Terry (eds), *Social Identity Processes in Organizational Context* (Ann Arbor: Psychology Press), pp. 249–264.

Veggeland, F. and S.O. Borgen, 2005, 'Negotiating International Food Standards: The World Trade Organization's Impact on the Codex Alimentarius

Commission', *Governance* 18:4, 675–708.

Vibert, F., 2007, *The Rise of the Unelected: Democracy and the New Separation of Powers* (Cambridge: Cambridge University Press).

Wagenen, R.V., 1971, 'Observations on the Life of an International Civil Servant', in R.S. Jordan (ed.), *International Administration: Its Evolution and Contemporary Applications* (London: Oxford University Press).

Warleigh-Lack, A. and D. Phinnemore, 2009, 'Conclusion', in D. Phinnemore and A. Warleigh-Lack (eds), *Reflections on European Integration: 50 years of the Treaty of Rome* (Houndmills: Palgrave Macmillan), pp. 212–223.

Warwick, D., 1975, *A Theory of Public Bureaucracy: Politics, Personality and Organizations in the State Department* (Cambridge: Cambridge University Press).

Weber, M., 1983, *On Capitalism, Bureaucracy and Religion* (Glasgow: Harper Collins Publishers).

Wessels, W., 1998, 'Comitology: Fusion in Action. Politico-administrative Trends in the EU System', *Journal of European Public Policy*, 5:2, 209–234.

Wessels, W., A. Maurer and J. Mittag (eds), 2003, *Fifteen Into One? The European Union and its Member States* (Manchester: Manchester University Press).

Wille, A., 2007, 'Senior Officials in a Reforming European Commission: Transforming the Top?', in M.W. Bauer and C. Knill (eds), *Management Reforms in International Organizations* (Baden-Baden: Nomos), pp. 37–50.

Wilson, J.Q., 1989, *Bureaucracy* (New York: Basic Books).

Wolf, P., 1973, 'International Organization and Attitude Change: A Re-examination of the Functionalist Approach', *International Organization*, 27:3, 347–371.

Woolcock, S., 2000, 'European Trade Policy', in H. Wallace and W. Wallace (eds), *Policy-Making in the European Union* (Oxford: Oxford University Press).

Wrong, D.H., 1970, *Max Weber* (Englewood Cliffs: Prentice Hall, Inc).

WTO Staff Regulations

WTO, 2004, *The Future of the WTO: Addressing Institutional Challenges in the New Millennium* (Report by the Consultative Board to the former Director-General Supachai Panitchpakdi).

Yi-Chong, X. and P. Weller, 2004, *The Governance of World Trade: International Civil Servants and the GATT/WTO* (Cheltenham: Edward Elgar).

Yi-Chong, X. and P. Weller, 2008, 'To Be, but not To Be Seen: Exploring the Impact of International Civil Servants', *Public Administration*, 86:1, 35–51.

Zurn, M. and J.T. Checkel, 2005, 'Getting Socialized to Build Bridges: Constructivism and Rationalism, Europe and the Nation-State', *International Organization* (Special Issue), 59, 1045–1079.

Index

CPSIA information can be obtained at www.ICGtesting.com
Printed in the USA
BVOW08s1522150814

362960BV00003B/31/P